The Education
of
Jennie Wang

Memoir of a Good Student

Jennie Wang

Bilingual Academy

2015

FIRST EDITION

Library of Congress Cataloging-in-Publication Data
Wang, Jennie. 1952-
The Education of Jennie Wang / Jennie Wang.
a.   cm
Includes a Reading Guide.
1. Jennie Wang. 2. Lin Jian (林 涧, Chinese pen name).
3. Asian Americans--Biography. 4. China.
5. Shanghai Memoir. 6. Chinese American Women.
7. Cultural Revolution (1966). 8. Education.
9. ESL. 10. World Literature.

PS   2015
813'54-dc19
ISBN-13+978-0693588031
ISBN-10-0692588035
LCCN: 2015916622

Printed in the United States of America

DEDICATION

To Jessica, Pan-Wen, Liu Yong,

Justin, Amy, Paul,

all my students in Asia and America,

their students and children.

ALSO BY JENNIE WANG

License Plate Number One:
Stories of Old Shanghai
Lin Jian (林 涧)

The Iron Curtain of Language:
Maxine Hong Kingston and American Orientalism

Novelistic Love in the Platonic Tradition:
Fielding, Faulkner and the Postmodernists

China Men's American Dreams:
Stories and Poems
Ed. Lin Jian (林 涧, Chinese pen name)

Querying the Genealogy:
Comparative and Transnational Studies in
Chinese American Literature
Ed. Lin Jian (林 涧)

Smiles on Washington Square:
A Love Story of Sorts by Raymond Federman.
Trans. Lin Jian (林 涧)

CONTENTS

Author's Note

Introduction   *Déjà Vu*!   1

Chapter 1   Overture   6
Chapter 2   August 18, 1966   16
Chapter 3   "Store in your Brain!"   34
Chapter 4   A Self-Education Curriculum   66
Chapter 5   Life in the Countryside   99
Chapter 6   Father, Mother, Grandmas   130
Chapter 7   Back to the City   152
Chapter 8   English Studies   188
Chapter 9   Love and Duty   204
Chapter 10   Legacy   227

Acknowledgement   244
Reading Guide   245
About the Author   247

AUTHOR'S NOTE

For the most part, the material in this memoir is drawn from my diaries and notebooks from 1966 to 1979, when I was an adolescent growing up in Shanghai. Those pages were written in Chinese.

The author is limited by time and space, identity and difference, also alienated by sense and sensibility, both cultural and linguistic, in speaking of China, especially when politics are involved. As most bilingual readers may understand, sometimes the barriers are insurmountable. Therefore, a third person narrative point of view is adopted to render certain ease and distance, objectivity and reflective space, as used in *The Education of Henry Adams*.

Published as a memoir, the author is only accountable for her own remembrance of things past—people and events as she could recollect, reconstruct, translate, and deliver with her own ideas, imagine to be, and possibly reason.

To protect the people who are still living, their names are fictitious, made up as close as possible to the original, either by sound sense or by character. Naming in Chinese, mysteriously, often reflects one's character or destiny.

INTRODUCTION

Déjà Vu!

Teaching Chinese American Literature, I was often asked by my students to tell them my own stories. They got the impression from my lectures that I might know more about China and Chinese culture than that in the books they read. They wanted to know the dark secrets I heard from old people, the Red terrors I witnessed in China, and the silent blues I endured in white America. They were interested in my life and career from Shanghai to San Francisco, from Buffalo, New York to Cedar Falls, Iowa, and from Boston back to Shanghai, then out of Taiwan, back to northern California, where I stay in my writer's cabin, summer and winter, which I call my "home" in America. My mentors and colleagues in America advised me to writer a "memoir" of sort. "A Chinese woman," as they called me, escaping China, and being saved in America.

I had been putting this project off and off, first because I had to write academic books and articles for my work, personal writing seemed to be a leisure activity. Subconsciously, after ten years of research and study on the writing of Maxine Hong Kingston and American Orientalism, which became the subtitle of my last book—*The Iron Curtain of Language* (2008), I had my fears. I fear of being stereotyped left and right, as Kingston was, such an exceptional writer, labeled as either "Chinese" or "American," and misinterpreted by readers, popular and academic; attacked by jealous rivals, male and female; and worse, reviewed by critics who were acclaimed "politically correct," yet literally incorrect. These concerns were enough to hold me back.

1

I hesitated to call it a "memoir," lest my product, like Kingston's post-modern fiction—"Memoirs of a Girlhood among the Ghost" (鬼佬群中的女童回忆录), being classified in the literary market as "autobiography," "confession," "slave narrative," "women's writing." Who am I to write an autobiography? I am neither a star, nor a celebrity. In the eyes of my family and friends, I am not a "success" in today's world, where success is measured by wealth and fame.

In the eye of my students, however, who were mostly English majors, I seem to have accomplished what they wished to venture—go abroad, get degrees in American universities, major in Liberal Arts, instead of science or business, and become a professor, a writer to write books. If for my students' sake, I must tell a "success story," at least I could say, I succeeded in my education as a good student, as an autodidactic, in and out of school. I am a lifetime student, still keep my mind alive, my spirit high, and my eyes open to good and evil, right and wrong, true or false on the globe. I still cherish a will to make America a better place, with knowledge and books, with my unique transnational heritage. Maybe in this respect, this book shall benefit my students and some of the good students to come. Therefore, let me call it *"The Education of Jennie Wang: Memoir of a Good Student."*

Personally, to write this book was a painful experience, to recall past events that I wished to forget—the atrocities of mob violence during the Cultural Revolution, house searching, public humiliation, poverty, suicides, close of schools and universities, and going down to the countryside. Especially damaging to me, as to a generation of my kind, was the deprivation of school education, social respect, and self-esteem. Ten years went by, wasted in endless waiting for a change of government policy, for "day light." Let the bygones be bygones, I often told myself. Or, "Let the sleeping dog lie." Who cares now about the Cultural Revolution? I never looked back since I left China in 1979.

I do not have nostalgia. I have let go and forgotten so much—my naive, adolescent self, my innocent belief and love, the people dear to me, as well as the nightmares in a world full of "sound and fury," where I had no control of my life, no choice of action. Emotionally, I have overcome my "Hamlet Complex," let go and forgotten "the slings and arrows of outrageous fortune . . ./ the thousand natural shocks/ that flesh is heir to/ The oppressor's wrong/ . . . . the law's delay." I even do not have dreams in my sleep after I came to America.

So it was impossible for me to recall past events and retrieve my old self emotionally in its "subjectivity," as might be expected in the popular mode of writing, with the expectation that the oriental woman must play the role of "supplicant." Nor was it my wish to retrieve my past and an introverted self in writing this memoir, but to reconstruct the values of education for my students and the future generations of my kind. I have them in my mind.

When I open my diaries of those youthful days, about fifty notebooks, large and small, I couldn't relate to the writer any more. I saw a faithful but naive adolescent. I have difficulty in calling her "I." I have moved far far away intellectually and emotionally from my old self. Therefore, only in a third person narrative, with certain distance, objectivity, and transcendence, would I feel comfortable to face the past, study my old self, a lost self. So I call her " J." She is and isn't me, the author writing the book. "J" is only a sign, a sign of someone, sometime ago, somewhere, some say.

Those diaries were written in Chinese; whereas, the book I am writing is in English. Thus, much of the writing is translation from Chinese into English. Chinese/English translation is what I was taught to avoid from the start. English has become my primary language now, fortunately and unfortunately. Maybe language has transformed my identity. I wish I could write in Chinese as well as I did at eighteen, or twenty-five, but that was another part of an irretrievable past and self. That special skill—English/Chinese translation, which I mastered so well when young, without use for decades, is also lost now.

American English, or what I call "the Iron Curtain of Language," couldn't deliver the truths and sentimentality in Chinese, or convey the revolutionary passion and idealism dominating the spirit of the age in post-revolutionary China when I grew up. In English, my tone might sound cold, cynical, and stoic. I must caution the reader that as often as not, I am being ironic, as expressive of my present self. That ironic distance helped

3

to hold my tears, and control my emotion in recollecting past events. So it goes.

What made this project came out of my closet, pressed on my shoulders, and couldn't wait, was the development of current events among college students last year (2014), namely, the student demonstration in Taiwan in the spring, and the prolonged student protestations in the streets of Hong Kong last fall. Slogans, big letter posters, Samsun cell phones, yellow umbrellas in the hands of arrogant youth leaders, ignorant mob, innocent victims, and fanatic activists, blocking traffic, fighting the security guards, attacking the administration, "down with" the government heads, catching the camera eye and news report, media exposure and media coverage on TV—enacted another "democratic" movement in Asia under Western eyes.

I suffered from a "*déjà vu*." It made me dizzy. I was teaching American Literature in Taiwan. Most of the students were at a loss, really did not know what was going on. Only a few students and a few strange faces in class, pulled by off-campus religious groups, "gender equity" organizers, "environmental" activists, were chosen to go to Taipei, to demonstrate, to ask the government head to step down, so on and so forth. I thought Taiwan was a democracy, the government head was elected by a popular vote. How could a group of students possibly bring him down?

Gradually, students reported to me there was blood shed in Taipei as I had cautioned them earlier. I noticed multiple absences, those students neglecting course work. Those strange faces came back frustrated, demanding undeserved grades for participating in political action. They displayed disruptive behavior to threaten teachers and classmates. I was incensed.

I told them, my own experience as a student participating in political action during the Cultural Revolution had caused the death of an innocent teacher. (Subsequently, millions of innocent people were persecuted, tortured, jailed and died. Plenty of history books in the library could teach them the bloody lessons if they wished to know.) Later in my life, I realized the value of a teacher. Without the many teachers who gave me knowledge, wisdom, and guidance in my life, work and career, I couldn't have made it. If my

4

students wanted to go into the streets, demonstrating, participating in politics beyond their knowledge and comprehension, and be used by politicians and terrorists, I would stop teaching, because I was not prepared to go through another "Cultural Revolution."

It was not hard to remind the students in Taiwan about the value of a teacher, as they grew up in a traditional Chinese society, where teachers were still respected. Some of them had tears in their eyes. For those students, I felt I ought to tell my stories. That is why after the "Overture," the Chapter begins on "August 18, 1966," instead of my childhood memories and my family background, as might be expected. The truth was, in 1966, I really did not know much of my family history as I learned in recent years. That will be the material for the next book.

The "Overture" was written in 1995. It stands as a "Preface" of sort here, to establish the voice of the author, identify the subject, and create the author's relationship with her audience. The narrator is a college professor, a modern woman in the West. She teaches American Literature and Multiethnic Literature in English classes. Her voice is distanced, mute and ironic. In her mind, Toni Morrison's Sula embodies a universal human condition for many "Bests" coming from Asia to America. She is thinking and questioning the value of a modern education, what education is and is about throughout the book.

At present, the student demonstration in Taiwan has escalated to violence and even suicide. It is hard to believe youthful activists would threw away their precious lives like suicide bombers. The media and "counselors" might have their modern theory of interpretations—depression, repression, anxiety, peer pressure. Parents are helpless and panic. I believe if they go to the library and read books, they won't be depressed. I wish this book will reach those innocent students, confused and alienated amidst chaos and violence, and their parents who wish to protect them. While I tell a "success story"of a good student, who went to college in America, I wish to share with them all the tragic lessons from the "Education" of Jennie Wang.

Summer 2015

CHAPTER 1

OVERTURE

That night J came home she had just taught Toni Morrison's *Sula* in a summer course "Contemporary Fiction" in a college near Albany, New York. The intense love and bond between the two women, Sula and Nel, growing up girlfriends in the isolated "Bottom" of Medallion, touched her probably more deeply than her students. The students, regardless of their diverse background, took Morrison's heroine, a black woman growing up in 1920s and 1930s, as though she were their peer. They had no problem understanding Sula, a modern woman, who went to college, wandered all over the white world in Nashville, Detroit, New Orleans, New York, Philadelphia, Macon, and San Diego. . . a free spirit, only to return home ten years later to break the marriage of her best friend. "And you didn't love me enough to leave him alone," Nel said. Sula, the modern woman, has every ready answer: "If we were such good friends, how come you couldn't get over it?" Such good friends, such good friends . . . She was still chewing that question, when the phone rang.

"I am coming to New York." It was Klever, long distance from Hong Kong. "Best got admitted to a good high school in Boston. She wants to prepare for MIT. I'm bringing her over." What a joy! Mother's dream, father's pride--the top student in a top school, the "Number One" girl! Best was always "Number One" in school, she went to the best private school in Hong Kong, where English was her first language, French by choice her second. Cantonese, the regional dialect she spoke in the streets of Hong Kong, she took as her "native tongue," while Mandarin, or "the common language" taught in school, that she could "sort of get by." To Best, Chinese was only the language of her parents. Her mother had prepared her for a Western education, for Europe and America, for the modern world. Klever wasn't wealthy, but she wanted her daughter to have the best education—something she herself missed when she was her age. . .

Twelve years had gone by, Klever and J had not seen each other, though they kept in touch once or twice a year, now and then a picture, but always a Christmas card. The day Klever left for Hong Kong, Best in her arms, was the day J got her student visa to America. "Come abroad soon," Klever said. They kissed each other good-bye at the Shanghai Airport. Drawing her even closer, Klever whispered into her ear: "Get the hell out of here." Yes, J did have the good fortune to get out of China soon after. Following Klever's departure, J left Shanghai, only drifted farther away.

She came abroad to study Modernism and Modern Literature. Literature wasn't a hard subject for her. Literary language, bookish English, British English had been her "native tongue." Growing up in Shanghai, she had been trained by teachers who were educated in Europe, and who wrote English prose in the style of Thomas Hardy. She had read a lot, read together with Klever. It was Klever who first opened her eyes to the Western world, Western literature, and Western style. During those "underground" years when they were out of school, Klever and her friends, some professors' daughters and college age "big brothers," had secret access to the books, books stolen from burned public libraries and confiscated from private collections, circulating underground all over Shanghai.

Klever shared with her novels, books of philosophy and poetry. They read Pushkin, Lermontov, Shelley, Tolstoy, Roman Roland, Balzac, Goethe, Dickens, Dreiser, the Brontes, Thackeray, Hardy, Hazlitt, Galsworthy, Maugham, Jack London, and many more. Because the books were in high demand, they often had to finish reading several books in a week. Not infrequently she'd devour a big volume overnight, which meant, she had to pull a light into the closet and sleep there, not to disturb her mother.

Her mother at that time "worked in the fields," undergoing political persecution, not because of any wrong-doings herself, but because of "ancestral sins." Her mother, unfortunately, came from a "sinful" family of compradors, bankers and real estate owners--

the wealthy class before 1949. The Red Guards had taken away almost everything from their house including her watch, bicycle, jewelry and birthday gifts. So it goes. Books became her jewelry. She read every book she could lay hands on. But she had never read Joyce, Conrad, T. S. Eliot, or James until she came to college in this country.

An expatriate in the modern world, free to enjoy modern freedom, individual liberty, she fell in love with Henry James' novels. She loved *The Ambassadors* with its impressionistic landscape on the Parisian lake. San Francisco was Paris to her. She was dazzled by the strange shapes of Modern architecture, the colorful Spanish houses in residential areas, and the picaresque street scenes. Breathing the fresh air from the seaside, near Sea Cliff, for the first time in her life she was free from political movements, free from government control, free from family and parents, free from her "ancestral sins." Here life is what one can make for oneself. "Live all you can, it's a mistake not to."

How often she wished she could have shared those books with Klever! When her parents were going through a divorce, she asked Klever, how a child might live without the hell of parents. Klever's parents left her for Hong Kong when she's only five. "Don't you worry," Klever assured her, "they'll give you enough pocket money, and you'll be free without them." When she was ten, and Klever twelve, Klever took her to movies, all foreign movies, Richard III, The Idiot, The Wanderer. . . Klever could repeat the stories, and memorize all the names of the characters, actors and actresses, foreign names, which she couldn't. When J was thirteen and Klever fifteen, they both got "wheels"—bicycles, a luxury for girls of their age. They used to ride into the countryside just by themselves to explore "Nature."

After all, they were city girls. They knew every fancy store in town. They would spend their afternoons loitering through every busy street of Shanghai, window shopping, or exploring good restaurants. Like most Shanghai girls, they liked pretty dresses. Unlike many Shanghai women, they never went after fashion. Fashion came after them. Klever used to wear whatever her parents sent from Hong Kong, and J had to use some of her mother's clothes made before 1966 that her mother couldn't wear to work anymore, anything that looked fancy would be criticized as "bourgeois." So together they looked "modern," or "Western," in the fashionable streets of Shanghai. Sometimes they went to visit friends, playing cards, not Mahjong. Mahjong was old fashioned. Bridge was in vogue then. Sometimes they went to movie or theater for drama, not opera. Opera, too, was old fashioned. J used to go to opera with her father, all kinds of opera—Shaoxing Opera, Suzhou Pintan (Ballad), Peking Opera, where she learned the best of classical Chinese. Klever never liked opera, she couldn't stand the high pitch of regional dialects.

Often the two girls would come home late, around midnight. No one in the house ever bothered. Grandmas, uncles, nannies trusted that they were good girls. The Chinese believed that "those who read books know manners." The books educated the two girls and taught them how to behave themselves. They were "by nature" good, not in a vulgar sense of being "well-bred from respectable family," but in a blessed way, they never lacked self-discipline and self-esteem. Manners they seemed to be born with; lies they had never known any. They were polite to the elders and modest before poor neighbors. Grace and courtesy were part of their sweet nature. Happily they were above girlish virtues that others had to be taught by parents.

They were not "ladies," but tomboys. Both excellent athletes, they played basketball for their respective schools they attended. Sometimes they met in a District championship, she always admired Klever. She admired Klever's graceful jump and beautiful touch. In school, they weren't really hardworking, but they never failed to maintain decent records. J was the so called "Number One" girl, way ahead of three hundreds of her peers. Klever was also a top student. Even the teachers let them go by themselves, respecting their intelligence as well as their independence.

Then came the long nightmare when the schools were shut down. "Well, to hell with it," Klever said, "we'll educate ourselves. Great people educate themselves." So they continued their own education at home. Klever played violin; J practised calligraphy. Klever took interest in photography; J studied economics and world history. English was their common subject, they took lessons from private tutors, those "returned students" from England and

Germany. Though they chose different masters, they helped each other to learn, never competed, one was never jealous of the other's accomplishments. Klever had a knack of learning foreign languages, she could spell every word precisely once she saw it. Amazing memory.

No wonder she could pick up Japanese quickly when she first arrived in Hong Kong and had to work for a Japanese company. Within a few years she had learned enough from the Japanese to start her own business. Now she was fluent in French, trading with some French and Italian companies. She knew that life in Hong Kong wasn't easy for Klever. But as though watching Klever playing basketball from a distance, she never doubted for a moment that others might fail, Klever would make it.

"How are you doing in Hong Kong?" She asked Klever.

"Oh, busy busy. I have my own business, sell custom jewelry, you know."

She knew nothing about custom jewelry, didn't know what to say. So she changed the topic:

"Why do you want to send Best to attend high school here? And why Boston?"

"Well, most of her classmates applied to the three best known high schools on the East coast, two in Boston and one in New Jersey."

J got the picture of the type of prep schools that Klever was talking about. It happened that she had taught freshman writing at Cambridge the year before. She had some idea of the kind of education in Boston prep schools. There were rich boys and girls from India, Taiwan, Mexico, South Africa, Canada, boarding in those expansive prep schools. There the English classes were still teaching Milton and Hawthorne, and the students were still writing essays to prove that "Man's sin was caused by the sin of Woman." They came here to receive an "American education," yet they only learned how to put up with the punishment by the puritans and share the guilt of white "ancestral sins." She doubted those were the "best" schools by her own standard.

"How much will you have to pay, Klever?"

"Around twenty-thousand a year."

"Twenty-thousand! That's a lot. I paid nine thousand a year for my Master's in 1984. I paid with the money I had made from waiting tables, you know, in Auntie Cecilia's restaurant."

"Yes, I know, I know it was hard for you those years when you first came abroad, wasn't it? I couldn't imagine that your mom and dad thinking of you waiting tables."

"Well, it wasn't too bad. I had a good time there. Auntie Cecilia was fond of me, although she thought it's silly of me to want a Ph.D. She was a writer in Hong Kong herself, you know."

"I don't know any writers in Hong Kong, J. Anyhow, we are the unfortunate ones, you and I, we had to make it for ourselves. Best is fortunate just as now I have been doing well for the last two years. Otherwise I couldn't afford it."

She couldn't understand why Klever would want to spend her hard-earned money this way. She thought she might want to warn K for what she was getting into.

"Are you sure the high school education is better here than that in Hong Kong? It might be better for Best to finish her high school in Hong Kong, then come here for college later."

"I wish she could have waited. The kids in her school are all from rich rich family, and most of them go to America, Canada, or England for high school. So she wanted to go, too. I couldn't deny Best the kind of opportunity the other kids have. What they have I have always managed to let Best have it too."

"Did we have what the other kids had, Klever? Mom and Daddy? Aren't we good enough for what we are today?"

"Yes, we are good enough because we knew who we were when we grew up. But who are we now, J? We are nobody here in Hong Kong."

"I see. I know Hong Kong is a pretty exclusive and snobbish society, isn't it?"

"Oh, yes. We are outsiders here. Aliens from the mainland. We don't have family names, social connections, school ties, friends we grew up with, as others do, so we have to do the best for our children. Well, I let Best talk to you."

"Hi, Best."

"Hi, Auntie J."

"I am glad you got admitted to a good school in Boston. You must be very intelligent, like your mother. I hope you'll like America, like your school."

"I am admitted to all the three schools I applied. But Mom and Dad want me to go to that girl's school, which is not the best of the three."

"Do you like that school well enough yourself?"

"I don't know. I must say that school is lucky to have me."

The girl's immodesty did not surprise her at all. She was rather pleased with Best's confidence and honesty. Like mother, like daughter, she thought.

"What do you want to study in America?" She was on the point of saying to Best: "You could study Literature and read all the books you don't have in Hong Kong once you come here. Your Mom and I loved Literature so much when we were your age, and you can make your mom's dream come true." But what she heard from Best was:

"Chemistry."

"Chemistry?! Why not Literature?"

"No way." Best's voice sounded just like an American teenager. "I hate English."

Klever's daughter would hate English! And growing up in British Hong Kong! She couldn't believe her ears. It was a shock more than a surprise. The picture she had envisioned of the mother in her daughter shattered instantly. She wished she could ask her: "Then why do you want to study in America where everything is taught in English?" She expected K's daughter must have a ready answer to such a question. She wanted to know. So she proceeded to get a picture of her knowledge of English.

"What do you read in English?"

"Shakespeare and Bronte."

"Which Bronte?"

"*Jane Eyre.*"

"Why do you hate English?"

"'cause. . . 'cause it's boring."

Before J could discuss this with her further, Klever at the other end took over the phone and explained protectively: "Her English is all right. She's got all straight As in English. If you want to know, she is more like you than like me. She likes books. But I don't want her to become a bookworm like you, in the end cannot make good money and cannot get a good job. She will get a degree first, and then a well-paid job in business or industry. That's what we have in mind."

"Sure she'll get a degree, sure she'll get a well-paid job, here in America. That's not hard, for a girl as talented as your daughter, Klever. For most Chinese in America, it's probably the easiest thing to do here. But are you sure if that's the best for her, that will make her happy, and make you happy, and ultimately happy? Do you hear what I say? You'd better come here and live here and see for yourself before you send a teenage girl all by herself to grow up in this country."

"I cannot stay in the States for long. I have to come back. Can't get away from business." She could sense that Klever was disappointed with her and a bit unhappy. But it was Klever who asked: "Are you happy with what you are doing there?"

For a moment she failed to answer Klever's question, though she trusted that Klever meant well. Then she decided to give it a try:

"Well, I suppose I am happy with the books, some of the books we read together, do you remember that book *Gone With the Wind*? 'Tomorrow is another day'?"

This time Klever failed to reply directly. "Well, well, that's a long time ago. '*Gone with the Wind*,' indeed. I don't have the time to read those books now. The happiest moment in my life now, J, is at night when I look out of my window, I can see across the water, across the bay, 'Up the Sea.' I'll see you in New York."

"Up the Sea" in Chinese stands for "Shanghai," their hometown, their birthplace. She closed her eyes in a vain effort to recapitulate the pictures of that city. From Lake Erie she couldn't see "Up the Sea," as Klever still could, across the Pearl River. Migrating from the West coast to the East coast, she has drifted even further away from the Pacific, the water that flew from East to West, and the air that blew her over. She had come to see the Atlantic, thought that she might go to Europe someday. But now she feared to cross the ocean once more. Distance did make difference; it weighed. Every step one took determined one's destiny.

Even though the rains and storms during the ten years of Cultural Revolution had diminished and disappeared at the back of her mind, she knew if she looked back, she wouldn't see what she wished to see--her grandmas, her uncles, her old nannies, her playmates, and her playgrounds. Klever was not there anymore. "What one loses one loses." What one gained, the opportunity of coming abroad, for instance, one gained by a loss that one even didn't know it was a loss, and even years later, still couldn't recognize.

It took fifteen years of life experience abroad to understand the double irony of James' art. She thought of that James' novel *The Portrait of a Lady*. What she didn't understand as an undergraduate she began to understand now, she could understand what her professors didn't, or couldn't, explain satisfactorily--the ending of that novel, the question why Isabella Archer, an immigrant woman, chose not to come home to Albany, New York, but "took her wandering feet" back to Rome. Home is where one makes for oneself.

Between Rome and Shanghai, New York was only a middle ground, Whitman's "Passage to India," if only one would look the other way around. She opened her eyes, and she could see now the rising skyscrapers, neon lights, highways, and new bridges, there "Up the Sea." She could imagine its thrill, its excitement, its prosperity. But for her it was the thrill of love and death in "The Jolly Corner." Was Shanghai to become another New York? Or another Hong Kong? Then the coming of Best and Best's generation might bring home closer. A home that was not home any more.

She thought of Sula, who came from a place called "the Bottom," quite a different world, a different culture, as one could imagine, from that in Shanghai, "Up the Sea." But tonight after Klever's phone call from Hong Kong, she was lost in her thoughts wondering what it was that made her feel ever so close to Sula, this modern woman who died on the National Suicide Day. She smiled a bitter smile, putting down a quiz question for her students to answer: "How do you interpret Morrison's evocation in the opening chapter of the book: 'The heavy trees that sheltered the shacks up in the Bottom were wonderful to see'?"

CHAPTER 2

AUGUST 18, 1966

It all started on August 18, 1966, a dark, rainy night, still summer, but chilly in the rain, the students marching in the streets. On that day, Chairman Mao viewed the parade of Red Guards on Tiananmen Square. That was in Beijing. In Shanghai, it was raining and chilly, August 18, school had not started yet. Normally school starts September 1st, but it never started that year, not until years later.

Indeed, it was chilly and cold for a summer day, J was shivering in the rain. When she eventually got home, it already passed midnight. PoPo had to feed her with hot boiled, fresh ginger soup, to take the chill and the wetness out of her body. PoPo had tears in her eyes, was glad to see her back. She was so worried that J might be mugged or trampled in the streets. How could a girl go to school in the afternoon, did not come back till past midnight! There were no cell phones then!

In the afternoon, she was called to come to school, to join the lines of student parade, already gathered in the school courtyard. Shanghai No. 2 Girls' School was a large middle school, including both junior and senior high, with a student body and faculty about two thousand people. A brief announcement was made that middle school students in Beijing were gathered on Tiananmen Square, to see Chairman Mao; therefore, all middle school students in Shanghai must be gathered to march towards the People's Square, to show support, or pay a tribute. No one knew what to expect there and then, or the days, months, and years in store. No one knew that was the end of school for all.

Not till the next day when she read the newspapers did she learn what was going on the day before. Chairman Mao had made an appearance on the Tiananmen Square, red ban on his right arm, waving to thousands of Red Guards, mostly high school and college students in Beijing. Mao honored the Red Guards as the rightful revolutionary force, encouraged them to challenge the status quo, the education system, social values and hierarchal power at every level. It was politically correct to rebel against the authorities, Mao said, "造反有理"! So it goes.

Not until years later did she understand what Mao meant for the students then. Not until years late did she witness the aftermath of that student movement, what it meant for the students to go into the streets, and how the political movement arrested the growth of their minds, and affected the common destination of "The 60s' generation." So it goes.

Not until after she came to American Universities through course work, research and study, did she learn the far-reaching impact of student demonstration, East and West, worldwide, the student movement in the 1960s; only that in China succeeded with seizing government power. What she experienced as "Red Terror," in the white world was "heroism." So it goes.

One way or another, it was that historic moment that ended her school education in China, after the first year of junior high (7th grade). School was closed for the next two years; as a matter of fact, for her generation, ten years after. No class, no instruction, no school, youngsters were left in the streets, smoking, playing crickets, or idle at home.

At school, the Red Guards held political meetings to torture teachers, beat them, cut their hair off, post big letter posters all over place from classroom to teachers' houses. Then without teachers and classroom instruction, they all graduated on time—the 1966 junior high and senior high, the 1967 junior high and senior high, and the 1968 junior high and senior high—all graduated on time, no one left behind.

Upon graduation, the majority of the students were assigned to go to the countryside, to settle down in remote villages and deep mountains, in every corner of China. Another student movement was under way. It was called "Go up to the Mountains and Settle down in the Countryside." Mao wanted them "to be reeducated by the Peasants." Mao was a great poet.

The railway stations were packed, train after train, day and night, thousands of young people, junior and senior high school graduates, leaving home, leaving their parents, siblings, relatives and friends, who were seeing them off. Many people bursted in tears, crying, sobbing, wailing, like at funeral scenes, as trains after trains, one by one, honked away. Those assigned to go to the North to be "planted" on military farms wore military uniforms and heavy padded hats. So it goes.

In her memory, that cold, dark, chilly night in the rain, students marching in the streets, marked the onset of dictatorship, mob violence, nihilism, chaos, ignorance, and a decade of nightmare thereafter... That night in the streets, she did not know, a "Revolution" was coming, "the Big Cultural Revolution," which would last so many years. She couldn't remember how old she was, because life did not make any more sense for her age since then.

Overnight, she had to be responsible, bear the historical burden of her family's class origin for the past hundred years, face the present ordeal that her mother, all relatives, and herself had to go through under the Red Terror, take over housekeeping and worry about the survival of her family, protect them in a hostile social environment, and play the role of mother to her five year old brother, Jimmy, taking him to hospital, attending parents' meetings; that were her inescapable duties for the next ten years. So it goes.

The People's Square was situated in the center of the city, by The People's Park, formerly The Horse Racing Court, in The Bund District. From her school, which was located in the western part of the city, formerly the French Concession, in Xuhui District, it was some distance to reach The People's Square, half an hour by bus, at least an hour or two to walk.

Yet, they did not have to walk far, they never did. They never reached the People's Square. Only a few blocks out of the school gate, the march was stopped. The streets were held up, with lines of students pouring into the cross roads from other schools—the Shanghai No. 51 School, the South Sea School, the South Sea Model School, the Turn Bright School, the Huaihai School ... Down the road, the schools in the Luhui District already marched their students to Huaihai Rd.—the road in between the city center and the West End. Students stopped there, occupied the crossroads, stopped the marching of other students coming from the Xuhui District.

Fortunately, the lines of Shanghai No. 2 Girls' School were stopped on a fancy street, Shanxi Rd., a couple of blocks from Huaihai Rd., where there were fancy bakeries and candy stores. Some "brave souls" began to sneak in and out of the lines to buy candies and cookies, feed themselves. J wouldn't dare, being well disciplined, a good student.

Good or bad, all got stuck there hour after hour. After dark, the rain ruthlessly fell. Though under the impressionistic, heavy French maple trees, leafy in August, the girls still got wet, their clothes were dripping. J was shivering, kept wiping away the water in her face and from the hair. By six o'clock, dinner time, most students grew hungry. The school administration managed to pass out some plain steamed buns, while they were still standstill in line shoulder by shoulder, crowded, hardly moved a couple of blocks. There was still no hope to go forward after it passed 7:00pm, 8:00pm, 9:00pm, 10:00pm, and 11:00pm. Like most of her peers, at first, she was anxious and impatient. After 8pm, she got bored, and felt dreary. She did not like those steamed buns, Northern style, not the kind of food she had at home, so she passed her bun to the girl next in line.

Then came two girls, well dressed and friendly. They handed her some chocolates and shortbreads, without saying a word, left her with a knowing smile, like angels. Their smiles she always remembered, as they retreated into the darkness among the crowds, "Apparition of these faces in the crowd/ Petals on a wet black bough." They must have stolen out from their line, a couple of blocks ahead of where her class was standstill, to approach her, and make friends. How kind, how sweet of them, she was touched.

These two angels were not from her class. She knew them, but had never spoken to them before. They were top students in their class, Class No. 4. Hers was No. 5. They were on the Dean's Honor List at the end of last school year, distinguished across board of the six classes of the same grade, the first grade in junior high. As there were at least about fifty students in each class, "top students" were those above three hundreds of peers.

J had noticed them in another parade in the spring that year at the Shanghai Airport. The Romania Head of the State, 齐奥塞思库 (Nicolae Ceauşescu), who later was beheaded in a mob violence in his own country, came to Shanghai for a visit. Shanghai No. 2 Girls' School was honored to send a group of students to go to the airport to join the welcome ceremony, waving flowers and dancing in a parade. The opportunity was not for everyone though, only the good students, well behaved, also good looking and well-dressed, were selected to go to the ceremony.

Yes, she recalled, these two angels were there, one of them was wearing a Scottish wool skirt, that looked imported from Hong Kong; and the other was in a mini skirt. How pretty! J admired them for their courage, or boldness, whether it was confidence or naivety she couldn't tell. She herself never dared to wear anything fancy to go to school, as anything fancy would be judged by her peers as "bourgeois." She might get beaten up or spat upon. She was used to that kind of abuse when she was in grammar school. Girls or women were taught to be thrifty and simple (艰苦朴素). Simplicity was valued as virtue itself. Nobody would care, or dare to brag about "brand name" purses or shoes those days. Nobody even knew those brand names from the West.

Not until a week or two later, did she get to know these two angels personally. They called upon her at home. Bellring, the one in Scottish wool skirt, carried a heavy leather bag, imparted to her what happened to her family. The Red Guards had already "visited," searched her house, took away every valuable they could

A fancy bakery on Huaihai Rd. 1962.

lay hands on. Her parents were dragged out into the streets wearing tall paper caps (戴高帽子游街), to be humiliated, attacked and beaten in public. Bellring escaped from home.

Olympia, the girl in a mini skirt at the airport parade, was a school basketball player, a tomboy sort of a tall girl. Brave and protective, she tried to comfort Bellring. They were planning a trip to go away. They came to give J a friendly warning of the "house searching movement" approaching, from Beijing to Shanghai. They also told her that the day before, their friend Pinnacle, another top student in Class No. 3, went home only to find the Red Guards already occupied their big Western style mansion, her aging parents were kneeling in the front lawn, forced to plea guilty, hair already shaved by the Red Guards, faces covered with bruises, having been beaten up. Pinnacle tried to reason with the Red Guards, they smashed her in the face, her glasses broken into pieces. "Pinnacle needs another pair of glasses now, but does not know where to get them these days," Bellring said sympathetically. J could recall Pinnacle's stylish frame in school. Of course, nowhere could she get another pair as stylish as the one she used to have. Her parents couldn't leave the house.

J thanked Bellring and Olympia again for the goodies they passed to her the other night. By then she knew why they chose to be nice to her and befriend her—they took her as their kind. Shanghai No. 2 Girls' School was a top high school, with an average of 85% graduates annually admitted to universities. Considering the admission policy then, which prioritized "the family factors," the class background of the students; and which strictly excluded students from the former ruling class, counter-revolutionary and wealthy family, one would imagine, the majority of students must have come from government favored, privileged or proletariat family.

Yet, the school, being located in a wealthy district at the West End of the city, the former French Concession, where the old residents were upper class people before the Revolution, and the new were mostly high class cadres, educated professionals and celebrities, actually housed a student body more elitist than proletariat—a majority of cadres' children, some from the educated family, famous medical doctors, professors, celebrities, actors and actresses; and about half from ordinary family.

Remarkably, only a handful of girls from family of the former propertied class were admitted for their superior scholastic aptitude, teachers' recommendations, and high scores from the citywide entrance examination. Among the over three hundred students of the first year junior admitted in 1965, there were only about four or five of them, even less in previous years. In American language, they were the "minority" students.

"In school, they call us 'Black Puppets' now," Bellring candidly told her, without panic, or self pity. Later, J learned from Pinnacle that Bellring came from a family of a big name, the Guo's. Her grandfather was a very successful business man, owned large estates and businesses overseas, in Hong Kong, South Asia, Latin America and North America. Originally from Canton, he had moved abroad, immigrated to America, currently lived with his many children from several wives.

Bellring's father was his eldest son, handsome, gentle, and well-educated. He married a woman of his heart's desire—

Bellring's mother, beautiful and intelligent. She did not enjoy the social life in Hong Kong, where they lived. Instead of emigrating to Latin America to join her husband's extended family overseas, she wanted to return to China. So Bellring's father took his whole family, three school age children, one son and two daughters, left Hong Kong against his parents' wish, first went to his wife's hometown in Yunnan, soon came back to Shanghai, lived in the house his parents had left. That was in 1958. Only once in a blue moon any propertied man would make such a choice. So it goes.

Olympia's family also had a Western style house all to themselves. Her maternal grandfather was a modernist architect, educated in England. He bought the house in Shanghai in 1930s for one of his wives. This wife gave him three sons and one beautiful daughter—Olympia's mother. He did not take the family with him when he emigrated to England in late1940s. Olympia's own father, a medical doctor, was the son of a Minister of the Supreme Court under the former regime. After its downfall, all his brothers in the military followed his father to Taiwan. He alone stayed with his wife, three sons and one daughter, Olympia, a happy family. By 1955, he was arrested and put into jail not for what he did, but for who he was. He was jailed for thirty years. So it goes.

Olympia's mother remarried. This time, she married a son from working class family. Olympia's stepfather worked in a factory. When the Cultural Revolution came, he joined the "rebels," wore "Red Guards" band on his arm, very macho. When he came home, found his own house was searched by the Red Guards, who stayed for a week long, day and night, torturing his mother-in-law, three brothers-in-law and their wives, at least, he managed to protect his own wife and five children.

J decided not to go to school. Olympia was not afraid. She was prepared to beat up anybody physically, if she were challenged. But school was soon closed. They had no school to go. In the streets, Olympia made friends with a group of truck drivers, who took her on rides, traveling long distance to other cities and small towns, having fun. So it goes.

Immediately after August 18, 1966, student body were instantly divided into "Rouge et Noir," either Red or Black. The Red ones must be born in and from the family of the proletariat—the workers, peasants, soldiers, and revolutionary cadres, if still in power. As many cadres were persecuted before and after August 1966, their children immediately lost their Red status. The "Black Puppets" were children born of parents who were landlords, affluent peasants before 1949, counter-revolutionaries, criminals, and politically "right wing," not self declared, but identified as "nonconformists" in the 1950s and 1960s.

Mao had a theory on the classification of the people in Chinese society, in which he identified the enemies and friends of his regime. The "bourgeoisie" in China (former industrialists, capitalists, property owners, business men) was left out from the black list, the category of "class enemies." Instead, the "bourgeoisie" was included in "the United Front," not in the Red category, its status was sort of in a gray area. Not until forty years later, did J get to know why the Communist government did not kill, instead patronized the "bourgeoisie" when they captured Shanghai in 1949. That was another story.

That original classification, so called "The Black Five Categories," constitutionally deprived these people of their citizen rights. After August 1966, "The Black Five Categories" were unconstitutionally added a "Black Sixth Category," to include the bourgeoisie (the propertied class before 1956). Only in a couple of months, the black list was extended to "Nine Categories," targeting "the traditionalists," "the revisionists," "the reactionary academic authorities" (university professors), soon rapidly, extended to all celebrities—writers, actors and actresses, movie stars, and the like. These people were called "The Stinky Nine," which became the label of all well educated, intellectuals and performing artists. The whole intelligentsia as a class was overthrown by the Red Guards. So it goes.

The "Black Puppets" ten years later. J ((R).

The day of Bellring and Olympia's visit and friendly warning must have been between August 23 to August 31, 1966, because looting in the streets, personal attacks, and mob violence first started in Shanghai on August 23 in front of the Peace Temple, at West Nanjing Rd. and concurrently on Central Huaihai Rd., the two main streets in Shanghai. There the Red Guards stopped pedestrians wearing tight leg pants and pointed shoes (小包裤，尖头皮鞋), humiliated them in public, and burned their shoes.

The Red Guards house-searching movement in Shanghai immediately followed. It was on August 31, 1966, the Red Guards came to J's house for the first time "house searching," and they stayed for three long days and nights. A nightmare for everyone in the family and the neighbors as well.

It was in the middle of the day, her mother came home from work, escorted by over thirty people, wearing the Red Guards band on their arms. They came to J's house, which was only a three bedroom flat, on the second floor of a house in a lane on Wuyuan

Rd.. At that time in Shanghai, most family only had one room, two rooms were considered to be comfortable, three bedroom housing was a luxury. The Red Guards came in with her mom from work, and they were all her coworkers and colleagues, who must be born from Red family, the "Proletariat," as they were called. Those people took her mom home in the middle of a working day, because they wanted to search her house, for what she had. Some were out of sheer curiosity to see the interiors of her household.

They started house searching, cross-questioning everyone in the family, packing, and taking away as much as they could, that were their job. At first, they wanted "gold and green," (green was US dollar, which few had ever seen one bill after 1949.) At least, J had never seen one. Then they wanted jewelry—diamonds, jade, chains, earrings, pins, which J had never seen either. Then they wanted the silk, the furs, the blankets and clothes, even the spring mattress, which was considered a comfort luxury. Except for four bench chairs, a table, three beds, they took away all the furniture.

In the master bedroom, there was a large closet, built when J's family moved into this place only four years before, after her mother divorced her father and moved with her mother, two children, and her nanny PoPo, from another district of the city. Most of these trunks were left by J's grandma, who passed away two years before. What a blessing in disguise! She was a wealthy lady, born in a well established family in old Shanghai. After she passed away, J's mother inherited her title, therefore, classified as a "capitalist" at her work place.

In the closet, stored over thirty wooden trunks and leather suitcases. J never knew how many trunks in that closet, till the Red Guards counted and took them away. The leader of the Red Guards asked her mother what necessities she would like to have, her mother only begged them to leave the children enough clothes, which they agreed, and they did. As a result, for the next six or eight years, J still had over a dozen of wool sweaters to use. One of her girlfriends later counted for her, and called her "a girl of eighteen wool sweaters."

The second day after the Red Guards came to search the house, they took her mother out in the lane in a public space, put a pointed paper cap on her head, put her on stage—standing on a

J's Mom, 1966.

covered well, which was in the lane close by their house. They began to criticize her bourgeois family background and life style, showing some material objects that they found in the house, to justify their search, things that could be identified with the "Old Four" cultures: the feudal, the superstitious, the bourgeois, the revisionist cultural artifacts. There was a bright red wool carpet, for instance, the Red Guards asked what it was for. PoPo told them, traditionally it was to be thrown in front of the bride and bridegroom, when the new couple came to perform the ceremony, kouto to their parents and in-laws. The Red Guards identified it with the "traditional" and "feudal culture," must be displayed to educate the public. So it goes.

The Red Guards were to come to destroy the Old Four, but they did not burn the objects; instead, they took them away in their big trucks. What they displayed to the public, if she could recall, besides that red wool carpet, were Western style clothes, traditional embroidered gowns, trunks of silk gowns, Qi Pao, pairs of her mother's leather shoes, because the style was pointed (尖头皮鞋), and pants with tight legs. Those things looked modern, Hong Kong style; hence evidence of bourgeois life style. So it goes.

Then they put J on the stage, asking her to expose and criticize her mother's bourgeois values, how she was influenced by such values and life style, and now came to realize and reject such values. That was school language, J had no problem to make a "confession" of sort. Standing on the well, bowed her head, she confessed that her mother's bourgeois life style did have bad influence on her; for instance, her mother once took her to the largest beauty salon in Shanghai, had her hair permed.

"More," the Red Guards demanded, she recalled, when she was in grammar school, her mother had her hair cut in a style called the "duck's behind," different from other girls' hair style. (That was because she joined the District swimming team, her mother had her hair cut in an athletic style. When she went to school, she was followed by a group of urchins, calling her "duck's behind!" "duck's behind!" They spat on her.) So she made another confession, and soon got out of it, off the stage, and off the well. The Red Guards liked her, some were her mother's office mates. J used to go to office with her mother on some weekends, when her mother had extra work to do, J helped her stamp and stuff envelops; so they knew J was a good girl. They let her go. So it goes.

When the Red Guards put PoPo on stage, standing on the well, barefoot, it was a different story. The Red Guards wanted her to criticize J's mother for having exploited her for a life time as a servant in the house. To their surprise, PoPo started arguing with them, asking what crime her "young lady" had committed that they could torture her like this. She started asking them if J's mother had done anything wrong at work, or was unfriendly with her coworkers, that would cause them to search the house. If she committed any crime, did anything wrong, PoPo said, if her "young lady" did not behave well in society, they could tell her and she would educate her to behave herself. It was her responsibility. As far as she saw to it, she knew J's mother had never spoken one ill word of anyone, never hurt any one. In recent years, she was a model worker, the most efficient bookkeeper in her office, wasn't it, PoPo asked. Her young lady did not even take leave from work when her mother was dying, did she, PoPo asked. The Red Guards failed to answer her questions. They did not want to argue with her, and they couldn't touch her, because PoPo was classified as a "proletariat." As the Red Guards took her inside the house, PoPo kept arguing and protesting. . .

PoPo was her mother's nanny, brought her mother up. Then her mother married her father, PoPo came with her mother to live in her father's house. She raised J and her brother Jimmy. PoPo was really "the fire and hearth" in the family. When J's Grandma, her mother's mother, was young, PoPo was her companion. PoPo was a vegetarian. On PoPo's sixty birthday, Grandma gave a banquet party in Gongdelin (功德林), the only well known vegetarian restaurant in Shanghai. That was in 1959, hard times, the whole

PoPo, 1972.

country was undergoing "three years of natural calamities" (三年
自然灾害). Everywhere there was a shortage of food supply.

At the party, J's Grandma ordered everyone in the house call
her "PoPo," instead of "mama" from now on. "Mama" was the
address for nannies in Shanghai; whereas, "PoPo" was a respectful
address of grandma's generation. After Grandma passed away in
1964, PoPo was the only Grandma to J at home, because by then
her mother already divorced her father, left her father and J's
paternal grandma in the old house in another district of Shanghai.

J never got to see her paternal grandma much since they
moved out. She was a church going Christian. She hung a large
and heavy framed portrait of Jesus Christ on her small bedroom
wall behind her bed. She was a widow, tall and heavy, with lily feet.
She seldom fell ill. However, whenever she had a little ailment, she
panicked, moaning and crying. She was fearful of death. She was
always fearful of Death, as J recalled.

J was afraid of her. "Ar Niang," as she called her, was hot-
tempered. She was a passionate woman, assertive and self-
possessed. Sometimes she would argue with the servants in the
house. Once she argued with her sister-in-law, who came to visit

her from the countryside. She was mad at her, and threatened to throw her out of her house. The other Grandma offered money to appease them and send the relative home. "Ar Niang" did not even appreciate it. With her wealthy in-laws, "Ar Niang" would never give in an inch, or lower her head. She was always uptight and dignified. She did not have any sense of humility before wealth and distinction. In all family photos, she was always in the center.

While her son pursued ambitiously a "good life" with his wife, a college educated modern woman from an upper class family, "Ar Niang" remained to be "incorruptible." She refused to change her life style to be "modern" or "Westernized." She even preferred her own cooking to the much fancier family dinner served daily by servants. She chose to have her meals in her own bedroom, and eat at a small desk by herself.

"Ar Niang" used to take J to her church when she was little, put her on stage, singing with other children. J did not enjoy chorus singing. She did not like the people there. They were mean, ignorant and superstitious people. J liked to go to the Buddhist temple, where the kids had fun. Children were free to run around, watch fireworks, eat good food and fruits. J got to meet the relatives and their children, as the occasions of meetings were mostly family gatherings, birthdays and death days of some ancestors. Children had to learn courtesy to perform rituals, pay tribute to their family ancestors. The Buddhist classics were full of wisdom and mystery.

J's maternal grandma was a Buddhist. In addition to those family gatherings held in the Peace Temple or the Jade Buddha Temple, those large temples several times a year, when J had to be dressed to go, during summer time, she often liked to retreat into a small temple she donated to her master nun in the suburb of Shanghai. J was allowed to visit her when she stayed there. The nuns entertained them with seasonal fresh fruits and vegetables, fed J with stories, and showed her books of classics. Those nuns were courteous, learned, soft spoken, sweet souls. They had a peaceful good life inside the temple.

The vegetarian banquets were elegant, fanciful and tasty. At the feast, J was taught to taste and be able to tell the ingredients of the vegetarian fish, vegetarian duck, vegetarian goose, vegetarian chicken, etc., for instance, the vegetarian fish was made of potato and bean curd skin, the vegetarian chicken was hard bean curd stew; and the vegetarian goose was made of thousand layers of bean curd skin.

PoPo was a Buddhist too. She did not like school, couldn't even write her own names. J used to write letters for her to her husband, son, and in-laws at home in the village. She was a child bride. After her marriage, she gave birth to a son, who was about J's mother's age. She did not like to have sex with her husband, so she became a vegetarian, left her family, and came to work to support herself in Shanghai.

She could recite a couple of books of Buddhist classics from the beginning to the end, with the book open in front of her! J couldn't believe she could read and recite all those words, half Indian, half Chinese. So she tested her once, stopped her in the middle of her recitation, asking PoPo where it was in the book. PoPo pointed a finger on the page, and it was the right place! Another time, J turned back a few pages, when PoPo went to do something in the kitchen. When she came back, PoPo turned the pages back where it was, told J not to mess around. J could not believe her eyes. PoPo must be a Saint.

By the second day in the middle of night, passed 2:00 am, the Red Guards were still busy searching the house, taking the trunks out from the closet and opening them one after another in all three rooms. The house was lit all nights long. J went into the bathroom, saw her little baby brother calling her from the window of the building across the lane, where his kindergarten was, a teacher was with him at his side. That afternoon, J had sneaked out of the house, went to her brother's kindergarten to ask the teacher to let her brother stay there overnight, not to come home, because there was this house-searching situation going on at home. The teacher could see from the window across the lane facing their side. The kindergarten accepted kids who stayed there daily, as well as weekly, so there was company for her brother, a place to sleep, and be safe. The teacher was very nice to agree to let her brother Jimmy stay for a day or two.

Jimmy wouldn't go to bed. After midnight, he climbed to the window, to watch what happened to his mother and the house. The teacher, curious and sympathetic, watched with him too. "How's mom?" he asked J, he did not cry. "Go back sleep, you go back to bed," J ordered him. He slipped down off the window without crying. Maybe the five year old had already been taught by his teacher that under the circumstance, it was "politically incorrect" to cry for Mom.

By the third day, J couldn't stand the big mess in the house. She found an excuse to get out of the house. She told the Red Guards that she had to go to school. They agreed to let her go. J was prepared she might have to go through some self-criticism, or "confession," or be humiliated by those Red Guards. When she went to her classroom, to her surprise, the Red Guards were friendly and happy to see her. They were having a meeting, planning how to criticize their teacher, Teacher Wang. They were glad to see J come, because they needed to write an essay, listing all the wrongs of Teacher Wang, theoretically speaking, against Mao's education policy. J had written "best essays" in school, so they were glad to see her come to class, and asked for her help.

Teacher Wang was a woman with five children. Her husband was in jail. She belonged to the criminal class. The Red Guards named all the reasons why they did not like Teacher Wang. Some disliked her grading. Others disliked her goggle glasses, too thick, too many circles, her shabby, ugly appearance; and others for something she said or something she ate. J organized the material, theorized a bit, drafted the essay, and even wrote the calligraphy for the Red Guards to make big letter posters. Then she went home.

A week later, J's classmate, Currie, came to her house. Currie told her what happened after she left. With the big letter posters J had brushed, the Red Guards went to Teacher Wang's house, and posted them on her door. Teacher Wang lived in a former garage with her five little children in stricken poverty. There was not much to search about in her house. The Red Guards pulled her out into the lane, cut her hair off, zigzag, ordered her knell down, slapped her, tortured her, and humiliated her in front of her five little children, her neighbors and the Red Guards, who were all her students. Next morning, Teacher Wang was found dead in the garage. She had hung herself inside.

Though J did not go with the Red Guards to search Teacher Wang's house and persecute her, she felt guilty about writing the essay. She felt as though she had participated in a murder. She felt worse than seeing her mother tortured by the Red Guards, and watching the Red Guards taking away their furniture, blankets, clothes, furs, silk, silverware and household utensils. Trunks after trunks—thirty-six of them, the Red Guards counted. While they moved them out from their second floor flat of the house, and loaded on their trucks, they drove away with red flags and arm bands, singing revolutionary songs, and shouting slogans.

J never went back to her classroom, never wanted to see those Red Guards, who made her write the letter. She never participated in those political activities in school afterwards. She was disgusted. She did not know, who would know anyway, even those Red Guards did not know what they were doing. They did not know some of their own parents were soon to be purged, persecuted, and sent to prison. They did not know that from now on, there would be no teachers, no school, no class for them, till they "graduated" in 1968. Teacher Wang was the last teacher J had in school. So it goes.

CHAPTER 3

"STORE IN YOUR BRIAN!"

J's Birthday Wish

The next spring, 1967, J made a birthday wish, she would "complete her own education." Following the student demonstration, mob violence, looting and house-searching, persecution of thousands and thousands of intellectuals and professionals, all schools were closed down. No one knew when it would open.

It never opened. Three years later, one day in 1969, all the students of J's grade level found themselves graduated. J's grade ought to have graduated in 1968, so they were identified as the graduates of 1968, the last grade of the five grades above them. Those who had entered high school the earliest in 1960 might have received some education before the Cultural Revolution. These six grades of graduates, the 1966, 1967 and 1968 junior high graduates and senior high graduates were later labelled in society as "The Old Three School Graduates" ("老三届"), a cynical label in status quo, acknowledging those "graduated without schooling."

On that graduation day in 1969, everyone received a diploma, which states, so and so graduated from Junior High. During the three years of Junior High (1965-1968), all students only received one year classroom instruction, had a few months of participation in political movement in 1966, the rest of the time were spent at home, left alone, uneducated.

J, as a good student in school, educated in Marxist, Leninist Theory and Mao's Thought, possibly could rationally understand the rhetoric, or the rationale of house searching, mob violence, personal attacks, and even the persecution of the "class enemies," including her families and relatives. These actions were justified by a theory. She did not know much about theories then. She knew that her families owned some real estate property before 1949, and "exploited" people. So the Red Guards came to take their assets away. Because her families and relatives belonged to a class which "exploited and oppressed" people before 1949, the Red Guards tortured them, "to avenge the oppressed people." Since J's first day of school, she was indoctrinated in such a theory.

In theory, she could take it for granted for all the personal attacks and personal disasters her family went through. She could even accept the deprivation, humility, and the stricken poverty her family had to face for the next decade. She could endure the hard times with forbearance, courage, transcendence and hope, hope for a correction of government policy, which was eventually realized in 1976.

What she could not understand, she couldn't put up with, and she definitely couldn't accept was the disruption of school education, when ignorance became the destiny of the young generation, and more than one generation. Since she entered public school at the age of seven, she was taught a good student must live up to Mao's expectation for children: "Study hard and make progress every day" (好好学习，天天向上). She had followed Mao's words, to be a good student, (who was not?!) self-consciously tried to make progress, and improve herself every day. She knew, there was no theory, classical, modern, or revolutionary, Chinese or Western, that could justify that young people did not need to go to school, study math and science, learn about society, people, history and humanity. Something was definitely wrong with the government policy.

So she made that birthday wish in 1967. She was determined, as she put down in her diary: *"I will not let the mistake of government policy stop my education! If school will never open, I will have to complete my own education one way or another, sooner or later, to the highest level attainable. No one shall stop me."*

Mao's Education Reform

A good student.

Mao had written on theories—实践论，矛盾论，辩证唯物论 (*On Practice, On Contradictions*, and *On Dialectic Materialism*). He even had an agenda for education reform before the Cultural Revolution had started. His presumption was that knowledge must be examined through practice in reality, like science, to prove whether it was true or false, valid or mere logical fallacy. Like Marxism and Leninism, the communist ideology was put into practice in social reality to be testified. The theory was tested by the revolutionaries, particularly in Mao's hands. It was modified when necessary, to adapt to the special condition and historical circumstances in rural China. In other words, theories have to prove true and effective in reality to be acceptable and convincing.

Marx and Lenin did not have much to teach about the post-revolutionary Chinese society, which was faced with the contamination of the West and especially in the cities, under the threat of "restoration" of Capitalism. ***It is easy to destroy an old world; it is not easy to construct a new world."*** This is one of the few quotations from Mao that J readily accepted, and always remembered, whenever she had to take a position between the old and the new. This might be the root of her conservatism, occasionally. She learned to look beyond a destructive action to what could possibly happen. Later she had a good attitude at work, not to criticize without finding constructive suggestions.

Yes, it is easier to fight a war than to maintain a revolutionary power and manage a new system, as no one had experience or rules to follow before. Mao was concerned about the education of the young generation—his revolutionary successors (革命接班人). He compared the young generation to "sunrise at eight or nine o'clock." Mao said to the youth: *"The world is ours as well as yours; but in the end, it is yours."* Mao started his guerrilla wars from the mountains and villages in rural China, where millions of peasants supported his revolutionary ideal. Mao was afraid that in easier circumstances, the young generation began to enjoy the luxuries in city life, and they tended to forget the revolutionary ideal, the welfare of the poor peasants in large part of China. Gradually, his successors might lose touch with the foundation of his power, the grassroots people, who supported his regime. In the city, bourgeois values and life style might change the identity and class consciousness of the young people. It would corrupt their revolutionary will (腐化堕落).

Class Struggle during Peaceful Transformation (和平过渡时期的阶级斗争)

In order to preserve the young generations' revolutionary spirit, their "Red Blood" inside and out, Mao proposed the concept of "class struggle during the period of peaceful transformation." Mao ascertained that under the socialist economic system, the propertied class, or the bourgeoisie, was eliminated, but socialist China was not yet a classless society. Until China reached the ideal state, class enemies still existed at home and abroad. Abroad, China was faced with nuclear arms race from the West, military conflicts on boarders north and south, the potential dangers of "Restoration" from pretenders in Taiwan, international coup d'eta, as happened in Eastern European countries, collaborated by right wing and underground counterrevolutionary forces in certain regions in China (里应外合). Therefore, class struggle must go on, at least, in the superstructure of culture and society (思想意识形态领域), beyond economic ownership.

During the Cold War period, Mao was informed that his enemies attempted a "conspiracy through peaceful penetration." They could and would bring down the Red regime without fighting a hot war, only a "cultural war." Through cultural penetration, advertising and promoting bourgeois values and life style, fashions, decadent music, songs and blues, the capitalist and imperialist power could easily corrupt the mind of the young, gradually, the young generation might lose their faith in revolution, and give up class struggle. Gradually, while the popular mind changes, the socialist system and the government power should deteriorate by itself.

Therefore, Mao insisted, class struggles still existed during "the period of peaceful transformation" in a socialist state, if not in the form of armed forces, but reflected in popular culture, in "the superstructure" of culture and society (上层建筑, 思想意识形态领域). Popular beliefs might change the value system in society and public consciousness, challenge orthodox socialist theory and ideology. A bourgeois social and ideological superstructure could and would bring down the socialist system by "peaceful conspiracy" (和平演变) in the hands of imperialists and capitalists, class enemies and their collaborators at home.

It was Mao's idea that the city people—college students, intellectuals, professionals, celebrities, as well as cadres and office workers—all need to be reeducated by the peasants (接受贫下中农的再教育), meaning they need to go down to the countryside periodically, live there and labor in the fields together with the peasants, to have a first hand experience of country life, to renew their revolutionary will. (That movement had started already in 1964, before the Cultural Revolution was well underway.)

Therefore, the education agenda for the 1960s' generation emphasized class consciousness and class struggle. Students were taught to "remember the bitterness (poverty and misery, exploitation and oppression) of the past, while tasting the sweetness of life at present." All the movies, drama, performing arts and books were centered on that theme (忆苦思甜，不忘阶级斗争).

Furthermore, Mao was determined that an education reform was necessary. Mao himself was a teacher. He studied at a teachers' college and worked in the library before he became a revolutionary. He was a voracious reader, an autodidactic, and an independent thinker. He distrusted the classics, the traditional authority of knowledge and the traditional way of learning. He even did not have much respect for Confucius, as most of his peers did. Instead, like most of the modernists in earlier 20th century, he believed in an alien God—Marxism and Leninism.

He was not necessarily the best student in school. However, he became the leader and teacher of all those educated under the traditional education system in China, or universities abroad. Now after he established his regime, he immediately and boldly abolished all classics and its traditional curriculum in education, as no one did in the history of China. In order "to build a new world," to build socialist China, he began to teach the people, especially the young generation, his revolutionary ideas, new beliefs and myths, an alien system of thought in theory and practice. He distrusted the old masters in traditional schools. He criticized the traditional system of knowledge. He encouraged the students to destroy the system of education, traditional curriculum and way of learning, such as reciting.

The Shanghai No. 2 Girls' School was one of the few pilot secondary schools benefited from the experiment of education reform in 1965, the first year and only year J was in school. The students were told that they must be ready to accept innovations in curriculum instruction. For example, instead of Algebra, which was traditionally taught the first year, they had to study two semesters of Geometry before they got to study Algebra.

Six principals were appointed to the School Board to work out an experimental curriculum for secondary education reform. One of the honorable Principals was Professor Su Buqing (苏步青), a distinguished Professor of Mathematics, on faculty at Fudan University. It might be his idea. The School Board trusted his expertise. Geometry before Algebra was put into practice immediately the first semester when J entered junior high. School ended after her first year. As a result, J never got to study Algebra. (Fifteen years later, J took Algebra as a sophomore, to fulfill the requirement of General Education at San Francisco State University, she received a C grade for the course. She must be too old for Algebra, or lack of high school prerequisite.)

The next year, at the onset of the Cultural Revolution, Professor Su Buqin was identified as an "anti-revolutionary academic authority" and targeted for criticism. He was exposed to public humiliation at Fudan University. Radical college students at Fudan cut his hair zigzag, beat him. He was terribly abused and tortured. He committed suicide immediately. So it goes.

The most challenging experiment of education reform was for the students to go down to the countryside to work in the fields. In the spring semester of 1966, all the students in school were assigned to go to the countryside in the suburb of Shanghai, to live there and labor in the fields. Each class took a period of two weeks in turn. The students from No.2 Girls' High were shuttled to a village in the suburb of Shanghai. They were put up in a dark cottage, about twelve of them in one room, without modern bathroom facility.

The next morning the whole class were sent to the rice patty fields, to plant rice seeds (稻田插秧). As the girls toiled through the muddy rice patties, they screamed at the sight of snakes and incests in the water (蜈蚣百脚). They soon began to catch the incests, escape from being bitten (蚊叮虫咬), or went to take care of the bites. In the end, some stayed planting in the fields with tears, others simply went ashore and sat on the narrow field paths to let time pass.

Another ordeal was that after three days, J found her bowel movement couldn't adjust to that old fashioned communal wooden toilet bowel, that sat in a corner at the end of their beds. Five days passed without normal function, her system revolted. She got sick. Some other girls had their problems too—skin rash, stomach ache, vomiting, red eye, fever, etc.; some kept crying. Though she did not cry, together with these "problem" girls, J was sent back home after a week.

Though it was too hard for the city girls to work in the rice fields, at least the idea was for them to learn what kind of work was involved to have rice on the table that they ate everyday, so that they would not forget but respect the peasants who planted it, and provided for the city people. The experience was not enjoyable, but valuable. How many students really benefitted from the experience in the fields, it was hard to tell, as they never reported back to class after they returned.

Personally, J recognized the truth that a good student in the classroom might not be a good "revolutionary successor." To be a good revolutionary successor to the Red regime, one must be capable of facing hardship and dealing with real life situations in the countryside as well as in the city. Obviously in the practice of physical labor, she fell behind of her class. Such self-knowledge turned out to be a blessing in disguise three years later, when Mao called all the graduates to go "up to the mountains and settle down in the countryside." J at least knew her own limit.

Housekeeping before Coming of Age

Whether she liked it or not, only a year later, J had to face hardship. She had to deal with poverty, emergencies and real life situations. She had to take on the responsibility of housekeeping, learn to do all kinds of housework, such as cooking, sewing, knitting, shopping and cleaning. Those "hands-on activities" might be called "Home Economics" in modern education.

Fortunately, the household was very simple. After three days and nights house-searching, the Red Guards finally drove away several trucks loaded with thirty-six trunks of "luxuries" and "四旧 物件" ("Old Four" material objects), things that could be identified with old, traditional, religious, or bourgeois values. They left J's family only the necessities, no chairs, but four benches and a square table for meals, beds without mattresses, and some clothes for four seasons.

From then on, J's single parent family of four—PoPo, J and her brother, headed by her mother, lived on her mother's salary of fifty-four RMB a month in stricken poverty. J's mother had divorced her father in 1960. He used to give them twenty RMB a month of alimony which, in PoPo's eye, was only enough to buy fruits for the kids. Now he stopped his alimony. The Red Guards searched his house too, took away all the valuables he had such as banknotes and jewelry. His salary of fifty RMB was only enough to support himself and the two mothers he had.

One day, a group of Red Guards came into his house. They were from Beijing, a terrorist group called "The United Actions" (联动). The Beijing United Actions Red Guards had a horrid, nihilist reputation in Shanghai, as they attacked people from house to house. When they came in, they would smash everything in the house, cut clothes into pieces, whip people with their leather belts. They rode away others' bicycles. When those terrorists came to the neighborhood, vulnerable family turned off their lights, shivering in darkness. So that name alone already scared J's father to death. They pushed him against the wall in his bedroom, took away his Rolex watch, expansive camera, semiconductor, all fancy items that they could play with. When J's father asked them for a receipt, they slapped him in the face. Fortunately, they did not whip him before they left in a hurry.

J's mother was going through all sorts of persecutions and tortures at work. Frequently beaten up by the Red Guards, she came home exhausted, sometimes with bruises all over her face. She told J what she went through during the day was exactly like what they saw in the movies of Fascist persecution of the Jews. The Red Guards threw her body against the wall. Most of the time she still had to stay late to write confession after confession overnight, to be turned in the next day. She had to report to the Red Guards either on Monday, Wednesday, Fridays, or on Tuesday, Thursday, Saturdays. People worked six days a week instead of five days at that time. Sometimes she would ask J to write for her, which J did week after week.

Under the circumstances, J became the housekeeper in the family, going to the vegetable market every morning, budgeting how to survive with the meager income at night, and taking some leftover clothes to exchange for cash in a state owned pawn shop. That pawn shop was located on Central Huaihai Rd.. After she got three or five RMB in exchange for a pair of old pants or a wool jacket, she would save that money to pay utilities.

She was nine years older than her brother Jimmy. When she was sixteen, he was only seven. J took upon herself the duty of half a mother. Whenever he had a fever, even at night, she had to put him on the back of her bike and took him to the hospital. She had to protect him from being bullied by other kids in the lane. After he entered grammar school, J was the one, instead of her mother, to attend the parents' meetings, because she would be better respected than their mother at such public meetings.

On Sundays, J would take him to the Bund to watch the ferry, sometimes took a ride for fun. More than once they saw bruised corpses floating on the river. People had thrown themselves into the Huangpu River the night or days before. Too many people died too soon, took their own lives too easy. J did not know how to explain to her brother, or protect him from the horrid sight they saw. So it goes.

"穷人的孩子早当家" ("Children from poor family serve as housekeepers before coming of age") was a well broadcasted line in a revolutionary model play of Peking opera, *The Red Lantern*, which was played on stage, broadcasted on radio during the Cultural Revolution, dominating the national stage for a decade. The heroine was a young adolescent girl, Steel Plum. She grew up in a single parent, revolutionaries' family, raised by her grandma. She had countless uncles, her father's comrades, come and go, busy with their underground tasks. She knew she had to keep secrets for them. Her father bid her to help her grandma with housekeeping —"Children from poor family are housekeepers before coming of age." Steel Plum was created as a role model for the 1960s generation. Ironically, J could very well relate to and identify with the role of that Red heroine.

PoPo no longer received pay from her mother, so she started looking for work outside of the family, to have some income. Once

PoPo found a full time job to wait on a woman after child birth. PoPo's ex-daughter-in-law, who lived in another city, Wuxi, wrote to J's mother saying that it was inappropriate for PoPo to take care of an infant baby at her age, and to work outside of the family. She would like to take PoPo back to live with her family. PoPo left, and J became the housekeeper in the family. So it goes.

PoPo's Admonition

Before she was to leave, PoPo encouraged J to keep reading and studying, learn as much as she could from books, definitely, to continue and complete her education as a lady. "Listen," PoPo told her: *"People can take away what you possess in the house, but they cannot take away what you possess in your mind. They cannot take away what you learned and stored in your brain. Yes, keep reading those books."*

PoPo's words must be true. Now some fifty years had passed, J had moved from place to place, no less than over forty times, left behind and let go of so many things, homes, furniture, clothes, jewelry, personal belongings, material objects, yet she could still recall PoPo's admonition as though it were yesterday, because she had listened to PoPo, and stored in her brain. Nobody, no circumstances could, or did, take that away.

PoPo's idea of a woman's education maybe came from J's Grandma, J's mother's mother. J's Grandma was born in 1900 in a well established family in Shanghai. They were business people. Her grandfather had built many houses on the Bund and in the British section. He was one of the few business people who could speak some English and help the foreigners deal with some transactions in real estates in Shanghai. He built a garden mansion in the center of the city for his family, where Grandma was born. In her childhood, she was sent to grammar school, but she did not like books, homework, and school. After grammar school, she refused to go to missionary school to learn English. She liked more

44

practical work, such as handcraft and management. Her grandmother was a capable and successful business woman, managing real-estates for her husband, had quite a reputation in Shanghai in the 19th century. J read it from an article Klever gave to her, published in 1990s. Grandma never told J anything about her family history.

Grandma herself must be a modern woman in her own ways. She resisted foot-binding. She did not care for pretty dress or fashion. By character, she was strong, willful, and self-centered. Indulged by her mother in her maidenhood, she refused to get married at the right age. After her mother passed away, she had passed the normal age of marriage. At her uncle's will, she married J's Grandfather, a widower with three children, two daughters and a son. Though he was only a few years of her senior, she did not have a happy marriage. Her independent and willful character failed to please and win the heart of her husband, a traditional scholar from a traditional family.

After she married into her husband's family, living among ladies from traditional aristocratic family, who were mostly versed in 琴棋书画 (harp, chess, calligraphy, and painting)—the four classical feminine art-crafts for women in traditional Chinese society, and who were born and raised for the company of traditional scholars and statesmen, knew how to talk, how to please, and socialize in society, she found herself inadequately educated. After she gave birth to a daughter, J's mother, she separated herself from her husband, and went back to live with her own family.

Her three daughters were all educated in missionary schools. All were admitted to universities in Shanghai in the 1940s. All studied Law. To the disappointment of their parents, only one daughter completed her college education. The other two dropped out of college, and got married following their own will. The one graduated from college, even had a job with the Central Bank, moved with the bank to New York.

Grandma was too preoccupied with herself to take care of her daughters' education. She sent J's mother to an American boarding school, and kept her there from her husband's visitation and custody. Grandma of course couldn't be happy with the outcome of missionary education. It failed at least in her family, not only with two of her three daughters, but also with her eldest son, Uncle Quixote. Uncle Quixote was educated all the way through St. John's in Shanghai to St. John's in New York. He came back an alcoholic, joined the communists!

Grandma must have been a British feminist of sort, serious about her economical and legal rights. Her father used to represent a British company in Shanghai, and pursued British life style, enjoyed automobiles, cruise and horse racing. After the Liberation, the new government issued a new marriage law in China. Grandma immediately asked a friend to draw papers and filed for divorce. Her husband was shocked. Who could imagine? He called J's mother to complain that an old lady over the age of fifty, especially after all her daughters were married, and grandchildren born, would ask for divorce from a marriage of thirty years?! Grandma meant what she said. It was not a threat. She did it anyway.

After the divorce, she had better control of her life, more time and energy to focus on her family and her various creative projects. For a while, she was focused on J's education, as J was the only grandchild she could lay hands on. J usually stayed in her bedroom after school and before going to bed.

"The girl is too articulate. Do not let her talk back," she warned J's parents.

"It is after Liberation now," J's mother replied, "we are all liberated, Mom."

"In a democracy," J's father added, "everyone can talk back."

In his heart, he was amused that his three year old daughter was able to talk back to adults. Grandma warned him, someday he would be sorry, and suffer from the consequence of his indulgence.

It was true, when his daughter grew up, he found she was too much to handle. J's mother, however, was never sorry for her daughter's ability to talk and talk back. She relied on her daughter to talk back to the Red Guards, the neighbors, the neighborhood committee, the local police station, her son's teachers, medical

J's mother (L) and her Aunt May Fourth (R) at YWCA in 1940s.

doctors, and the authorities. She found her daughter always had good reasons to talk back, and made herself right.

When J grew to five or six years old, her mother followed the idea of Grand-Aunt May Fourth in girl's education. Grand-Aunt May Fourth, Grandma's youngest sister, was a couple of years younger than J's mother. Her daughter Alice and J were same age, same grade. Alice was sent to a studio to take ballet lessons and play piano. J's mother took J to join Alice. J did not like ballet because it was painful to raise her legs on the rail in the ballet studio. J was not the type who could put up with modern "foot-binding."

After a couple of times, she was saved by her father. "Why ballet?" he blamed his wife; "you want your daughter to become a 'dancing girl'?" Though there were no more "dancing girls" after the Liberation, as Broadway was closed, it was true that before 1949, "dancing girls" were viewed as high class prostitutes in Chinese society. No decent family would accept a "dancing girl" for marriage. So J's mother had to stop sending her to the ballet studio. So it goes.

Grandma, on the other hand, was opposed to the practice of piano. "Why piano?" she asked. This time it was her turn to talk about "Liberation now." "It is after Liberation now, no more foreigners and no more Western cultures, please." She always had her own good ideas, creative and ingenious. "For musical instrument, let the girl play PiPa. Yes, the girl is hot tempered, red haired, and needs discipline. Let her practise calligraphy. That will give her some patience."

So she passed word to her ex-husband, to find a good tutor of PiPa and another one of calligraphy for J. Her ex-husband immediately followed her recommendations, and did what she wanted. He found J the best tutors, who were his friends. Then once a week, regularly, he would come to J's house on time, and take J to a tutor's house to learn to play PiPa and practise calligraphy.

J could never forget the little scene Grandpa made with her the first time they went. When they got off the tricycle, J offered money to pay the tricycle driver, because she was under the impression that Grandpa needed money. Grandpa had money in his pocket that day. He was terribly hurt, turned red. He told J, a child should not offer to pay for an adult. J looked down, was embarrassed and guilty. She felt so sorry for her Grandpa, and sorry for herself too. How insensitive she was! The old man wanted to have his dignity and self-respect in front of his grandchild. Strangely, that guilty feeling never left J whenever she thought of her Grandpa.

In practice, there were two different schools of PiPa. The school that accompanies ballad singing belongs to performing arts,

Alice (L) and J (R)

which J's grandpa's concubine played on stage. She was a successful singer of Suzhou Pintan. Even Grandma enjoyed her performance. Grandma often took J to the tea house where Po, as J called her, performed on stage sometimes, with a male partner, who played another musical instrument. Grandma definitely was not a jealous woman. She never blamed the concubine, never said a word bad about her. After her divorce, the two became friends. Po and one of her two sons sometimes came to visit Grandma. Grandma liked her son PangPang. He was a good student, went to medical school somewhere in the north, and became a surgeon. In 1965, he had an accident during surgery. The patient was the wife of a high officer in the military. With his unfavorable family background, he was punished severely. He was sentenced for fifteen years in prison. His newly wed wife divorced him. So it goes.

Grandpa obviously did not want J to learn performing arts. He took J to a nationally distinguished master of PiPa. His art belonged to the school of "national music" (国乐，大套琵琶). That school of PiPa

J and Grandma, 1958.

came from a classical tradition, pure music without singing. Under the tutorial of this master, J learned to play the high tunes of 阳春白雪 (*White Snow in Bright Spring*)，十面埋伏 (*Besieged in Ten Directions*) and 春江花月夜 (*A Night of Flowers and Moon Light*). These were national classics.

J's practice of PiPo lasted at least for a couple of years, till 1963. One day, the master suddenly left to go to Hong Kong. At first, his son, also a good musician, took over J's tutorials. Before long, the master got arrested at the border Customs House in Shenzhen. He was caught with a book manuscript, that he intended to carry out of the country, to be published abroad. His house was in chaos. J's mother told J not to go there anymore. Police might be there, it was dangerous. Less than a month or two, J's Grandpa was arrested too in Shanghai, being involved in his friend's case. There was a group of scholars caught writing books together, crying for freedom of speech. Grandpa died in jail without trial. J's mother did not go to see her father in the end. Grandma did not cry, she did not shed tears. So it goes.

Only a year or two later, in 1964, Grandma passed away. Six black limousines escorted her body to the funeral house. It was the neighbors who counted the number of vehicles, as they watched the big array of the moaning families coming out of the house in the lane. They counted the celebrities too, among the throng of relatives and friends. One of Grandma's brother-in-law was the son of a former vice-mayor in Shanghai. He was heard sobbing: "Sister! Sister! Why cannot you wait! I'll follow you, follow you, I do not want to live in this world any longer." He was a cadre, joined the communists before 1949, and worked underground in Shanghai. The following year, he was found having liver cancer and passed away indeed! Old ladies in the family blamed his wife: "Why would she let him say something poisonous like that?!" Others believed that he and Grandma were very fortunate to go before the Cultural Revolution came in 1966. PoPo said to J: "The breath between teeth could be poisonous. Words out of a mouth could kill a man."

J's mother did not know how to arrange the funeral as she had no experience before. Grandma's stepmother, who was six years younger than Grandma, was still alive. She and PoPo instructed J's mom step by step from the funeral house, through the seven weeks of memorial ceremony to the burial. Grandma was buried in the Shanghai Buddhist Cemetery.

When mob violence started in 1966, the Red Guards attacked the Buddhist Cemetery, and looted the tombs, Grandma's newly buried coffin was dug out. J's mother did not want to go to the cemetery to take care of the remains. PoPo went by herself to see the horrid aftermath in the cemetery. She came back cried and cried her eyes out. J's mother said there was nothing she could do about it. So it goes.

PoPo must have shared Grandma's wish to have J better educated than they had done with her mother, when she left her with the admonition: "Store in your brain! No one can take it from

Grandma's tomb in Shanghai
Buddhist Cemetery, 1965.

you." The two of them were really a pair of post-modern, post-colonial feminists.

Life in the Closet

Fortunately, immediately after the house-search movement in 1966, Klever discovered an underground library, books looted and stolen from scholars' studies, school libraries, or hidden and left over from house-searching. Quantities of books were passed around from house to house, through friends and relatives' hands, circulated underground among readers of all age. These were books that would have been forbidden, burnt, criticized and labeled as containing Western thought, bourgeois taste, reactionary or revisionist viewpoints.

The books were stolen or passed out directly from the ruined libraries, the searched houses of those famous intellectuals in arts and letters, translators, authors, musicians, movie stars, actors, actresses, and celebrities. As many of them took residence in the former French section, there were more books than that in other districts circulating underground in their neighborhood.

A first rate translator of French novels, Mr. Fu Lei (傅雷) and his wife, lived near by. They committed suicide together after the Red Guards discovered a photo of Madam Song Meiling in their house, and began to torture them. Many books, at least, many Balzac's novels that he translated, were scattered from his library, circulated in the streets, to the benefit of avid readers of French novels.

Another celebrity, a first rate Beijing opera actress, Yan Huizhu (言慧珠), lived only a couple of blocks down the street. She hang herself in the bathroom in her Western style dancing skirts and high heel shoes, as though mocking the Red Guards and their accusations. (It was on September 11, 1966, according to her son's memoir published recently). Their nanny, Aunt Precious Prose, who used to work for Grandma before 1949, often came to visit PoPo. After that tragedy, she came with that actress' teenage son, to ask PoPo for help. The boy's father, Yu Zhengfei (俞振飞), a first rate Beijing Opera actor, was arrested by the Red Guards, under custody. Like many people under persecution, he was "isolated for interrogation" (隔离审查), couldn't come home to take care of his son. He was a learned man, had a big library at home, that was looted too.

J could recall the last time she saw Yan Huizhu and her husband Yu Zhengfei acting together on stage. They played a classical piece of 昆剧 (Kun Opera), called "墙头马上" (*Over the Wall and on Horseback*). It was around 1964. J remembered them not because they were celebrities, as people adore movie stars nowadays, but because the stage image of that play stayed in her mind's eye. After the Cultural Revolution was over, Mr. Yu was restored to his position. He served as the President of the Shanghai

53

Opera Academy. What a pity his wife was no longer there to play his counterpart! So it goes.

Klever had a bosom friend, Lily, who was her grammar school classmate. Lily's father used to be a very important, progressive, revolutionary author. He was a novelist and playwright. One of his books was made into a movie called *The Diaries of a Nurse*. When the Cultural Revolution started, he was severely persecuted, put in prison for years. Because of his father's persecution, Lily was attacked by the Red Guards in school, got her hair zigzagged. When J ran into her in the street, Lily looked like a ghost. J was shocked, could never forget that horrid look, that zigzagged mess of hair. Lily wore hats for a long time after that.

Mere from Lily's hands, Klever borrowed at least dozens of books, books Lily got out of the house and passed to her friends. Otherwise, the books would have been taken away or burnt by the Red Guards. The Red Guards had no use for books, except for that little Red Bible, Mao's Quotations, which they carried as a regalia wherever they went. Those who liked to read books wouldn't go into the streets, attacking people and looting houses. The books the Red Guards did not burn got scattered, stolen, and passed around underground too.

Klever's house was not searched, so the books were there safe for a while. The books were in high demand. Every cousin, neighbor, schoolmate, relative or friend, wanted to borrow those books. J went to Klever's house everyday, sometimes twice or three times a day, as they were neighbors and best friends. J had the privilege from Klever's library.

Klever was like an elder sister to J since 1963, when J was eleven years old, and Klever thirteen. Klever used to take J to movies, mostly Western movies, or movies from Russia, Hong Kong and India. Klever had a knack for names. She remembered accurately all those foreign names of the characters, as well as the names of movie stars. Klever could talk about movies, books, or paintings, as though she knew everything. In school, Klever played basketball, she was a marvelous player, played the position of left power forward. Later, Klever played violin, studied photography, also English and Japanese languages. She easily mastered the vocabulary, did not need to memorize or recite as others did. She

Klever and her Grandma, 1972.

was so talented and so smart! J admired her, and followed her around.

Once J was worried that her mother might get married to another man, and life would be difficult for her. Klever told her not to worry, just ask her mother to give her enough pocket money, then she would have a good time, living by herself. Life would be better than living with parents. Klever herself was left by her parents in early 1950s, when her parents moved to Hong Kong, taking her only brother with them. They left her alone in Shanghai under the care of her paternal grandma. Her grandma was delicate and soft-spoken. She always stayed in a dark small room at the back, while Klever had the master bedroom in front. As her grandma was getting old, Klever became her own boss, and boss in the house.

As soon as the house searching was over, and the schools were closed, Klever told J that they must find ways to educate themselves. Maybe it was her mother's idea. Klever's mother used to be a high school teacher in Shanghai. A good "teacher" she must be. If her husband went gambling, lost money, came home late at night, she would make him sleep on the floor. If he won, he had to turn in the cash to her to sleep in the bed. In Hong Kong, Klever's mom became a housewife, stayed at home for the rest of her life. She wrote to Klever frequently from Hong Kong, sometimes sending her American fashion magazines. No books though, maybe books were not allowed to go through the customs without passing strict censorship.

Besides Klever's library, J also got books from her relatives and schoolmates. She made notes in her diary, one day her Grandma's best friend, Grandma Eura, sent her daughter to deliver a book for J to read. The title of the book was 《新珠》 (New Pearl) written by a Japanese author. She need to return the book in a few days, that was why she sent her daughter to make a special trip, let J read it and got back on time. Grandma Eura had passed the age of sixty. She was reading those books herself. Her daughter was disabled, could not speak, but she could read and was reading as well.

Another time, J went to visit Grand-Aunt May Fourth. Her family was thrown out of her large apartment by the Red Guards. Now five people lived in a shabby slum, in someone's kitchen. She was not depressed, but gay as ever. J found Grand-Aunt May Fourth was drinking Saki and eating pig's feet for breakfast in late morning! She was so excited after reading Emily Brontes' 《呼啸山庄》 (*Wuthering Heights*), mimicking the whistles of winds in the wildness, and blowing her drunken breath into J's ears. Of course J begged her for the book. Grand-Aunt May Fourth said several people were waiting, but she would let J have it first. Why? J had been of great help to Grand-Aunt May Fourth the other day.

A few days before, Grand-Aunt May Fourth received signals that her elder brother, one of J's Grand-Uncles, three years older than J's mother, like a brother to her mother, was going to commit suicide. The Red Guards came to his house, the leader fell in love with his wife, a celebrity of beauty. They gave him a hard time, whipped him and tortured him cruelly, more than usual. They also posted a big letter poster on his door, saying he was a playboy, had raped one hundred eighteen women in his life! They made him confess that he did.

That day, Grand-Aunt May Fourth could find no one around to help. She came and grasped J to go with her to her brother's place. Her brother's family had also been "swept out of the house" (扫地出门), as it was called as part of the house-searching movement), living in a shabby garage. When they got to the door, no one answered the door. Grand-Aunt May Fourth was so strong and powerful, that she kicked the door open. They found her brother half-dead with a bottle of sleeping pills at his side. The two of them pulled him out and managed to take him to the hospital. He survived at least this time, only to die in another suicidal attempt a couple of years later. That was not his second attempt, but a third time. So it goes.

It was from reading *Wuthering Heights* that J dreamed of someday she would write about PoPo, and the stories PoPo told her when she was little. J started reading those novels with great joy and excitement, day and night. She tried to get every book she could lay hands on, borrowing and sometimes begging friends and relatives to let her have the book for a day or two. As the underground library had a high demand, sometimes she promised to return a book the next day, which meant she had to finish reading a thick novel over night.

At first, J was not allowed to burn her midnight oil. After the house searching, J's family of four slept together in one bedroom, letting go of the two other rooms. The local housing agency assigned two other family, that moved in one after another. One was a family of five, another a newly wed couple. The couple were both high school teachers. The husband was born in a bourgeois family, so they were "swept out of the house." Theirs was a big house in the same lane, that the husband's mother owned. Now three family shared one bathroom. As her mother had to sleep and got up to go to work in the morning, she wanted J to turn off her lights after bedtime.

J kept reading her books with her bed lamp on over her pillow. Soon she got an idea to solve the problem. In their bedroom, there was a long corridor of closet, built when they first moved there, as storage for Grandma's trunks. Now with thirty-six trunks gone, there was enough space to move in J's twin size bed. J pulled in a wire to have her lamp lit, closed the closet door only halfway, so that she could let in some air to breath. Thus she created a space for herself, reading the books night after night in the closet.

During 1966-1971, J read many novels, as mentioned in her juvenile diary, which she left with Currie before her departure for America in 1979. In 1996, after seventeen years, when for the first time she returned for a visit, Currie handed her back her suitcase, that contained all her diary, notebooks and personal letters. She brought these back to Iowa, put them in a paper box, and left it in her closet. Since then, that box was moved from closet to closet many times. It was another two decades.

Why would she want to touch a painful past? Let bygones be bygones. In J's heart and mind, China was a past—"Gone with the Wind!" America offered a future, a paradise regained, a rightful place to forget history and past wrongs. For anyone who could forget who she was in the old country, and make a fresh start, work hard, this person could create a new self, new identity in American society. She was proud of being self-made in America, free of "ancestral sins." She had no nostalgia. She was not sentimental, reminiscent either. On the contrary, she was too rational, too objective, and too detached from the personal. Her career in America set her on the path of academic work and academic writing. She had no time for personal stories or creative writing. It had been thirty-five years since she came to this country. So it goes.

J reading in the closet, 1969.

June 3, 1989, Buffalo, New York

In 2014 J saw history repeating itself, stark naked before her eyes. *Déjà Vu!* Once more! This time it happened in Taipei. Last time it was in Beijing, 1989. "Massacre on Tiananmen Square" with collage of bloody body images on television screen and report of increasing casualty every day created tremendous emotional trauma in overseas Chinese communities and on American campuses.

J was writing her doctoral thesis in graduate school at Buffalo, New York. She followed the event on television and newspapers, newspapers published in English as well as in Chinese from New York City, San Francisco, and overseas communities. Different languages, different discourses fabricated different stories, which challenged the critical and analytical skills of an English major. At any rate, student demonstration in Beijing escalated to confrontation with police and armed force. National security was at stake.

What did the students want? They wanted a Premier to step down. J sensed something was wrong. The movement started in the name of "anti-corruption," yet this Premier did not have any record or report of corruption. Whereas, the other leader(s) who supported the student demonstration had some exposure of corruption. It suggested, a power struggle was going on in the Central Committee, using the students to support one party against the other. Those students must be mis-oriented, couldn't follow reason or logic.

Rumor had it that a twenty-three year old student leader at Peking University was promised to have a Nobel Prize award. Her mentor, a right-wing professor, was protected by the American Embassy, already left China by then. This young woman was the one who went back to the People's Square on June 4, to tell the students to stay, hold on. J heard her tape recording on a television program, in which she was presented by her American boyfriend, who brought her out of China. She herself was in hiding, did not appear on television. On the tape she said that her husband did not know where she was on June 4. J's acquaintance, a Chinese American woman in Long Island, recognized this American "boyfriend" on television, who was her ex-husband, a "bad guy" she knew, and knew him inside out. So it goes.

Some demonstrators kept fasting for days. Blankets, food, camping and aid equipments were shipped in from Hong Kong overseas. The most radical mob were not regular college students at all. They were unemployed people, some former criminals out of prison, some desperadoes. Chaos ruled the People's Square. After a prolonged period of demonstration, a martial law was declared by the government.

On the evening of June 3, 1989, Professor Liu Bingyan and his wife, who were the initial organizers, advocates and supporters of the student movement in China, came to Buffalo from Harvard. The State University of New York at Buffalo had many exchange programs with China. It hosted a large student body from China, Hong Kong and Taiwan. With hundreds of students and faculty, research fellows and visiting scholars present, Professor Liu encouraged those from mainland China to send letters home telling their families and friends that the government already opened fire in Beijing; "be prepared, a Civil War is coming." He predicted that the armed force, which was called in from another province to maintain order in Beijing, would revolt against the government in Beijing, and start a Civil War.

Emails were not as common as nowadays. When asked if the letters carrying political messages from USA would reach their addressees in China, Professor Liu assured them, he and his wife had received postal parcels from USA before he came abroad. There was no problem. He received them integral. His wife thanked the Church in Boston for its support. She was full of gratitude.

Some student leaders jumped on stage, shouted "Down with the communists!" "Down with Li Peng!" (China's Premier). J knew a couple of them, their parents were communists, not capitalists in China. The one who shouted "Down with the communists!" just came last year, a college student from a military institute. His parents were officers in the military. Their friends took pictures of them shouting slogans on stage. Someone told J, they could use the pictures as evidence to seek refuge, applying for a green card at US Immigrations and Naturalization Service.

The "black puppets" of 1966, like J, did not get on the platform and shout such slogans. Maybe they did not wish to see another August 18, 1966. Maybe they never had a voice on such occasions. Most of them were not there, not participating. They were real students, preoccupied with their academic work and research. The good students got jobs after graduation, wouldn't need such pictures taken. They knew who they were. No one had the heart to take revenge upon their own nation in a foreign country. As a foreign student, J had her courtesy, behaved as a guest in a host country. She never criticized American culture and policies, not until she was naturalized to exercise her right as an American citizen.

Professor Liu gave his microphone to a student, who was calling long distance to Beijing. "Listen, listen, the government opened fire. Let's listen to the gunshots." Silence reigned for two minutes, J did not hear a spark. "Hello, how are you? What do you want?"—was all that said at the other end. The audience was relieved.

Like most of the students there, J was worried about her family and friends in China. What would happen to them if a Civil War broke out tomorrow? Her friend Joan sitting next to her was from Beijing. Her parents and five siblings were all there. She started crying. Joan was the wife of a research fellow. She worked as a janitor in a local motel, as she needed the income to support her son going to elementary school. She donated her last week's wage to support student demonstration. J was touched.

J stood up, asked Professor Liu: "Are you really the leader of this movement? A Martial Law is a Martial Law. It means, if the students do not retreat, the government will take martial actions. The Chinese say: '全军覆没，首斩将领' (If the entire army was destroyed, behead the leader first). If the students were to be killed on the square tomorrow, you shall be responsible for it. Are you ready to take the responsibility for what you did tonight? If you were the leader, I suggest you tell the students to go home." Before she was going to ask him: "Where are your own children? Are they on the Square?", someone on the platform interrupted her.

Professor Liu did not take offense. Instead, he approached J afterwards when they met in a small meeting. He asked J to serve as his interpreter. J was recommended by the Chinese Student Association on campus, because some felt his wife's English was inadequate and sometimes problematic in interpreting his talks. He himself did not speak English. His wife learned English in missionary school in 1940s, did not speak the language living in China throughout the 1950s and 1960s. They just arrived in Boston recently. Professor Liu himself was not satisfied with his wife's interpretation. He found things were not as his wife interpreted to him when he came abroad. J helped him for a while. Then she put down a five dollar bill to support the student association, left the room.

A few days later, J ran into William, who was a doctoral candidate and a good student. J asked him why he was not participating, he said he couldn't make sense of those mob *"demons-taitors"*; at least, it seemed to him that they did not know who they were. J asked him if he knew many students were killed on Tiananmen Square on July 4, he replied flat: "If those people did not die, there would have died millions. Didn't you hear they wanted to start a Civil War?" J knew what he was talking about. Soon afterwards, William got a professorship at New York University, while those sons of bitches shouting slogans dropped out of graduate school, became unemployed. They went to apply for refugee status, all got to stay in the United States. Uncle Sam was very generous indeed. So it goes.

After the trauma was over, the Chinese government protested against US media misrepresentation of the "massacre" on Tiananmen Square. The report of casualty on the Square was reduced from "thousands" to six hundreds including demonstrators and soldiers on both sides. The Chinese newspapers told a different story that some of the villains attacked the soldiers with knifes. Brutal pictures were exposed in the papers. Ted Koppel wrapped up the event with a change of rhetoric. Instead of "Massacre" and "Crash down," he gradually toned down, called it a "Tragedy" on Tiananmen Square. A tragedy must have a "tragic necessity." Was William talking about that tragic necessity the other day?

In the following years, "China" disappeared from the center of US mainstream news and public media. Only that picture of a single handed man stepping back and forth before a tank was played time and again, standstill in American popular consciousness. That photo did not make sense to a critical reader. Why would the tank slow down and stop before a single handed young man? Did the tank roll over this man's body? J watched this scene on TV when the tank was moving, she did not see any clear picture of tank(s) roll over students' bodies. Most of the bloody body pictures she saw on TV were collage, juxtaposed broken arms or legs that were bleeding, or injured bodies were rushed into the hospitals.

Immediately, diplomatic relation between US and China broke for a decade. "The honey moon was over. . . . Uncle Sam 'lost China' again, after General MacArthur." These words were dated June 1989 in the "Preface" of J's doctoral dissertation. J had tears writing these words. It was unfortunate, indeed tragic on both sides and for all around. Afterwards, Chinese students lost their good reputation on American campuses.

When J went on the job market in 1991, once at a campus interview, she was asked about her opinion of the student demonstration in China in 1989. J knew, on campus, professors who did not support student movements would be unpopular; students might not take his or her classes. However, she spoke the truth. She replied that she was not part of it and did not support it. As it turned out, the search committee wanted to make sure she was not a troublemaker, as most search committees would. "Good," the professor who asked the question apparently did not share the point of view of the mainstream media, "we did not like it."

Later in a private conversation, he told J: "We called those students 'speed-bumpers.' We were not sure what was going on, so we asked." J even did not know what a "speed-bumper" was, or how he meant it. He explained, a "speed bumper" was something that stood in the middle of the road, slowing down the traffic. He saw those ignorant students stood in the way of progress—China's modernization, the normalization of US-China relations, and American liberal politics since the war in Vietnam. J could only think of that man in the photo, tumbling in front of the tank, dancing. His body must be a real "speed bumper," crystalized in that metaphor.

Hong Kong, 2014

Déjà Vu! It happened in Hong Kong this time. Students left school, went into the streets, marching, camping in the rain under yellow umbrellas, fighting with the police. "Speed bumpers" blocked the busy traffic in the "middle" of the city, "occupying" the "middle" highway in the "middle" of a global financial city center.

The media played with the pun of the word "middle" in Chinese ("占中"), as though the students were marching towards Beijing to take over the "Middle Kingdom," occupying the center of the Tiananmen Square.

The students were "demonstrating" and demanding for rights they did not even know how to exercise, and against government leaders with whom they were far from being equals. This time even worse, it was supported by an underground, sinister, violent, global, terrorist movement. Self-abusive and self-destructive racist mobs attacked the common people and tourists from China physically, using a racist language, such as "Go back to China!" It sounded so familiar. On the social media, however, senior citizens from Chinese communities in the United States were calling the demonstrators *"de-mob-traitors"* and *"de-mob-crazy!"*

Professor J was stunned, realizing why some of her students were eager and even demanding that she write a memoir. The coming generation, the good ones, good students, who wanted to study, wanted to receive a sound education, were puzzled, torn and lost. They wanted to know: How did J survive the Cultural Revolution? How did she transcend the harsh circumstances, peer pressure and popular culture? Where did she found the right path in darkness to be enlightened? After all, what "lessons" had she learned in her time? What books she read? All boiled down to the question of the "Education" of Jennie Wang.

J talked to people around in school and society that she felt higher education in Taiwan was "ruining children." J used a Chinese proverb to describe the situation that it was "误人子弟." Surprisingly, everyone agreed, and couldn't agree with her more for that expression. But who were ruining the children? The omitted subject in that proverb was "the teacher" who ruins not his or her own children, but "other people's" children. The Chinese, while they respect the teacher above the authority of parents, hold the educators responsible for their children's future. In a situation where ignorant politicians control campus life and curriculum instruction, how could J possibly save her students from "national suicide" and international terrorist movements?

Maybe she ought to write a book as they wanted, show them the depth of an education received from print books, beautiful words and intelligent thoughts, wisdom accumulated for centuries in humanities; how different it was from the slogans and cliches, the skin deep, vulgar, racist images in movies, power point lectures, social media, online sales and advertisements, information penetrated through video games, cell phones, popular music and songs. Who would believe, a street revolution in Hong Kong organized by the distribution of "smart" phones and "yellow" umbrellas could pull down the five star red flag flying in Beijing? How smart were those "smart" phones and fanatic youngsters? How strong were those yellow umbrellas in a global village, where black is beautiful and white is might?

CHAPTER 4

A SELF EDUCATION CURRICULUM

Western Literature

From the underground library, the most popular books were novels. They were world masterpieces since the 18th century, mostly French and Russian, some German and English, a few American novels, all available in Chinese translation. Those "translated novels" were much in demand, circulating among city people old and young. Borrowing from her friends and relatives, J read as many as she could lay hands on.

From the notes in her diary and notebooks, she could recall those books at best by genre, nationality, to a certain extent by chronology, and the time period she read them. There was no alphabetical order in her memory of the authors' names, as regulated in the printed world in the West. Author's names were less important than the titles of the books then in China. Western copyright law came in later, which treated the book as an individual intellectual property; therefore, the authors' names went before the title of the book. In China, a book title went before the author's name as usual. Besides, different editions of translations could easily have different spellings in Chinese. So the writer of this memoir couldn't recall or regulate them in an alphabetical order. That would be unreal. She could only add English titles and the authors names wherever she could find them, and as much as she could, to benefit the monolingual reader, the bilingual parents, especially those students who asked her what books she read when she was young.

She was not alone reading those novels. During that period, most literate people she knew—cousins, friends, neighbors, relatives and schoolmates—were all thirsty in reading those translated novels with sterling titles:

《悲惨世界》 (*Le Miserable*)

《包法利夫人》 (*Madame Bovary*)

《娜娜》 (*Nana*)

《红与黑》 (*Le Rouge et le Noir*)

《基督山恩仇记》 (*Le Comte de Monte-Cristo*)

《安娜.卡列尼娜》 (*Anna Karenina*)

《复活》 (*Resurrection*)

《战争与和平》 (*War and Peace*)

《罪与罚》 (*Crime and Punishment*)

《白痴》 (*The Idiot*)

《父与子》 (*Fathers and Sons*)

《罗亭》 (*Rutin*)

《害怕的人》 (*The Man Who Was Afraid*)

《浮士德》 (*Faust*)

《少年歌德之烦恼》 (*The Sorrows of Young Werther*)

《约翰. 克里斯朵夫》 (*Jean Christophe*)

《唐·吉诃德》 (*Don Quixote*).

The French, Russian, some German and Spanish novels were most popular, as those above mentioned. The English came later. At first, someone discovered a series of Dickens' novels and passed them out. J got to read—

《雾都孤儿》 (*Oilver Twist*)

《荒凉山庄》 (*Bleak House*)

《大卫·科波菲尔》 (*David Copperfield*)

《艰难时事》 (*Hard Times*)

《匹克威克俱乐部》 (*Pickwick Club*)

《双城记》 (*A Tale of Two Cities*).

Those novels told stories of poor boys in the city, their poverty, theft, orphanage, the dark side of London. "Fog, fog everywhere." These works offered a picture of the society as Engels criticized, to justify the theory of revolution.

Although they read and talked about 《傲慢与偏见》 (*Pride and Prejudice*) and 《简.爱》 (*Jane Eyre*)—these two most popular books for female readers in the 21st century American popular culture and curriculum instruction—J and Klever did not take them seriously as "woman's writing," or "female models." Klever laughed at Mrs. Bennett as well as Mr. Darcy. She called them "phony," like some of her neighbors. J disliked Jane Eyre's character, called her "that little woman," too calculating and self-centered.

(Years later in 1980, she took a class on the 18th Century English Novel at San Francisco State. The first day when Professor Solomon began to teach Austin's *Pride and Prejudce*, he asked if the students had read the book and what the opening lines were. J raised her hand, without looking at the book, she recited: "It is a truth universally acknowledged that a man of property must be in want of a wife." It was definitely not a "truth universally acknowledged" in San Francisco in that time—early 1980s.)

The English novels J liked better were those later ones—

《岛国的法利赛人》 (*The Island Pharisees*)
《福尔赛世家》 (The Forsyte Saga)
《刀锋》 (Razor's Edge)
《孽障》 (My Son, My Son).

Galsworthy's trilogy reminded J of those prudent Grand-Aunts, Grand-Uncles and their beautiful wives married into the family, yet always outsiders. 《孽障》 (*My Son, My Son*) was a novel she was eager to read completely, because she remembered that dim corner in her neighbor's house in a rainy day when she was little. One afternoon in Nana's home, she sat in a sofa and happen to see that book at the side tea table in front of the big radio. She started reading it, curled up in the sofa for several hours when Nana's elder sister Angel came in. Angel was a senior high school student. She was surprised that J was reading that thick book. She grabbed it from J abruptly, and said: "This is not a book for you a little child to read!" J begged her, but she would not let J touch it again. J remembered the title of that book at least.

American novels were relatively few. 《红字》 (*The Scarlet Letter*) and 《佛洛斯河上的磨坊》 (*The Mill on the Floss*) were scary books in a dark society. 《珍妮姑娘》 (*Jennie Gerhardt*) and 《嘉莉妹妹》 (*Sister Carrie*) were about young women making their way in the city. The characters invited sympathy, but they were not interesting, admirable female portraits for J. She found Dreiser's 《金融家》 (*The Financier*) and 《斯多葛》 (*The Stoic*) more challenging.

Dreiser was received as a socialist on the left bank. So was Jack London. Therefore, quite a few of his novels were translated, such as the following noted in J's diary—

《马丁. 伊登》 (*Martin Eden*)
《荒野的呼叫》 (*The Call of the Wild*)
《铁蹄》 (*The Iron Heel*)
《海浪》 (*The Sea-Wolf*)
《白猿》 (*White Fang*).

Those were powerful novels, but crude and alien to J's sense and sensibility. Books by American authors such as 《大地》 (*The Good Earth*) and 《红星照耀中国》 (*Red Star over China*), on the contrary, were too familiar, not of much interest to J.

《战地钟声》 (*For Whom the Bell Tolls*) was the only Hemingway J read. Everyone thought 《飘》 (*Gone with the Wind*) was the best American novel, especially with that felicitous one-word Chinese title, which sounded so romantic and uplifting, made every translator envy. (Only in American universities was she taught that Mitchell's novel was not Literature, only a bestseller. Hemingway was major and master of the American novel. He dominated the canon of American Modernism. After graduate school, J did her independent research to rediscover a number of American Woman Writers during the Modernist period, and began to teach their works in her course on 20th Century American Novel. That was another story.)

Many of Balzac's novels in the series of *La Comédie Humaine* were available in Chinese. The most popular ones, that circulated fast and frequently, were—

《高老头》(*Père Goriot*)

《欧也妮·葛朗台》(*Eugenie Grandet*)

《贝姨》(*Cousin Bette*)

《邦斯舅舅》(*Cousin Pons*)

《夏倍上校》(*Le Colonel Chabert*)

《于絮尔·弥罗埃》(*In Xu Er · Mi Rohee*)

《搅水女人》(*Study of a Woman*).

Thanks to Klever's ambition in reading and her social network, J got to read some less popular ones—

《赛查·皮罗多盛衰记》
(*Rise and Fall of Cesar Birotteau*)

《都尔的本堂神父》(*The Vicar of Tours*)

《比哀兰德》(*Pierrette*)

《发明家的苦恼》(*Inventor's Distress*)

《幻灭》(*Lost Illusions*).

The last one, J noted in her diary, she had to wait for a long time to get a copy. Klever liked to sneer at those stingy, small-minded, petty bourgeois hypocrites in Balzac's novels. J could still recall her exciting gestures and the funny faces she made when she talked about them. She was fun.

There were collections of short stories by Guy de Maupassant, O'Henry and Conan Doyle. Thirty-five years later, J still remembered the irony in Maupassant's story "Uncle Jules." As she couldn't find anything better to describe the contemporary philistine mentality in Shanghai in reception of Chinese American writing, she used that story as an allegory. One of her students found a copy of that book in a local used bookstore! There was a blue stamp at the back of the book, which cried: ***"Used books have a life, bring used books alive!"***

There were many other books that were less known, but no less serious and important, as mentioned here and there in J's notebooks. They might be forgotten today, therefore, worth listing, saving them as souvenirs. "Used books have a life, bring used books alive!" Some readers might want to read them someday. Some might come across the titles in libraries, or would like to look them up, as these listed below. Who knows but in lower frequencies some of the books wouldn't change some people's lives?

普希金,《上尉的女儿》
(Pushkin, *The Lieutenant's Daughter*)
果戈理,《小说戏剧选》, 满涛译
(Gogol, *Selected Works of Fiction and Play*)
赫尔岑,《家庭的戏剧》,《赫尔岑主义》
(Herzen, *Family Drama, Herzenism*)
科普塔伊娃, 《伊凡·伊凡诺维奇》
(Koptayeva, *Ivan Ivanovich*)
车尔尼雪夫斯基,《怎么办? 》
(Chernyshevsky, *What Is to Be Done?*)
拉齐斯,《走向新岸》
(Lacis, *Towards New Shores*)
高尔基,《福玛》,《我的童年》
(Gorky, *Foma Gordyeff, My Childhood*)
列夫·奥瓦洛夫,《我是11-17 号》
(*I'm No. 11-17*)
哈克尼斯,《城市姑娘》
(Harkness, *City Girl*)
雷马克,《生死存亡的时候》
(Remarque, *Spark of Life*)

高尔斯华绥，《苹果树》
(Galsworthy, *Apple Tree*)

奥尔德里奇，《外交家》
(Aldridge, *The Diplomat*)

帕乌斯托夫斯基，《金蔷薇》
(Paustovsky, *The Golden Rose*)

莫泊桑，《如死一般强》,《漂亮的朋友》
(Maupassant, *As Strong as Death, A Handsome Friend*)

菊池宽，《 新珠》
(Prefecture, *Mrs. Pearl*)

《小林多喜二选集》
(Takiji, *Selected Works*)

威廉，《带枪的黑人》
(R. Williams, *Negroes with Guns*).

Most of Western poetry, essays, plays and drama J read in Chinese translation. Moliere's *The School of Wives*, *The Miser*, *The Imaginary Invalid* and *The Bourgeois Gentleman* were humorous and interesting. Wilde's *Lady Windermare*'s Fan was witty. Ibsen's *The Doll's House* did not appeal much to the contemporary Chinese women as it might to J's grandma's generation. For Shakespeare in Chinese translation, she read *Hamlet*, *King Lear*, the *Merchant of Venice*, *Romeo and Juliet*, and *Much Ado about Nothing*. The translator's name was 朱生豪 (Zhu, Shenghao). (*Macbeth* she did not know till after she came to America, and once lived in a "Shakespeare Room" for years, that was another story.)

As for poetry, unlike her peers, she did not care so much for Byron and Shelley, who were considered to be revolutionary poets in their times, therefore much translated into Chinese (Keats was less translated). She preferred Lermontov, and had a passion for Pushkin. After reading, reciting and recording Pushkin's *Eugene Onegin* and another *Collection of Poems*, one night in the closet, J wrote in her diary that she "would be willing to give up [her] left arm if she could read *Eugene's Onegin* in its Russian original!"

She did know a little Russian. Her Junior High School assigned four classes of the first-year students to take English as a second language, and two classes to take Russian. J was assigned to take Russian. After two semesters, she mastered the alphabet, the pronunciation, even succeeded with the roll of her tongue, but she only learned a limited amount of vocabulary. She found it easy to memorize the vocabulary in Russian, which was close to pinyin. English pronunciation was often irregular. She was not able to read poetry and fiction yet. She always had a fancy for that language. Now out of school, she never had a chance to learn Russia, as the Soviet and China relations turned sour in early 1970s. So it goes.

Her passion for Pushkin's *Eugene Onegin* was not for the love story, but for the beauty of Pushkin's poetry. J seldom trusted poetic translations. Nevertheless, whoever translated that book must be first rate. Of all those great novels of love, the best one was by a Spanish novelist, Prosper Mérimée's *Carmen*. To J's taste of love, Carmen was more elevating than Alexandre Dumas fils' *La Dame aux Camelias*, or Tolstoy's *Anna Karenina*. A drama of *Lady of the Camille* was staged in Shanghai before 1966. J could still remember a couple of scenes. One scene was a love-seat on stage, so comfortable and romantic for an afternoon intimate chat with a bosom friend. That special piece of furniture was a luxury, not seen in ordinary household in Shanghai at that time, only on stage.

In public sphere, Love was a forbidden subject. In private, when people exchange notes, and discuss those great love stories, no one talked about sex and Freud. Love in those books or in those days were purely spiritual, innocent, romantic, or idealistic. Maybe the cultivation of noble feelings and sentiments of love, the understanding of relationship between men and women, the exposure to various types of love in books, leading to tragedy or comedy, before the lovers entered the bedroom—was a good education, necessary in a classical education, as few could afford today, before the beauty of love was replaced by modern sexual education in school. So it goes.

The first book that exposed J to explicit sexual material was a paper back from America—Mario Puzo's *Godfather*. This book J read in its English original. Pinnacle's boyfriend Armstrong had a relative in Hong Kong, who smuggled the book into Shanghai.

Armstrong shared with Pinnacle to teach her how to make love. Pinnacle let J have it, because she had no privacy at home to hide the book from her siblings. Before long Armstrong broke with Pinnacle under the pressure of his mother. Among other concerns, his mother disliked Pinnacle's physique, thought she looked too thin, not strong enough to give birth to children. Was Armstrong attempting to get Pinnacle pregnant, so that he could persuade his mother? (Pinnacle married another man in Hong Kong, and gave birth to two big boys.)

The 1960s was still an age of heroism, so another popular type of books was biographies of great men and women in Europe. J had the opportunity to read the biographies of statesmen such as Bismarck, Caesar, Che Guevara, Churchill, Hitler, Khrushchev, Metternich, Napoleon, Pompidou, Truman, Zhukov; philosophers —Kant and Marx; artists and musicians—Beethoven and Michelangelo; and men of letters—Chekhov, Jack London, Romain Roland, Tolstoy, including Macaulay's Life of Samuel Johnson. As for scientists, J only read *Madame Curie*. Madam Curie impressed J with her simple life style, her selfless, sacrificial spirit and devotion to her scientific research.

From a biography of Catherine of Aragon, J learned so much of English history, that turned out to be very useful knowledge some twenty years later. When she was writing a chapter of her doctoral dissertation on Fielding's novels, at least she knew the cause of separation of the Church and the State. One of her dissertation readers commented that J was as familiar with the 18th century English history as though she were talking about current events in contemporary America.

(The subject of her doctoral dissertation was *Novelistic Love: A Postmodern Investigation of "Love Stories" in the English and American Novel*. It covered many novels across the centuries and time period in literary history from Fielding to Federman. Thesis writing was not as difficult for her as it could be for a non-native English speaking candidate. Having read so many novels in her youth, she was confident, and felt ready to say something about the way Western novelists write "love stories.")

J's hero was not any of those great statesmen, men of war, or men of letters; neither gentlemen from fashionable aristocratic circles, nor Bohemian artists, youthful, sentimental lovers, but a stoic, deformed Italian man—Arthur Burton, a fictional character in a memorable novel called 《牛虻》 (*The Gadfly*). That novel was written by a less known woman author—Ethel Lilian Voynich.

Arthur was born in a wealthy, propertied family. He and his mother were somehow different and alienated from his own families. He was especially close to his tutor and spiritual Father, Montanelli, his mother's priest and secret lover. Later when Arthur learned that Montanelli was his biological father, he loved him even more.

Beginning in 1840s, when Italy was dominated by Austria, Arthur joined the revolutionaries, became a member of the Youth Movement. While Montanelli was transferred to Rome to become the Arch Bishop, another priest took care of Arthur's confession. This priest was an informer, a government spy, he exposed Arthur's secret activities to the police, which led to the crash down of the Youth Movement. Arthur was suspected by his peers as an informer. Even his sweetheart despised him.

Betrayed by the Fathers and rejected by his beloved, Arthur was utterly disillusioned with his faith and politics in his time. Escaping from death and persecution, he exiled to South Africa, where he had to take mean manual jobs to survive. He suffered all sorts of hardship and humiliation. He was disfigured and deformed. With his deformed body, he worked in a circus to amuse people like an animal.

After thirteen years when he returned to Italy, he was a different man, bitter and cynical, his good nature changed. So was his figure, so that no one could recognize his feature, and remember him from his past. He became a brilliant writer and critic, nicked named "the Gadfly," vehemently attacking religious hypocrisy. He resolutely joined Marthni's revolutionary movement against the Church in Rome. He was arrested, put into jail, and finally sentenced to death.

There were three scenes that moved J so much, that she felt as though she could touch the depth of Gadfly's heart, the agony of conflict between faith and love. The first was before he left Italy, during a military action, Arthur, at the risk of his own life, refrained himself from shooting and killing Montanelli. The second one was on the eve of his execution, Montanelli came to the jail to see him. Author still loved his Father, and wished to plea for his understanding, and claim kin. How devastating was his naked confession, that destroyed the tranquility of the Archbishop completely, soul and body. Montanelli had a nervous break-down. The third scene was at the field of execution, while bullet after bullet went through his body, Gadfly made a passionate, eloquent, and cynical long speech. No novelist could ever produce such a brilliant scene of execution, penetrating the mind of a dying soul, and give him a voice, full of agony and love.

J passed that novel to Olympia. Olympia was touched by the story in that book too. Knowing J loved that novel so much, yet couldn't keep it, Olympia copied that novel word by word in two weeks, and gave it to J as a surprise! J could feel Olympia's love for her was as strong as Gadfly's! When Olympia went north to settle down in the villages, J wrote her many love letters.

Love between women or girls were common, did not have to be involved in sexual activities, or viewed as "abnormal." There were so many ways to express one's love in Chinese culture. Once J mentioned she did not like the pink skin of peanuts. Currie peeled more than one pound of peanuts' skin overnight, without going to bed.

She did not even think of frying the peanuts first, then crush the skin. When she gave the whole bag of peanuts to J, J was speechless. To accept such a labor of love was like accepting a diamond ring from a proposal. Was she ready to make a commitment to reciprocate? Yet she knew she couldn't give Currie back the bag of peanuts. If she did, it would hurt her feelings. Currie was profound in her heart of hearts.

There was no copy machine yet in 1960s. If she loved a book too much to let it go, usually she would take notes, or copy passages

J and Olympia, 1972.   ***Love between girls.***

by handwriting. For this book, Olympia copied the text word by word, line by line, over two hundred pages at least! Olympia did it in less than two weeks! Those precious pages J kept carefully with her personal belongings all these years. That book, which looked like a manuscript, was still in her closet together with her own diaries and notebooks.

Copying by handwriting, taking notes, reading and rereading, reflecting upon the beauty and truths of certain passages were the primary methods J used, in order to learn something from the books she could borrow, but couldn't keep during this initial period of 1966-1968.

During this period, when J and her friends read voraciously from the underground library, they read by themselves at random, without any guidance or structure, neither restrictions nor prohibitions, unlike in American schools, where books were categorized for students by age groups, as appropriate or inappropriate for teenage or adolescent readers, boys or girls. J was literally exposed to that masterpiece erotic novel 《红楼梦》

(*Dream of the Red Chamber*) when she was only three years old. One day the toddler creeped into her father's nightstand, and found two books. The other one was 《淑女》(*A Gentle Woman*). That was her first contact with books in her childhood memory.

Those were the only two books she found in her parents' bedroom. She was curious, interested, played with the paperbacks, read by herself. Later she kept going back to the nightstand, figured out the characters in black and white by herself as much as she could, skipped and missed a lot. That was how she learned to play with books by herself from an early age. When she reached twenty-two, one day her boyfriend asked her how she could have missed the sexual allusions in that great erotic novel, such as "men were earth, women were water," she began to realize she was too little to understand sexual allusions in what she read. So it goes.

Reading all the books and love stories did not spoil the innocence and virtue of good girls. All her peers were "good girls," no sexual scandal, no social enigma at all. In those days, out of school, the knowledge from the books served as her moral guidance, spiritual salvation, an intellectual reservoir. Ideas and lessons learned from the stories of the characters in the novels and biographies offered her directions as to how to think, what to believe; what was right and wrong; how to tell the character and intentions of people around; how to love, who to marry, or not to marry, not to be cheated by men, and so on.

As for the guidance of how to live one's life, J always followed Nikolai Ostrovsky's maxim in 《钢铁是怎样炼成的》 (*How the Steel Is Tempered*) :

> *Someday when you shall look back*
> *and reflect on things past, you shall not*
> *feel sorry, shall not regret for your*
> *decisions, for what you decide to do today.*

That book was the Bible of revolutionary youth in 1940s and 1950s, officially accepted, sort of a grown-up story about a revolutionary youth. J was not a revolutionary youth, or a revolutionary successor, nor meant to be, but those words she took seriously, as she jotted down in her diary. As it turned out, magically, that maxim helped her to make many important decisions in life, served her wisdom for a life time. Only remembering what she decided to do then, could she sit down to write this book today.

For J, as for many, the books were the rays of hope in the endless nightmare of political movements and mob violence, a lighthouse in her closed closet at night, a promised land, far far away, beyond the cruel realities of daily life. She knew the value of books, some of the books were written in prison, many authors had suffered from hardship and torture more than she could imagine. Genius were always alone, abnormal, alienated from society. Their lives might be wasted, but their works, the books, were immortal, belonging to all mankind with or without copy right, with or without permit and license to read. It was worthwhile to copy the words and passages by handwriting, so that she could read them time and again.

Chinese Classics, Poetry, Fiction, and Theater

It turned out that copying by handwriting had a physical effect of enhancing memory, as though it were another way of reciting. Recital was a traditional method of learning in old times. In traditional school, basic education was for students to read and recite the classics. In modern China, students did not have to recite the classics, or from the books. Mao simply eliminated the requirement of classics in school curriculum, the basic education of 四书五经, the so called "four books and five classics." The junior high language textbooks included only a handful of classical poems from ancient lyrics.

When J was taught one of those ancient lyrics, 明日歌 (*Song of Tomorrow*), she was fascinated by the rhyme, so she asked the teacher, who was an old man, to recite for her. The teacher happily did, turning his head round and round, reading the poem in a classical traditional manner. J learned from him happily, came home, taught her five year old brother to recite: "Tomorrow after tomorrow, how many tomorrow does one have? . . . If one spends a life time always waiting for tomorrow, things will never be done." The little boy, who had curly brown hair and blue eyes, standing on the dining table in their neighbor Nana's house, imitating an old man's voice and tone, recited that lyric, turning his little head seriously round and round, to please his sister, and made everyone laugh and amused.

That was the only time she had heard classical poetry recital in school. Later, she studied many classical poems by herself. She wished she knew how to recite out loud as the poets and scholars did in old times. Unfortunately, the tradition was lost. At least she copied many poems by handwriting word by word, and line by line. She memorized some poems as an educated person in Chinese society must know, such as the popular ones from the three hundreds of Tang poems, and others she particularly enjoyed herself. Years later she could still recite many of them, including the two longest narrative poems from Tang Dynasty——琵琶行 and 长恨歌 (*The Song of PiPa* and *The Song of Everlasting Regret*).

In fact, from her self-study, she had acquired more than the popular knowledge of Chinese classical poetry. She studied the literary history, the prosody of classical verse forms as well. She tried her hand, writing classical verses now and then. She did not like her own poems, what she wrote herself was not as imagistic as those she read. She got to know her limit. Her mind might be too rational and analytical. She was too philosophical to be a poet.

The reading of classical fiction were more interesting. Beside *Dream of the Red Chamber*, the major fictions most people knew and read were—

《列国志》 (*Annals of the Kingdoms*)
《三国演义》 (*The Three Kingdoms*)
《水浒》 (*Water Margin*)
《西游记》 (*Journey to the West*).

J was familiar with the stories in those classics since her childhood. When she was little, little enough to sleep in-between

Jimmy, 1962.

her dad and mom, her father used to feed her with those stories at bed time. From her father's lips, those legendary heroes were as familiar as her "grand-uncles" —刘备，关公，张飞，赵子龙，诸葛亮，曹操，董卓，孙权，吕布，武松，武大郎... (Liu Bei, Guan Gong, Zhang Fei, Zhao Zilong, Zhu Geliang, Cao Cao, Dong Zhuo, Sun Quan, Lv Bu, Wu Song, Wu Song's brother Wu Dalong ...). Nowadays, when she saw the names of these classical warriors appear on the paper napkins in Chinese restaurants overseas, J knew every one of them.

Later when she was five or six, she used to walk into the streets by herself, stopping by at a bookstand, renting serial picture books (连环画). Those were the stories extracted from the classics, with illustrations on top, and brief narratives underneath. Rent to read on the stand costed only a few cents a book. J would rent three to five at once, sitting on the bench by the bookstand, read them all at once. When she finished reading, she would go back to the man who owned the little street side bookstand, and rent more to read. One day, a passersby watched her reading, and offered her a piece of good precaution. He told J that if she held the book in a good position, in a good distance, she would not become shortsighted. J followed the man's advice. Indeed, later she did not have to wear glasses to read, which was rare for a bookworm.

At the bookstand, J was exposed to a variety of picture books (连环画). Only a few of them left in her memory. 《双玉蝉》 (*Two Cicadas*), 《霍小玉》 (*Yu Biography*) and 《杜十娘》 (*Madame Du the Tenth*) were classical love stories about the misfortunes of society women. 《十字街头》 (*At Crossroad*) and

《柳堡的故事》(*Liu Fort Story*) were stories about young people' search for career path and identity.

J also knew some woman warriors from the legends of 《杨门女将》 (*The Yang's Women Warriors*)--穆桂英，佘太君，杨八姐，杨排风，柴郡主 and the like. She got to know these heroines not from her mother, but from theater, from Beijing opera. *Mulan* (花木兰) came much later from reading and reciting the classical poem 《木兰诗》 (*Song of Mulan*)："唧唧复唧唧，木兰当户织..." These lines Kingston later translated in her book *To Be the Poet* (Harvard UP, 2002, 108):

> Jik jik jik. Jik jik jik.
> Fa Mook Lan is weaving.
> the shuttle through the loom
> when news of the draft comes.

Growing up in China, however, J never respected Mulan as a special heroine or role model. Mulan was regarded as a traditional model of a filial daughter, as such she received less attention in anti-patriarchal, revolutionary China. In school, J was always educated to "draw a line"—to separate herself from her class background, her family and parents. To fight in her father's place would be something like going to Hong Kong, politically incorrect.

Yet in America, it was a different story. The second day after J's arrival in US, she had to take an English placement test at the university. The last part of the test asked her to write an essay in fifteen minutes on a given topic of women's participation in the military. By instinct, J wrote about the story of Mulan, without knowing that Kingston's Mulan—*The Woman Warrior* (1976) was a best seller, had inspired the imagination of many American feminists. From that placement test, she got a score of 98 out of 100. Her English proficiency immediately attracted the attention of the authorities. She was suspected to be a "trained Mulan" from Red China.

A decade later, out of graduate school, she found herself terribly wanted in America academia not for her dissertation work, but for her knowledge of the "No Name Woman" in Kingston's *The Woman Warrior*. That book had become an American classic, a canonical text in World Literature. It was used as a textbook cross disciplines all over the world. J was approached by a couple of university presses to write a book on the controversies over Kingston's works. It took her many years of reading and research to figure out why Western readers misread and misinterpreted Kingston's texts.

When the book was done, the presses did not want to publish it anymore. By 2001, their publishing agenda changed with the change of a presidency. China became an "opponent," a menace. "Woman Warriors" were threatening images. What a waste of her education, waste of her scholarship and intellect to be marginalized as a "specialist" in a narrowly defined field of "Chinese American Women's Studies" in America academia, as though she knew nothing else better than an ordinary American scholar! J couldn't escape racial stereotyping in America. She had to "search for roots" in China to understand America. So it goes.

Beat the Golden Bowl (《打金枝》)

It was her father who cultivated J's love for theater, which was a significant part of her education in China. J's father was a theater fan and an amateur. He introduced her to the first rate actors and actresses, also their various roles and role play. The photos of 梅兰芳 (Mei Lanfang) and 言慧珠 (Yan Huizhu) were placed under the glass on the table in his bedroom.

His favorite play was 《四郎探母》 (*The Yang's Captive Son Begs to Visit his Mother*). The Yangs were a distinguished family of warriors in history. In the play, the Yang's Fourth Son (杨四郎) was captured by the enemy, a tribal King. He was forced to marry the princess. They had a son. Several years passed, his mother led an army to the front, to declare war against the tribe. She was camped just across the border. He begged his wife to let him go and pay a visit to his mother. His wife made him swear that he would return overnight, which he did.

As a theater fan and an amateur, J's father played on stage, and he played the role of the Yang's Fourth Son. J remembered his costumes, the long feather and fur stored in his mother's bedroom behind her bed. J knew as a theater goer, only barbarians wore furs on stage. Her father never told her why that play was his favorite.

Now decades passed after he had passed away, J just realized that her father might have been sympathetic with the character of the Yang's Fourth Son in that play, because he could identify with him himself. He pitied himself in a similar plight. At that time he just married J's mother, a woman across class and culture, alien to his mother, without traditional virtue and respect for his mother. In his mother's eyes, he was captivated by a "barbarian" woman, raised in an American school, lived in another district in Shanghai, a stranger to her family and relatives.

He himself, however, never cut off completely from his origin, his own folks, his indigenous culture and tradition held by his mother. On the one hand, it was the modern, bourgeois, good life he pursued earnestly with his wife, a willing captive. On the other, the natural inclination to family, blood relation, native culture and cultural values, the manhood of a son in a Chinese family and filial duty lured in his blood, always called him back, pulling him apart.

He loved his family and all his relatives. He could always get tickets, tickets with good seats, always in the center on the third line. Even if center seats in the first or second line, or before tenth line, he would not take home, but gave to others. So J was used to go to theater in a center seat in the third line. With a row of six big people in the family—J's two grandmas, her father and mother, her father's sister Aunt Phoenix Letter and her husband, all stout and heavy, whose broader shoulders blocked the view of the stage, sometimes the audience behind them would have trouble viewing the stage. How embarrassing!

Though he himself liked to play Beijing opera, he would often take his families to see Yue Opera, or listen to Suzhou Pintan (评弹, ballad), which the women in the family liked better. Sometimes he would take J to see other regional opera, such as the indigenous Shanghai opera (沪剧), Ningbo Opera (甬剧), Jiangsu Opera (淮剧, 黄梅戏). J learned to appreciate all types of regional opera and different dialects in her childhood, except that she had never seen Cantonese opera in Shanghai.

(Decades later after she came to America, one day she was waiting at a bus stop in Chicago near Chinatown. Behind her, there was a senior citizens' club, a group of men was watching Cantonese opera on television, the door was ajar. J stood at the door, watched with them for two hours. She was amazed by the stage performance of Cantonese opera. Its language, stories, acting and costumes were superb, superior to all regional opera. It was so elegant and sophisticated; ironically, almost a sharp contrast to the ugly images and primitive dialect in Chinatown. Although she lived in San Francisco for many years, J never learned to understand the Cantonese dialect. Strangely, with the written scripts on the screen, she enjoyed the language of the Cantonese opera immensely, its poetry, archaic sound sense, and exquisite sensibility.

It was from then on, she began to see the beauty of those people in Chinatown. Later, when she went to teach in Taiwan, she quickly learned to enjoy the Fujian opera (哥仔戏) and Taiwanese songs. She found herself very fortunate to be able to enjoy many different regional art forms, that had been preserved and passed down from ancient time to the present, as few of her contemporaries would appreciate now. The contemporary college students enjoyed popular songs, some were fans of Michael Jackson without understanding of the context. Even in Shanghai, when she wished to talk to her friends, colleagues, and students about those classical opera, no one showed any interest. They turned away, looked puzzled at J, someone who came back from the West, teaching American literature and culture, should be so "provincial," or "nostalgic" about classical Chinese theater. J told them she was a "Post-modernist," then they even did not know what that word meant.)

Except for the Cantonese dialect, J grew up with a variety of regional dialects at home and from her neighbors. Her two grandmas both spoke Ningbo dialect, and PoPo spoke Nanxun dialect. PoPo's families, who frequently visited and stayed with J, spoke Wuxi dialect. The cook in the family spoke Yangzhou dialect. J's mother spoke Shanghai dialect with a slight Suzhou accent, and her father with a very heavy Ningbo accent. The neighbors spoke Sichuan dialect, Shandong dialect, Hunan dialect, Fujian dialect, Shaoxing dialect, Subei dialect, and indigenous Shanghai dialect, which was very different from Shanghai dialect in the city.

In everyday life, what the old people spoke was most important, because they did not know how to speak "the common language," as it was called in the mainland China. (J did not know before she came to America, that "the common language" was called "Mandarin" overseas.) The kids had to communicate with them in their dialects. Be they grandmas or nannies, they were the bosses in the houses. J spoke the common language (Mandarin) in school, Shanghai dialect in the streets and at home, but she often had to mimic a variety of dialects, depending upon whom she spoke to in everyday surroundings.

"Shanghai opera" was not sung in Shanghai dialect. It was only an English name invented after 1980s to be accessible to the Western ear. In Chinese, its formal name was 越剧 (Yue Opera), and its popular name was 绍兴戏 (Shaoxing Opera). There was a type of opera sung in indigenous Shanghai dialect, which was called 沪剧 (Hu Opera). Strangely, even in Shanghai, the indigenous Shanghai opera—Hu Opera was less popular than Yue opera. J never learned to appreciate the indigenous Shanghai dialect, which was the dialect largely spoken in the East Bay of Shanghai (Pudong, it used to be a rural area.) The opera was more like modern drama, less poetic.

J's Chinese name came from a line in a well known classical Yue opera 《打金枝》 (*Beat the Golden Bowl*), meaning "punish the princess." In the play, a spoiled and indulgent princess was amusingly punished by her father the Emperor. In the opening scene, the princess sang snugly: "I am a golden bowl with jade

leaves—daughter of the Emperor" ("我本是金枝玉叶皇家女"). It was another way of saying: "Who would dare to touch me?" Yet she was slapped by her husband, because she was too proud to go to her father-in-law's birthday party, and bow to her in-laws. The Emperor ruled that even a princess had to pay proper respect to her in-laws, observe family values. Maybe the naming was a naughty trick her father played on his wife, as J's mother lacked respect for her in-laws, had no traditional virtues at all.

The Golden Bough

By sound sense, the two characters of her first name meant something else, as her father often reminded her, the first word meant "a gifted scholar and learned beauty," and the second, "a golden bowl with jade leaves." To her father, J's name brought back all those familiar, lovely, theatrical characters staged in Yue opera. J liked the idea for what she was named to be—"a gifted scholar and learned beauty." The second word, jade with a gold side, was a rare word. At first, she couldn't find it in the dictionary. Her mother told her she had to look it up in a special dictionary. There she found it was not as it looked, a type of jade, ornament of sort, but a type of rare metal, "the hardest to break." Indeed, by character J turned out to be as tough as that rare metal. Although she had to survive many adversities and endure all sorts of hardship in her life, being incarnated with the quality of that rare metal, her spirit could never be broken.

One day during the Cultural Revolution, J's father asked her to change her name, because those characters belonged to the aristocratic, feudal, traditional, leisured classes. Classical opera was abolished on stage now. J had better change her name to "a good soldier," since her brother's name was "the good people," the two of their names could make it "the good people's soldier," i.e. the "militia," which seemed to be more appropriate for the spirit of the age. J did not like the idea, and reminded her father of the fact that she was born first, she could not take a word after her brother. Since no family would name children in a reverse order, her father gave up the idea.

J loved words from theater. On traditional opera stage, there were slides hung from both sides, showing the verse lines sung on stage, like the translations on TV screen nowadays. Those were most refined classical verses in rhythm and rhyme. It was from those slides shows by the stage J learned many Chinese characters. Theater-going was her extra curricula of Chinese instruction. There she learned to appreciate the richness of Chinese language before she went to school.

When she was about five years old, she was admitted to a kindergarten, founded by the First Lady, Madame Song Qingling (宋庆龄), Sun Yet-Sun's wife. That kindergarten was a private school, few in China in 1950s. It was open to children from the family of former industrialists, capitalists, and propertied class. Since it was not a neighborhood kindergarten, it was quite a distance away from home. J had to take a bus for seven stops to get there.

It was her father's job to take her to kindergarten, and after school pick her up everyday, six days a week. After they got off the bus, there's a distance to walk. If she asked her father to carry her on his back or hold her in his arms to school, she would have to give him a dozen of kisses. That was too much, J complained to Grandma. The story became a scandal of "the spoiled daughter" complaining too much kissing by her father among relatives. Only the Grand-Grandma was sympathetic with J, blamed his father for his indulgence.

Seldom would he take J home directly after school. He would take her downtown, go to his favorite theater, chat with his lady friends in the ticket office. J would sneak in through the dark hallways, stood in the corridors, or found herself a seat, to watch the performance on stage, before the matinee was over by five or six o'clock.

Then her father would take her to dinner in those downtown restaurants, mostly for some special dishes in small restaurants, such as eel or "East Hill Pork Stew," a soy source pork stew named after a poet, East Hill Su (Su, Dongbo). Those restaurants were housed in old buildings, without modern toilet. J's father's friends praised J for joining them, their daughters would not come with them to visit the old city. J's mother wouldn't come.

Sometimes her father took J for Western food on the 14th floor of Park Hotel. J liked the double, triple and multiple mirrors in the bathroom on the 14th floor of Park Hotel, where she could have a panoramic view of the city in the evening. When nobody was there, she played in the bathroom by herself. The waiters were so nice to her, that if she and her father ordered the same dish, a piece of fish or veal, they would always place a better looking one in front of her.

Under the bridge on the Bund at a street corner, there was a little family restaurant run by a Russian family, well known for their borscht. People lined up outside waiting for dinner. One day J went in after six o'clock, saw another boy from her kindergarten seated at the next table, he told J he was punished for not closing his eyes during nap time, had to sleep for another hour or two when everyone was gone. At last he ended there. What a small world!

That Russian family closed its door and moved out of the country on the eve of the Cultural Revolution. When J arrived in San Francisco in 1979, Aunt Viva told her that that Russian family had opened another one right here on Geary Blvd. This was how the refuges, the remnants of an old regime, survived from Russian to China and to America. A way to go.

When J was seven, one day on the bus, a young man said to her mother that J looked fit to be a swimmer, with her plump body shape, which would give her strong buoyancy. If she would like to join the District swimming team, of which he was a coach in charge, he would be happy to take her. J's mother agreed on the spot. For the next year or two, J had to go to training three times a week in the evening, 7:00-9:00pm, after dark.

The Athletics Club was located next to the Park Hotel. By then J was old enough to take the bus by herself. Her father told her, before her scheduled training, if she happened to be outside in the streets, downtown, she did not have to take the bus home for dinner. She could just go to the 14th floor at Park Hotel, order her own dinner. She could tell the waiters that her father would come in later to pick up the bill. That J did sometimes. It was a class privilege in 1960s Shanghai, that she enjoyed. A couple of times she took her friends there to eat, her father did not mind.

In early 1980s, the government opened another kindergarten in memory of Madame Song Qingling in a nearby neighborhood where J's parents lived. By that time J had already left China. With the money the city government had by then returned to him, J's father made a huge donation. Maybe, taking J to the kindergarten and picking her up was the best time her father ever had in his family

J's Swim Team Id. photo.

life. That donation might be meant for the memory of his lost love, "the golden bough with jade leaves" was broken from its stem, and blown away from Shanghai, gone with the wind. "Like white doves set free, soaring to the sky," he often grumbled to his wife, "who knows if they would ever come back home?"

Envision the Globe

Reading at random was not enough, however diverse and inclusive. J felt she need a more structured curriculum. She wanted to learn, as part of education, what she ought to have learned as in school, know what every educated person ought to know. By 1971, J was nineteen, reached the age of a college student. She knew she needed to began college level education. Remembering her birthday wish in 1967—she *"will not let the errors of government policy stop her education. If school will never open, she will have to complete her own education one way or another, sooner or later, to the highest level attainable. No one shall stop her"* (quoted from diary in 1967), J began to look for textbooks used in college.

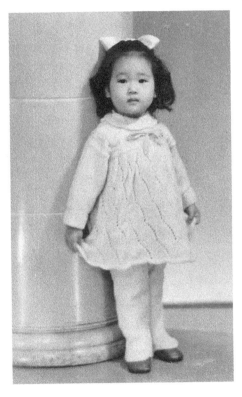

The little "white dove," pre-school.

A relative of hers, her uncle's wife's younger brother, was a college student before 1966. He let J borrow his three volumes of 《世界史》 (*World History*), which was the textbook he used at his university. J followed the textbook chapter by chapter, taking notes, trying to memorize as much as she could, in order to complete a curriculum that she thought was required for college students.

Mao encouraged the youth to "embrace your country in your bosom, and stretch your vision to the globe" (胸怀祖国，放眼世界). In order to "stretch her vision to the globe," she pored over maps (《地图册》), *The Dictionary of World Knowledge*, (《世界知识词典》, 1959版), *Introductions to Countries in the World* (《各国概况》), including periodicals, such as 《世界知识》 (*World Knowledge*) and 《地理知识》 (*Geography*). From the maps, she learned the various names of places in Asia, and around the globe. Then memorizing and identifying the places on blank maps, that she drew by handwriting, she gave herself quizzes and tests. Nowadays one could turn the world around on one's finger tip, all the geographical names would appear instantly on a smart phone. By contrast, those maps drawn by handwriting in her notebooks looked so primitive!

For college level study of World History, Western Philosophy, History of Arts and Letters, she studied whatever books and textbooks she could lay hands on. The following books, from which she took notes and/or copied passages, were still legible in her notebooks. For most of the books and textbooks, she couldn't trace the authors' names, and/or translators and editors' names, she could only group them by subjects, more or less chronologically.

Besides that three volumes of 《世界史》 (*World History*), J also studied—

> 《近代国际政治史》
> (*History of Modern International Politics*)
> 《波拿巴第三政变记》
> (*Louis Bonaparte Eighteenth Brumaire*)
> 《中东欧与世界》
> (*Eastern Europe and the World*)
> 夏伊勒，《第三帝国的兴亡》
> (W. L. Shirer, *The Rise and Fall of the Third Reich*)
> 《第一次世界大战简史》
> (*History of the First World War*)
> 《第二次世界大战回忆录》

(*Memoir of World War II*)

《印度对华战争》

(*India's War against China*).

The books she studied on Philosophy and Art History included:

《西方哲学史》

(*History of Western Philosophy*)

《希腊雕塑简史》

(*History of Greek Sculpture*)

《外国建筑史参考图集》

(*A Reference Album of the History of Foreign Architecture*)

《艺术哲学》

(*The Philosophy of Art*, 法, 丹纳, 傅雷译)

康德, 《宇宙发展史概论》

(Kant, *Evolution of the Universe*)

达尔文, 《生物进化论》

(Darwin, *The Origin of Species*)

普列汉若夫, 《论艺术》

(Plekhanov, *On Art*)

《赫尔芩主义》

(*Herzenism*)

柯切托夫, 《你到底要什么?》

(Keqietuofe, *What do You Want then?*)

《礼节性的访问 》

(Визит вежливости, *A Courtesy Call*).

Political Science was a main subject in university curriculum in China, one must study Marxist orthodoxy. So she studied:

《政治经济学教材》

(*Political Economics*, a textbook)

《雇佣劳动和资本》

(*Hired Labor and Capital*)

《马恩通信集》
(*Correspondence between Marx and Engels*)
《苏维埃政权的当前任务》
(*The Eminent Tasks for the Soviet*)
《列宁，斯大林论中国》
(*Lenin and Stalin on China* 陈元晖译)
《现代资产阶级的实用主义》
(*Modern Bourgeois Pragmatism*)
《马尔萨斯人口论》
(Malthus, *An Essay on the Principle of Population*)
《唯物主义和经验主义批判》
(*Materialism and Empiricism: A Critique*)
《与资产阶级斗争的新阶段》
(*A New Stage for Class Struggle against the Bourgeois*)
《国家与革命》
(*State and Revolution*)
《怎么办?》
(*What Is to be Done?*).

These books were orthodoxy, public and available in bookstores.

In order to have a survey of the history of Western Literature, she obtained a textbook used at Peking University—杨周翰编, 《欧洲文学史》 (*History of European Literature*), also a couple of canonical anthologies—周熙良编, 《外国文学作品选》 (*Anthology of Foreign Literatures*) and 《德国诗选》 (*Anthology of German Poetry*).

Chinese History and Literature

For Chinese history and the history of Chinese Literature, J studied both classical and modern, using the textbooks taught in universities. At first, another young uncle, who was also trying to complete his own college education, shared with her his textbook 《中国近代史讲义》 (*Lectures on the History of Modern China*), offered by East Normal University for distant learning (华师大函授部课本). J asked him questions and discussed a few topics with him, he was a great help. Afterwards, J tried to cover as many canonical texts as possible, as though she must know what a college student, or an educated person in China, was supposed to know. The following books she covered by self-study, now she might share with her reader as reference.

《中国近代史》
   (*History of Modern China*)
《中国历代哲学文选》
   (*Anthology of Chinese Philosophy from the Dynasties*)
《中国文学史》, 刘大杰编
   (*History of Chinese Literature*, ed. Liu Dajie)
《中国文学发展史》
   (*History of the Development of Chinese Literature*)
《楚辞》
   (*Chu Lyrics*, or *Songs of the South*)
《天问天对注》
   (*Annotations on Days of Heaven*)
《儒林外史》
   (*The Scholars*)
《古文观止》
   (*Classical View Only*)
《诗经》
   (*The Book*, or *The Book of Songs*)
《屈原和楚辞》
   (*Qu Yuan and Southern Songs*)
《文姬归汉》
   (*Wenji Gui Han*, *Cai Wenji's Homecoming*)
《木兰辞》

(Song of Mulan)

《古诗十九首》
(Nineteen Ancient Poems)

《唐诗三百首》
(Three Hundred Poems from the Tang Dynasty)

《白居易诗选》
(Selected Poems of Bai Juyi)

《宋词选》
(Lyrics from the Song Dynasty)

《宋诗一百首》
(One Hundred Poems from the Song Dynasty)

《诗词格律》
(Chinese Classical Prosody)

《读词常识》
(Common Sense in Reading Poems and Lyrics)

《稼轩长短句》 (辛弃疾)
(Ji Cassino Short Sentence, over 600 poems)

《逻辑》
(Logic)

《列国演义》
(Annals of the Kingdoms),

《战国故事》
(Sengoku Story)

《三国演义》
(The Three Kingdoms)

《西游记》
(Journey to the West)

《红楼梦》
(Dream of the Red Chamber).

She found in her notebooks, as she counted, at least five hundred classical poems she literally hand copied from borrowed books—nineteen poems were copied from 诗经 *(The Book of Songs)*, eight from 《楚辞》 *(Songs of the South)*, only one from 《天问天对

注》 (*Days of Heaven Notes*), another nineteen from 《古诗十九首》 (*Nineteen Ancient Poems*), one hundred seventy-nine from 《唐诗三百首》 (*Three Hundred Tang Dynasty Poems*), seventy-one from 《白居易诗选》 (*Selected Poems of Bai Juyi*), forty-nine from 《宋词选》 (*The Song Lyrics*), sixty-nine from 《宋诗一百首 (*One Hundred Poems from the Song Dynasty*), forty from 《诗词格律》 (*Chinese Classical Prosody*), eight from 《读词常识》 (*Common Sense in Reading Poems and Lyrics*), only five from 《红楼梦》 (*Dream of the Red Chamber*), forty-three from 《中国文学发展史》 (*History of the Development of Chinese Literature*), and so on. The number was not exaggerated, as it could be easily more than five hundreds, if those copied in her diary were to be counted and added.

J was not interested in modern Chinese literature as much as her peers. Some of her classmates used to carry huge copies of contemporary novels in their bags in and out of school. She only read a few most well-known ones at that time, as these titles appeared in her notebooks:

《老残遊记》
(*Travels*)
《矛盾选集》
(*Selected Works of Mao Dun*)
《鲁迅选集》
(*Selected Works of Lu Xun*)
《沫若选集》
(*Selected Works of Moruo*)
《巴金全集》
(*The Complete Works of Ba Jin*)
卜宁, 《塔利的女人》
(Bo Ning, *A Woman*)
徐讦, 《风萧萧》
(Xu Jie, *Winds Blow*)
张爱玲, 《十八春》
(Eileen Chang, *Eighteen Springs*)

唐人，《金陵春梦》
(Tang Ren, *Spring Dreams in Jinlin*)
老舍，《骆驼祥子》，《散文作品选》
(Lao She, *Rickshaw Boy, Selected Essays*)
萧红，《呼蓝河传》
(Xiao Hong, *Hulan River*)
秦牧，《艺海拾贝》
(Qin Mu, *Shells from the Sea of Art*)
鲁迅，《朝花夕拾》，《花边文学》
(Lun Xun, *NightPicks of Morning Blossoms,
Lace Literature*)
林语堂，《人间世》
(Lin Yutang, *In the Human World*, a periodical)
毛泽东，《毛泽东诗词》
(*The Poems of Mao Zedong*)
羽山、徐昌霖，《东风化雨》
(Yu Shan, Xu Changlin, *East Wind Rainfall*)
乌兰巴干，《草原烽火》
(Ulaan, *Prairie War*,
Tibetan Chinese Modern Literature)
玛拉沁夫，《茫茫的草原》
(Malaqinfu, *Vast Grasslands*,
Mongolian Literature)
欧阳山，《三家巷》
(Ouyang Shan, *Three Family Lane*)
康式昭，《大学春秋》
(Kang Shizhao, *Springs and Autumns in the University*)

Other books mentioned or copied in handwriting in her notebooks were miscellaneous. Though she sometimes came across books on science such as 《科学年鉴》 (*Science Yearbook*) and 《十万个为什么？》 (*One Hundred Thousand Whys?*, a popular book everyone read those days), obviously, she was less interested in science than in philosophy and literature. One book that caught her serious attention was 《刑事警察科学知识全书》 (*The*

Comprehensive Scientific Knowledge of Criminal Justice for the Police). She spent a great deal of time copying the categories of finger prints and blood types. That book was her first introduction to modern psychology.

CHAPTER 5

LIFE IN THE COUNTRYSIDE

"Settle down in the Countryside" (上山下乡)

The movement of "Go up to the Mountains and Settle down in the Countryside" (上山下乡) started in the winter of 1968. Schools received quotas from six provinces in remote, less populated, meagre regions—Heilongjiang, Jilin, Anhui in the North, and Jiangxi, Guizhou, Yunnan in the South (黑龙江, 吉林, 安徽, 江西 贵州 云南). With few exceptions, all the graduates of 1968, over twenty thousands had to leave the city. The graduates were asked to select a region and register for themselves. At first, it was voluntary.

Currie did not want to go. She asked J to come to class to speak up, to see if they could get away with the registration. J came, made a compliment to the Red Guards that they were the avant-garde of all political movements, always the first to answer the calls of Chairman Mao; they were the role models in school. Therefore, they ought to go first. She would like to think about it, and decide later. Then she pulled Currie up from her seat, and the two of them left the classroom. Other classmates followed them, sneaked out one after another. So it goes.

This movement affected the future of six grades of graduates, both the junior high and senior high graduates of 1966, 1967 1968. For the 1966 and 1967 graduates there were some quota for them to work in the city. For the 1968 junior and senior high school graduates, there was no quota to work in the city. All must "go up to the mountains and settle down in the countryside." It was called "All Red Assignments" ("一片红"). "All Red Assignments" covered the 1969 junior high, who had received no classroom instruction at all. Since school was closed in 1966, by 1969 there was no senior high graduates at all.

So the Red Guards went first. Some Red Guards, with favorable family backgrounds, born from the proletariat or cadres' family, had the privilege to go to military farms (军垦农场). They were honored to wear military uniforms. The rest were assigned group by group to specific villages, to join the "big teams of production" or "small teams of production" in people's communes in other remote regions. There they were welcomed to settle down in the villages (插队落户), work in the fields, and live with the peasants.

J got medical proof of a physical condition to be exempt from the draft. Pinnacle did not have to go, as her father was dying and her mother was seriously ill after the torture and house-searching. She had to take care of her parents and three siblings. Olympia was assigned to go north to Jilin (吉林). At the railway station, she met three boys from a nearby school, who took her as their sister on the way. When they got there, they settled down together in a village. After a few years, Olympia married one of them. Bellring chose to go south to Yunnan (云南), where her mother came from originally. She had some relatives there. Nana, a neighbor girl J grew up with, was assigned to go up to the mountains in Anhui (安徽). She went with all strangers. She wrote to tell J that there were no toilet paper in the mountains. They used leaves from the trees.

J saw her friends off at the railway station. Families, friends, and relatives swamped the platforms, sobbing, crying, and wailing, like at funeral ceremonies. Parting was not a sweet sorrow. Parents were reluctant to let go their children, but they couldn't stand the pressure from their employers, that forced them, day and night, to encourage their children to register, now they were heartbroken to see their loved ones off. For most of the children, it was the first time leaving home. They really did not know what to expect in future. They had tremendous fears. Some felt their families did not love them well enough to stand the pressure and let them stay at home.

PoPo and J, 1971.

Later, from the letters J received from her friends, the best news was that most of them received very warm welcome from the local people. The peasants loved them wholeheartedly. The villagers treated them with great hospitality, giving them the best they could offer in the house. For those "planted" in the villages, their peasant uncles and aunts, brothers and sisters soon took them in like families. The peasants were generous, kind, caring and curious about city people. As for the bad news, scarcity of food, water, deep snow, sickness, toilet problem, hopelessness, and worse, rape. Rape was not a topic discussed in public. After a year or two, some came back to the city, and stayed. They did not want to go back.

J's parents got pressure too. Her father came to deliver the message from his employer, that youth must answer the call of Chairman Mao. At least J ought to go out to work and "serve the people." Her mother agreed, she wished J could be independent, financially self-sufficient, and maybe could bring in a little income to help the family. She couldn't continue to support the family by herself. She had never supported anyone until the Red Guards took everything away. Then she had to provide for a family of four with her monthly small salary. She also feared that the Red Guards might come to their home, stay day and night, persuading her to let J go, as they did to some other family. So she asked J to register.

PoPo came to J's protection. "So what!" said she; "we'll go." PoPo came from a village in Zhejiang Province, a very nice region in the countryside, not far away from Shanghai. Her family, the Wu's, was well-to-do peasantry before 1949. After the Revolution, the household was classified as "middle class peasantry." Her family was well respected in the village. PoPo often said that she came to work as a servant in Shanghai not because "there was nothing to eat at home," but because she "had no patience" with her husband, who whined a lot. Her husband and son were still living in that village, they had a house. Her folks in the village used to visit her in Shanghai sometimes. J often took the folks out in the streets shopping. So they knew J well and liked her.

By then the government offered an alternative policy, which allowed the students to locate villages themselves, as long as they could find a place where they had relatives, and be accepted by local registra to settle down there. The policy was called "投亲靠友"—find shelter with relatives or friends. In Chinese culture, there was a tradition to turn to relatives or friends for a living, if one's family was in trouble, could not provide for the children. The children could be adopted by the family that would accept them, though adoption was not necessary.

J's father had no problem with PoPo's suggestion. When he was little, the Japanese bombarded Shanghai, his parents' home was destroyed completely, nothing left. "Not even one chopstick left," he used to say. His mother sent him and his sister to the countryside to live with their relatives in the village in Ningbo. He and his sister had a good appetite, devoured all the fish and meat on the table every meal. Gradually, his relative's family couldn't afford to feed them. They were sent back to their mother in Shanghai after a while. Later, when he became a successful businessman in Shanghai, he sent money back to the village. He always took the villagers as his kinsfolks, never looked down upon his relatives in the countryside.

When J's parents were going through their divorce, J's mother told J that the court might assign one child to one parent, which meant the elder one might have to go with her father. Jimmy was only two years old, and J was nine. Her mother told J that if she went with his father, his father might send her to the countryside, to live in the village where he came from. There was nothing she could do about it. J was scared, but she never counted on her mother to save her. J turned to Grandma. Grandma was determined that she would not go without taking J. After making a few phone calls, she arranged to have J speak to the judge herself, telling the court that she did not want to live with her father.

It was late at night almost around 9:00pm. J was on the bus for half an hour, coming back from her swimming class downtown. The court was still in session. It was held at a neighbor's house across theirs, Nana's house. Nana's parents were honorable people, well respected in the neighborhood. Her father, Mr. Comfort, was a model "Red capitalist," and her mother Mrs. Comfort served in Women's Union in the city as a representative of the capitalists' families. The Comforts had a living room (not every family had one) and a large, rectangular dinning table, which could seat ten people. Behind the seats, there were two sets of high-back chairs with two tea tables in between. So public meetings in the neighborhood were often held in their house. Between the living room and the kitchen, there was a dark corridor. J entered from the backdoor in the kitchen, stood in the corridor in darkness waiting to be called. Nana was with her, and told her not to be afraid.

When she was called, J went in. Her father turned around and said to her mother: "Look, your mother divorced her husband. Now if you divorce me, your daughter will have a divorce too in the future." How could he curse his daughter like that! J's mother did not care. She said: "合则留，不合则去." ("If we get along, stay; if not, go.") She sounded so easy and relaxed, that made things easy for all. She had married against her father's will, now she got the support of her father, who wrote ten pages of an appeal for her to divorce her husband. Even though the court found no substantial evidence of the charges, the judgment was in her favor.

The Judge asked J a question, and she replied. She was only nine years old, couldn't recall what she said. Decades later, she found a few sentences in the court divorce papers regarding the children: "This couple has two children, a daughter and a son. ***The daughter did not have a good relationship with the father. She expressed herself in court that she did not want to live with her father.*** The son was only two years old, it is only appropriate not to separate from the mother. Therefore, the court judges that both children shall live with the mother."

J's father appealed to the Supreme Court. When the Supreme Court's ruling came out, his wife already packed everything ready, ordered trucks to move to her new place the following day. J said good-bye to Nana. So it goes.

"This couple has two children," 1962.

One of PoPo's family's neighbor was a team leader, he could sign a letter of acceptance for J. In order to do so, J must be related to someone in the village. PoPo was not a relative, even though she was family since J was born. Besides, PoPo did not live there, was not a registered villager herself. She was registered as a resident in Shanghai. At first, there came a marriage proposal, which PoPo declined. Then the folks arranged for J to be adopted by a bachelor in the village, PoPo's nephew, twice distanced but related. J used to call him "uncle." His name was White Tiger. He wrote to J to claim kinship. J wrote back calling him "Qin Ba" (亲伯)—Godfather. He was happy. So it goes.

An Ancient River Town

On April 7, 1969, J packed to go with PoPo to live in the village. "Too many books you carry," her mother said. J took out some clothes from her luggage. She was heavy loaded this time, prepared to kill the dullness and ease the slow pace in the countryside. She expected there could be no privacy living in other people's house. The books must be Red and respectable, officially approved, to be acceptable by people around in public. She wouldn't bring anything "bourgeois" or "decadent." So she brought what was appropriate for a revolutionary youth in her time —three volumes of 《资本论》 (*The Capital* by Karl Marx), hardback, thick and heavy; over twenty volumes of Lenin's works; a collection of Mao's poems and some other works; and a copy of *Madame Curie*, that Klever let her have for a month, and some other books.

Thus, PoPo and J had two big luggage bags, which weighed about seventy-five pounds, and four small bags. They had to take the bus for an hour to reach the long distance bus station in Shanghai. From there, it took about four to six hours to get to Nanxun (南浔), that was the town where the bus stopped. PoPo's home was not in town, but in the countryside, quite a distance to go.

In 2004, Nanxun was rediscovered by tourism as one of those ancient river towns in Yangtze Delta. J wanted to visit PoPo's village, but she had lost touch with PoPo's families. Since PoPo passed away in 1974, thirty years had passed by. In the meantime, so much had happened in J's life. How could she remember how to get there? From a tourist center in Shanghai, she bought a bus ticket, thought she might just take a tour in town. Less than an hour after she got on the bus, suddenly the full address emerged in her mind, word by word, crystal clear, without any mistake! The address was: "浙江, 南浔, 南卅, 北里公社, 炬红大队, 泥水

斗" (Zhejiang Province, Nanxun, South Gate, North Lane Commune, Torch Red Big Team, Construction Village)! In English, the order of address would be in reverse, i.e. "Construction Village, Torch Red Big Team, North Lane Commune, South Gate, Nanxun, Zhejiang Province."

It was very strange. Maybe PoPo's soul were smiling in the sky, maybe somewhere on the bus, welcome her on board, nodding to her, pleased to see her back. Maybe it was because J had written many letters for PoPo with that address on the envelop before, hand-writing had "stored" that address somewhere "in her brain." *"People can take away what you possess in the house, but they cannot take away what you possess in your mind. They cannot take away what you learned and stored in your brain."* That was PoPo's admonition in 1969.

It was a "miracle" that happened not only once, but twice, and twice only in J's life. The second time was in the spring of 2014. J was planning a trip to do some research in one of those historical sites in the suburbs of Wuxi, a historical city in Jiangsu Province, in between Nanjing and Shanghai. She thought of PoPo's relatives, they used to live in Wuxi. She had visited them in 1962, fifty years before. J's mother had lost touch with PoPo's family after PoPo passed away. Spring Bell asked J's mother for a pension for PoPo's service. J's mother wouldn't give it to her. So it goes.

The night before, looking at a map, J happened to come across two words—"后祁". It was the name of a school. Instantly, it clicked! "后祁街，41 号" (Houqi St. #41)—that old address of PoPo's relatives came back to her mind even with a house number! "Ghost! Ghost!" J cried out; "Ghost here!" Was PoPo's spirit around? PoPo knew she was going to Wuxi tomorrow?! Or, was it because she had hand-written that address many times in her teenage days, sending letters for PoPo to her relatives that it was "stored in her brain," happened to pop up incidentally? It must be a "miracle," that brought back so many memories.

The trip to Nanxun was not the first time PoPo and J traveled together, they had travelled before. When J was eleven years old, they rode the train to Wuxi (无锡). PoPo took J to attend the wedding of her nephew. J carried a very large radio for PoPo, which was one of the wedding presents. They had a lot of luggage. PoPo was pleased with J's strength and alertness during the trip. They stayed for a couple of weeks. PoPo's relatives took her sightseeing and fed her with her favorite dim sum. Once she ate thirty-two small pork buns plus a bowl of won ton soup! It shocked everyone in the family when she came back. J had such a good time there that she did not want to come home. Finally, she brought back a dozen of sculptures, that was the special products of folk art in Wuxi.

Grandma was so pleased that J made a good guest in Wuxi. Following that trip, she sent J to visit her close relatives and best friends. She asked J to give them the sculptures she brought back as presents, and tell them about her trip to Wuxi. Such social activities were part of her education from Grandma. Grandma could have sent any adults around to run such errands, but she preferred to let J have some experience for practice. She meant for J to learn appropriate social mannerism by calling on people.

For each visit, J was given instructions as to what to say and what to do, how to make a phone call first, arrive on time, and do not stay too long, learn to listen, leave well before meal time. When she came back from each visit, she had to report to Grandma how it went, what she said, what the elderly said to her, and what so and so wished her to pass to her Grandma. Afterwards, when people called to thank her, Grandma would verify J's reports over the phone. She herself never went out, bedridden most of the time. J received high marks from most of those elderly she visited. One Grand-Uncle-in-Law was pleased with the sculpture J gave to him, it was a half-naked Greek woman. He let it stand on his bedside. His wife, Grand-Aunt Augustan III, called her elder sister to say that the eleven year old girl was bold.

It was not the only time Grandma had J ran errands. One year before the New Year's Eve, grandma put two hundred RMB in the ten year old's pocket, sent her to those special delicatessens （沧浪亭，鼎心园，乔家栅，哈尔滨，老大昌）to buy pork buns, rice balls, rice cakes, cookies, candies, chocolates, and flowers in a special flower shop. Another time, she sent J to Heng Shan Restaurant, that served Western food, to order a cream

One of the well known gardens in Nanxun—
Little Lotus flower Farm (小莲莊).

Chicken and mushroom soup to go. J had to take the bus for several stops. With the soup in hands, it was really not a pleasant journey for the twelve year old girl. So the second time, J asked Grandma if she could ride in a tricycle home. It costed only about twenty cents. Grandma said no, the bus only costed four cents. J ought to learn how to take challenges running errands, and save money. When J did take the bus home, soup in hands, Grandma gave her an award of two bucks. So it goes.

History, Culture, and Language

Nanxun (南浔) was a very special ancient town, situated right on the board of Zhejiang and Jiangsu provinces, near Shanghai. Its history could be traced back at least to the Song Dynasty (960-1279). Some say its best time was in Tang Dynasty (618–907).

It was one of those ancient river towns in the Yangtze Delta, known as "the country of fish and rice" ("鱼米之乡").

Blessed with its natural resources and ecological environment, the town looked content with its own prosperity. Teahouses, silk stores, groceries, gift shops and restaurants lined up on the water edge. River fish and river shrimps could be brought to the table alive, directly from the street markets. Its main transportation was by boat. Wooden boats sailing on the water inside the town and outside to the villages in all directions in the region. The region produced silk and tea. Other specialties were brush pen, fans made of birds' feather, and special paper for brush paintings and calligraphy, that displayed a high culture. The town was well-known for a long scholarly tradition with its rich collections of books, sculptures, poetry, paintings, and calligraphy, very elegant and exquisite, distinguished from orthodox court tradition.

The cultural tradition in this part of the country valued folk intelligence and wisdom, that had nurtured many learned wits and good brains in history. It was the excellence or the quality of people here that made this place "soulful" (人杰地灵). Many sons of the gentry from the region had held high offices, mostly served as "think-tanks" in court throughout the dynasties. During the Republic period, the national party's six of the twelve Prime Ministers were born in this region. Over the centuries, many distinguished family built their mansions here, with beautiful design, elegant pavilions, rock hills, bridges, and lakes, classical architecture (亭台楼阁). Unlike the mandarin quarter yards in the North (四合院), these mansions in the South were called "gardens."

In Nanxun alone, there were quite a few such "gardens." The best known were the mansions of the "Four Elephants." The "Four Elephants" used to be the distinguished family in the region. They were the Gu's, the Liu's, the Pound's, and the Zhang's (顾家, 刘家, 庞家, 张家). J learned from the villagers that one of Grandma's father's sisters was married to the Liu family. She came down from Shanghai and lived here in the Liu's mansion. She liked the local people very much, as they were very warm and hospitable. At one point, she brought a group of men and women from the local

"Benevolence and Philanthropy" (*"乐善好施"*).

villages back to her brothers' house in Shanghai, to be employed. For those villagers, it was "going up to the city and settle down" in the mansions of a wealthy and modern family.

PoPo was one of them. Her first name was 文 (Wen), the word in Chinese means "Literature" or "Culture". When she was introduced to Grandma, Grandma was pleased with her appearance and personality. She asked her to take care of her youngest daughter, J's mother, then only three years old, already weaned from her wet nurse. So PoPo stayed, left her husband and son at home in the village for the next thirty years. J's mother never missed her wet-nurse, PoPo said. When her wet-nurse came to visit her, she treated her like a stranger. What a forgetful lady she was!

PoPo got along with Grandma quite well. J never heard Grandma complain about PoPo, or vice versa. The worst Grandma said about PoPo was that if she complained, for instance, the tea was not strong enough, and PoPo did not think so, next time she would get something too strong. "She was very stubborn," Grandma said, she was obviously less stubborn between the two of them. Yet PoPo had an amiable reputation among the dozens of servants in the grand mansion. She never made any trouble, or gave trouble to others. She taught J's mother well enough not to make any noise in public in a large family.

Fortunately, all those years PoPo did not have to cook for the family, as the family always had a cook or cooks. After the house-searching, the cook left. PoPo had to cook for the family. She did not like it. PoPo was a vegetarian. She believed it was a sin for her to cook meat dishes. She never tasted anything she cooked, light or salty. Soon J took over. She learned to cook without tasting the food and make it right. PoPo was her first culinary teacher. Cooking was the most important skill in Chinese culture. As the saying goes for smart wives in folk culture, "hold his stomach will hold his heart." J's father couldn't live without his wife's cooking. He trusted his wife was the best cook in the world. J's mother never cooked at home before she got married. She learned at YWCA culinary school. She was a good student.

In addition to the "Four Elephants'" mansions, there were more than four gardens, at least seven or eight of them, in town. The Liu's built a separate garden not far from their resident mansion, called "Hall of Books" (嘉业藏书楼). This garden housed many finest and precious editions of classics, wood carved editions of Chinese history and literature, including the classics of 《春秋》,《史记》,《 前汉书》,《后汉书》,《三国志》 (*Spring and Autumn*, *History of China*, *Pre-Han History*, *Post-Han History*, *The Three Kingdoms*).

The Liu's family had spent twenty-two years (1902-1924), collecting and purchasing the books, fixing the pages, making new ones by carving, or copying by handwriting, and preparing for the construction of this library. When it opened, it had 600,000 copies of books to begin with. Remarkably, to encourage the love for books, the Liu's established a special rule—anyone who would like to read the books and who came from afar, must be welcome to stay, room and board free. This kind of hospitality was quite characteristic of the culture and tradition in this region—people were extremely generous, open, and very warm by courtesy. As

Hall of Books in Liu's Garden (嘉业藏书楼).

carved on that gateway, *"Benevolence and Philanthropy"* were characteristic of the wealthy people in this region.

Only a decade later by 1935, the Japanese bombarded the town heavily. The Japanese soldiers came to the spot, they bowed to the Emperor's calligraphy in exhibition, then looted the library, taking away mostly complete volumes, leaving behind the incomplete volumes. The Liu's knew the Japanese interest of collection, that they only wanted the complete volumes, not the incomplete ones. So the Liu's had taken out one copy from each complete volume, hid in a secret place, to fool the Japanese, thus some books survived the looting by Japanese invasion. After the fire and bombs and looting in Nanxun in WWII, the Liu's family declined. After 1949, the family donated most of the volumes to the Zhejiang Province main public library, let the books benefit more readers.

During the Cultural Revolution, the Garden was saved from looting and book-burning as the local government received orders directly from Beijing. The order relied on a legacy that this "Hall of Books" housed a valuable copy of wood carved edition of the most comprehensive index of Chinese herb medicine (李时珍的 《本草纲目》), which was recognized as a science book, there should be no harmful bourgeois ideology in it. Perhaps no one was capable of taking that book out from the rest, so the gate was closed for years. J had a chance to get in "from the back door," to have a peep of the interior, that was in 1971.

The folks here were loyal, patriotic, traditional people, but they were far from being narrow and close minded. Even Shanghai people wouldn't take them as "parochial." They were conservative in the way that they do not go after fashion or trends, such as revolution or street demonstration. Instead, they led the fashion or trends of their world in commerce, education, arts and letters, architecture, economics, industry and technology. They were very creative, adventurous and resourceful people.

For example, the Zhang's began international commerce as early as in the mid nineteenth century, trading silk with France. Later, a son came back, introducing the power of electricity, built his mansion with electric lights, which was in 1919. Another son of the Zhang's met Sun Yet-Sun on board of a ship to France, made friends. Zhang promised Sun to fund his revolution, which he did. Later when Sun succeeded in his revolution, Zhang became Sun's indispensable resourceful advisor. Sun honored him as "the Saint of the Revolution."

It was such a special place of countryside, that after so many years, as J reviewed her diary of those days she lived in the countryside, J wished she had never left that lovely village then and there. She loved the people, their culture and language, the dialect, also their special products, cuisine and food—凤箫(rice skin), 熏亲豆 (smoked beans), 大头菜(big head turnip), 肉粽(soy sauce pork rice cake), and 芝麻, 红萝卜, 熏亲豆茶 (a special tea mixed with sesame seeds, dried carrots and smoked beans). Their cuisine was much to her taste. Soy source was used for meat, chicken and fish. Green onion and ginger were used for seasoning. Sugar was seldom used. Hot paper and garlic were never seen, that sort of stuff were only for "barbarian" taste.

The special food in that region were 蓁鱼, 鲫鱼, 活虾, 河蟹, 蹄膀, 炒虾腰, 面筋箧肉, 千张包子, 笋烧豆腐干, 老母鸡汤 (Blue Fish, Jump Fish, shrimps, crabs, soy sauce ham, shrimp and kidney, meat balls inside deep fried bean curd cake, thousand layers of bean curd skin tightly wrapped with dry shrimps and pork, bamboo shoots sautéed with bean cakes, and chicken soup). Feast after feast, the peasants entertained her. She never heard of "chop-sews" or "sweet sour pork." Mixed meats was a scrambled dish called "Happy Family."

Above all, the people were so cultivated, warm, passionate, and hospitable. They treated J as a special guest, as well as a family. They would tell her all kinds of stories, secrets and gossips. They invited her to dinner from door to door. If she declined an invitation, as PoPo would warn her, people would take offense or feel hurt. So she might as well go. J went to as many neighbors' dinners as she could, and made friends with the families, old and young, men and women alike.

The peasants' family fed her with their best—bean curd stuffed with pork, pork chops, pork stew, soy source chicken, alive river fish, river shrimps and river crabs, fresh bamboo shoots, and ducklings! When she thanked the people saying they were too kind. People would say not at all, not at all. It was just the custom to entertain their guests. In this region, the further south, the more hospitable and warmer people were. If J ever got invited to dinner ten or twenty miles south, the people there world use their fingers, tear apart the large piece of pork stew, pile on top of her rice, and use their fingers to press hard over her rice, push down and down in her bowl!

They had their customs and traditions, they inherited the interesting ones, sensible ones, and humorous ones. There was no customs or so called "tradition" that made J felt oppressive or repressive, silly or dull. She did not hear or see any wife-beating incident. In her diary, J noted, a young husband, who was married into the wife's family, was abused by his hot tempered wife. In a fight, the wife poured a full stool of toilet over the head of the husband! The poor guy came out of the house crying for help. People just laughed at such folly.

For extramarital scandals, the community's response was civilized. There was no village raid, no public humiliation, abuses, or resentful punishment. The most laughable story was that of Gold Tiger. Gold Tiger was educated in the city, after graduation he came back, worked in a factory in town. Though he liked city life, he had to come home and maintain the household, because he was the only son. He got married to a peasant woman here in his home village, who bore him two sons.

Later he fell in love with a rich woman in another village. He divorced his wife, went away to live with the other woman in her family. That family took him in as an "adopted" son-in-law, put him to work in the field. After a while, field work was too hard for him. He couldn't get used to the food and life style in that village. He came back, asking his ex-wife to come to the other village, acting like a shrew, fetching him back from that family he was married to. His ex-wife did as he instructed her, brought him home. She forgave him and he was grateful. They had another son. They lived happily or unhappily thereafter, till his death did they part. In the village, for what she did, the wife was honored and respected by everyone as a good wife. Only the husband became a laughing stock.

One day, there was a wedding in the village, a group of men sailed on a boat with drums, gongs, drums and fireworks to welcome the bride from another village. J wanted to go with them. Normally by custom, only the bridegroom's brothers, best men and male friends were selected to go, no women were allowed. PoPo asked them a favor to take J. The guys got the permission from the Bridegroom's mother, and helped J jump on board.

When they got to the Bride's house, the men began to load the bride's dowry. The bride's mother handed J a red painted wooden toilet stool, and told her not to let it go. J thought she was given the toilet stool to carry because she was the only female on board. As soon as she got back to the Bridegroom's house in the village, she put it down by the bed in the new bedroom, and left. When she walked to the front door, the bridegroom's mother asked her if she had got the goodies in the toilet stool yet. J rushed back, the goodies were already gone. The villagers around knew the custom better, they already emptied everything inside—the candies, the nuts, small red envelops and whatever in it. J cried!

Those people were so quick, witty and resourceful, like PoPo. PoPo was the one J and her whole family relied on and turned to whenever they were in distress or had problems. On such occasions, PoPo used to say that her "uncle's family owned a store of ideas and strategies," she could always borrow some to help solve the problems. Of course she did not have any uncle. It was just a figure of speech.

J loved PoPo's language, the local dialect there. In that region, the diversity of dialects survived for thousands of years. As a result, it was unthinkable in modern society that out of thirty miles, people could hardly understand one another orally in their native tongue. They could communicate in written language though. Once put down in black and white, all dialects read the same, and became comprehensible. That was the magic of Chinese. A written language throughout centuries survived to unify the race all over the globe. J grew up with PoPo's dialect, the Nanxun dialect was like a native tongue to her, familiar and pleasing to the ear.

The dialect survived for thousands of years, it was rich with rhetorical tropes, similes, imaginative conceits, archaic expressions, and local color. Most interestingly, the peasants had such a rich sense of humor, every sentence they spoke could be a metaphor. If someone said to you: "棺材弯头踢一脚，死人肚里得知" ("go kick the head of the coffin"), it meant "you know it yourself, do not ask me." Or, if you are slow and couldn't make up your mind, people would say: "三娘娘嫁人，心不定" ("You are as shy as the tender lady, couldn't decide who to marry." Not to throw away something useless, people would say: "千年的文书好革药" ("A thousand year old piece of paper may be useful for a prescription of sort some day." Peasant talk was not illiterate or blunt, but humorous and artistic.

Once PoPo took J to a fortune teller in town. She was a blind lady. J fooled her with her Nanxun dialect so well so that the blind lady couldn't tell J was from city. She took J as a native from the village. She advised PoPo to let this girl leave home and go far far away. "This young woman is very special," she said; "her fortune says that she ought to be able to read and write before she went to school. She is made of good material, the kind of material that is to be used to make an altar, not a kitchen stool. At home, she might not be sweet and well liked by her families. But abroad, she will be appreciated. Do not let her stay in the house. Better leave home and go away."

Although J did not quite understand her prophecy, at least, J could tell she was right about her learning aptitude and literacy. J started learning characters as early as one or two years old at Grandma's. Grandma had a companion living with her. This lady was a school teacher. J called her "Sir Mammy." She was J's first teacher. She taught J characters. Sir Mammy had an admirer. He and his wife visited Sir Mammy frequently at Grandpa's place. The three of them were good friends, and friends with Grandma. It was this man, Sir Mammy's good friend, who wrote Grandma's divorce paper. Grandma also had a friend of handyman, who came often. He was extremely crafty and intelligent. He taught J songs, characters and paper-clipping. J called him "Sir Daddy Chen."

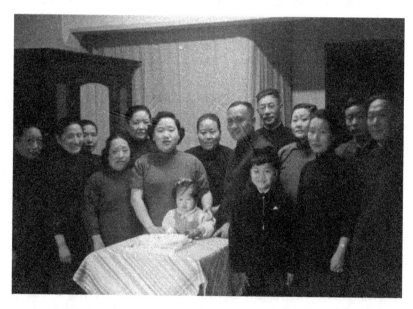

"Sir Mammy" (R3), "Sir Daddy Chen" (R1), GM's three classmates and her cousin (L), Ar Niang (C), Aunt Phoenix Letter, her husband, and their two sons (R).

When J was three, riding the tricycles in the streets from downtown home, on the way she would stick out her little finger, pointing to some of the characters she could recognize on some store sign boards. When her father took her out dining, he let J read the menu and order for herself. Before she went to school, she had already learned to read the stage scripts from the slides in theater, How did the blind lady know? It puzzled J. Fortune telling was a folklore passed down for thousand years in Chinese civilization, at least as ancient as 易经 (*Yijing*). (That book she did not know until she came to Berkeley though.)

PoPo's Family

Though J got adopted by White Tiger, her Godfather's house only had one bedroom upstairs, where he slept. So it was only appropriate for J to live in PoPo's house, the Wu's. PoPo's husband, Grandpa Wu, moved downstairs to sleep in a corner of the large living room, so that PoPo and J could sleep upstairs in a large, carved, redwood bed together. That room became J's study. J put all her books in it, used PoPo's dressing table as her desk. PoPo would not let anyone disturb J when she was studying upstairs.

PoPo's house had more than one bedroom, or bed. One was used by her son, Treasure Root, one used by Grandpa Wu, and one used by Treasure Root's four children. They sometimes came back in turn for a visit. They were J's age. They lived in the city of Wuxi with their mother and her parents. They seldom came for a visit. They were city children.

Their mother's mother, J called her Big PoPo, though she was tiny in her physique. Big PoPo originally belonged to the Wu's family. She was the daughter of the Wu family, sister to Grandpa Wu. PoPo was her adopted sister at first, and became her sister-in-law later.

PoPo was a child bride, came to the Wu family when she was little. The Wu's family had a son and a daughter. The son was a little older than she was, and the daughter younger. The child bride was to marry the son of the family when they grew up someday. In reality, the three children grew up together like siblings, "plucking blue plums and riding on bamboo horse." So the daughter of the family was like PoPo's younger sister. They were very close. She came to Shanghai frequently staying with PoPo. J knew her as though another grandma, she was extremely capable and confident, knew what to do, and she was less reticent and more affectionate than PoPo. J liked her a lot.

Snow Plum and his brother (L), J, Spring Bell holding Jimmy (R).

When she grew up, Big PoPo married a man from the city. Mr. Gold, who worked in the silk factory in Wuxi. They had a son and a daughter. It was her son's wedding in Wuxi that J attended with PoPo that winter when she was eleven. Their daughter Spring Bell also worked in the silk factory in Wuxi. Coming of age, Spring Bell returned to the village, married her cousin, Treasure Root, PoPo's son. After the marriage, Spring Bell went back to work and live with her parents in the city. She came back visiting her husband once a while, mostly as she liked, or had vacation during national holidays.

She and PoPo's son had two sons and two daughters, who were J's generation. Three of them were older than J, and one younger. Their elder daughter, sister Snow Plum, was friend with J. The two of them wrote to each other sometimes. Once Snow Plum broke her leg, had a cast for a long time. She came to Shanghai to go to hospital, and stayed with J for a while. Afterwards, she still had a little inconvenience when walking. So she did not have to go to the countryside to work in the fields, stayed in the city, and later got a job.

For all those years PoPo was away from the family and village, lived and worked in Shanghai, PoPo's husband never had another woman. PoPo sent him money when he needed. Her son had a mistress in the village sometimes. When Spring Bell came back, Treasure Root sent the other woman away. If his wife got angry with him, he would say, it was just because she was not at home. Who told her not to come back though! So it goes.

For many years the marriage lasted, till one day, Spring Bell got quite serious. She went to fight with the other woman, and called her bad names. When Treasure Root tried to stop her, she took action, divorced her husband. It must have taken place in the year of 1962, the same year J's mother divorced J's father. PoPo said it was too much for her. The two marriages both fell apart, one was that of her son and her beloved niece; and the other, J's mother, whom she raised like a daughter. She did not say yes or no to both divorces. She did not cry even. She was a wise woman, gentle and sensible. No one could find any fault with her. Or, she would not let anyone find any fault with her anyway.

Strangely, after their divorce, neither PoPo's son or her daughter-in-law ever married again. So they were sill family, PoPo's family. J's mother, on the other hand, couldn't endure poverty and hardship, supporting the family alone, remarried J's father after twelve years of their divorce. J was opposed to the idea, but her mother did not follow her idea. After they remarried, they were still not happy together. J found family life was a disaster. So it goes.

Whatever happened in the family, PoPo and Big PoPo remained sisters for a life time. Blood was not necessarily thicker than water. Under the same family name Wu, everyone belonged to the family in the village, including J. It was Uncle Gold Tiger's wife, Aunt Usher, imparted to J the little family secret. She explained to J how her family and PoPo's family were related, and why White Tiger agreed to adopt J. The truth was—White Tiger was Big PoPo's son! He was family! PoPo's nephew! J's Godfather!

Uncle Gold Tiger and Uncle White Tiger were cousins. Their fathers were brothers. Their last name was also Wu. How they were related to Grandpa Wu exactly J did not know. White Tiger's father grew up with Big PoPo as cousins in the same village. He was in love with her. When the time came, Big PoPo married a city man from Wuxi. He might be love sick, got pneumonia, which was a serious illness then in China. He chose to be alone, never married. One year, Big PoPo came back from the city, either because her husband lost his job, or they had an argument, she was going through a hard time. White Tiger's father let her stay with him, and took care of her. They had a baby, White Tiger.

As soon as White Tiger was weaned, however, Big PoPo left the baby, returned to her own family, the Wu's, across the river. Soon she went back to her husband in the city. White Tiger was raised by his father, without a mother. When he reached seventeen, his father passed away, left him a decent household, land, house and property, also a child bride. The young man did not like to work in the filed. Soon he spent all the money, sold his house, even sent away his child bride to marry someone else.

He did not want to get married and have a family. He only asked Gold Tiger to let him adopt one of his three sons. To adopt inside the family was a acceptable custom traditionally. However, Gold Tiger's wife, Aunt Usher, the good wife, declined his wish. She wouldn't want to give away any of her sons. A son was a son, it meant progeny, manpower, and household prosperity. Why would she want to let go any of her sons? Now as White Tiger was aging, he began to work hard, build a house, bought furniture, wanted to have a family.

PoPo's good friend, also a villager, Sweet Olive PoPo, found him a wife with a child of hers from a meagre region in Jiangsu Province. The woman was happy to move to Nanxun for a better life. Everyone was happy for White Tiger. The Chinese believed "败子回头金不换" —a prodigal son returned home, turned into a family man, which was something worth far more than what gold could exchange for.

Sweet Olive PoPo was a widow, had a son. She came to Shanghai together with PoPo to work for Grandma's family. She became Grand-Aunt May Fourth's nanny. She supported his only son to go through college. He joined the communists and worked underground in Shanghai. After 1949, his son became a cadre, held a top position in a factory in the northeast part of Shanghai. Happily he married a good woman, also a party member and a cadre in the factory. Her family was city people, well-to-do.

Sweet Olive PoPo's son was ashamed to tell his wife that his mother had worked as a servant, so he sent his mother back to live in the village. A widow from the countryside might make his family background look better, as though from the poor peasantry. Every year, Sweet Olive PoPo came to Shanghai, she would visit his son's family first, then she would say good-bye to her daughter-in-law and her in-laws, pretending that she was going back to the village. Then she would visit Grand-Aunt May Fourth's family, and come to J's house, stay with PoPo for sometime, as long as she wanted.

J liked Sweet Olive PoPo very much, she was delicate, gentle, and protective. What J could not understand was the mind of his son. How could he, a party member and a proletariat cadre, be ashamed of his mother being a working class servant? What kind of class conscious was that that he and his wife shared in common? Sweet Olive PoPo died alone in the village a few years later. So it goes.

Everyday Life in the Countryside

Life in the countryside was such a joy. It was carefree, tranquil, happy and healthy. Every morning, when she heard the roosters began "wuo, wuo, wuo," J knew it was about five o'clock. Though PoPo would let her stay in bed, she would get up, went downstairs, to say "good morning" to Grandpa Wu. She would ask him what errands he had for J to run for the day, such as picking up his herb medicine in town, buy some dim sum and tea, or get pills from the barefoot doctor in the village.

The Barefoot doctors' clinic was quite self-sufficient, well equipped and well supplied. The doctors could treat most of ailments, unless the patients need x-ray exams or possible surgery. The Barefoot doctors were literate young people, either youth from the city, or promising youngsters from local villages. They were selected to go through a short period of training, not as long as in medical school. They would return, or be assigned to the villages in

Grandpa Wu and Treasure Root's house, 2005.

Aunt Usher, Uncle Gold Tiger's wife
across the river, 2005.

most remote areas, which did not have easy access to hospital, to establish clinics.

Mostly they rely on a book 《赤脚医生手册》 (*The Barefoot Doctor's Handbook*), which was not like the little red book, Mao's Quotations, but a thick volume like an encyclopedia, thick and heavy. It listed all sorts of common diseases, the symptoms and possible treatments. If they had any doubt, they would look up references in that book to treat their patients. They even knew how to deliver babies.

The Barefoot Doctors' Clinics really functioned well to serve the peasants in the countryside, which effectively popularized modern medical practice and medical service in the mountains and villages. Moreover, as that handbook was available for sale in bookstores, it became the "Bible" in every family in the 1970s. In the cities, anyone who was literate would read the book. Every family had it. People could just look up their symptoms and go to the pharmacy to pick up a prescription. Ordinary people could treat small illnesses by themselves, such as fever, cough, cold, rash, high blood pressure, sleeplessness, headache, back problems and the like. In practice, the Barefoot Doctors program really helped the popularization of modern medical knowledge and medical practice all over China. It not only made modern medicine accessible in the countryside, but also in the cities.

J studied that book too, when she was in the village, so that she had a basic knowledge of common illness, and learned some treatments. She was not very good in medical science, not as good as her girl friend Apple. With that encyclopedia, Apple became a very knowledgeable medical consultant J could rely on. For years, Apple virtually served as a "Barefoot Doctor" for everyone around —family, relatives, neighbors and friends.

To come back to the day in village, while PoPo was burning the dried straw to lit the fire, boiling the water and making breakfast in that huge earth built stove, with a big chimney behind, J would go outside of the house, to let the ducks out, led them step down the stone stair way on the river band. J would stand on the stone stairs of the river band, watching them one by one jump into the water, and swam away for the day.

Each house built its own access to the water. People of the house stood on the stone staircase to wash clothes, brush their teeth, and draw water. Before dark, swamps of ducks and geese would come back to their own river bank, reach their own stone built staircases, and walk into their own house. To one's amazement, the ducks and geese would not make mistakes! For some ducks, that were lingering on the water, J had to call them home, as other family did. Grandpa Wu gave J the password. J learned to call Wu's ducks in a special Wu's tune, as Grandpa Wu taught her—" Ar—liuliuliuliuliu . . . Ar—liuliuliuliuliu . . . " The ducks would recognize the password, and follow her voice, as though it were Grandpa Wu's calling, to come back. J had to count the numbers till the last one made it in. The ducks would not lay their eggs outside, only in their own home nests.

The peasants did not go to the fields the first thing in the morning. Instead, men would go downtown to sit in the teahouses, drink tea, smoke cigarettes, read newspapers, talk about politics, and share the news of the day, or news in the world, inside or outside of China. Then they would go to work in the fields. The teahouses in town were quite a distance from the villages. For most of the peasants, it was several miles. It was five or six miles from PoPo's village, at least half an hour of walk. Back and forth it took one hour. In the countryside, people were relaxed, not pressed by the clock. Most of the peasants even did not look at the clock, they went by sunrise and sunset, as though their life were as immortal as the sun and the moon, and as ancient as the town itself. On rainy days, people just took a break.

PoPo's son, Uncle Treasure Root, wouldn't take breakfast at home. He usually would have his breakfast on his way to the tea house or in town. There were all kinds of delicious rice products and breakfast dim sums in the streets. He took J to the tea house once or twice, just for J to have an experience. He liked to show off his "city niece" to his friends there. There were many square tables in a tea house, each sat eight guests. Each guest would have an individual tea pot, unlike in the teahouses in Shanghai, there would be one tea pot on the table for the guests to share.

Between five to seven in the morning, the place was most crowded, busy and noisy. There were newspapers, radio, story

126

By boat or by foot to go to town. "The Third Restaurant" on the flag.

A vegetable garden at the backyard. Boats as main transportation.

telling, and sometimes singing and playing of musical instruments. People talk, talk, and talk, a house of smoke and laughter. J loved the stories there, but she was too lazy to walk miles to town and miles back every morning. Uncle Treasure Root would bring her back the newspapers.

J worked in the fields with the women in the Torch Red Big Team. Aunt Usher took J to work in the fields, with her team. It was harvest season, their job was to thresh the husk of the rice. It was easier than planting the rice in the spring, when the fields were all water. Now the fields were dry. The heavy rice ears were cut from the roots, lay by the field paths, bunched side by side to be threshed. J was assigned to take the bunched rice ears from the fields to the machines for the other women to thresh. People could talk at work, happy and loud. They laughed at J when they saw husks got into her hair and necks, J felt itching, and started scratching.

Aunt Usher took her away to water the vegetable gardens. There were all sorts of vegetables— 莴苣， 蚕豆， 茄子， 青菜， 土豆， 西红柿， 冬瓜， 南瓜 . . . (asparagus lattice, cocoon peas, eggplants, everyday green vegetables, potatoes, tomatoes, southern melons, Winter Born melons, yams . . .). There was one special product of the region, called "南浔大头菜" ("Nanxun Big Head Turnip"). It was like beets, dark brown colored inside out, with a huge head and 绣花茎 (silk embroidered vessels) on its long leaves. J inspected, the vessels on the leaves indeed looked as though embroidered with silk. Aunt Usher taught J the value of saving toilet, which could be used as the best fertilizer. That was why the peasant wouldn't mind its stinky smell.

Next to the vegetable garden, there laid many pieces of tiles, still wet. Aunt Usher told J that these tiles were made of earth, later would be used on roofs. Next year when they would use these tiles to build a new house. Though those darksome stuff looked dirty, J learned, roof tops were made from the bottom of earth from the land.

Then Aunt Usher took J to water their 自留地 (Self-Maintained Fields), which belonged to her own household. Whatever she chose to plant and grow here, she could cut any time.

She could use the vegetables to cook, or sell on the market, just like the hens, ducks, geese, and their eggs, or the rabbits and pigs she raised at home. Those were her own produces. In due course, she had to ask men to slaughter the pigs. She would put the rabbits, the chickens and ducks in a cage, take to the market to trade for some money. With the money, she would buy cotton cloth to make clothes for everyone in the family for the new year. This year, she made a couple of new blankets, blankets stuffed with cocoon silk, which was very warm. This kind of blankets was considered a luxury elsewhere, peasants couldn't afford it. Here it was their local specialty. She invited J to sleep over.

Each peasant household was allowed to have its "Self-Maintained Field," as separated from the common fields. The common fields belonged to the Big Team and the commune. The team members from each household in the village work by 工分 ("scores"). A man would receive higher scores than a woman, as he usually took care of the hard labor, and women were assigned to do lighter and easier work. A man who worked hard full time could receive 10 scores a day, and a woman perhaps 7-8 or 9.

At the end of the year, each family would add up its total scores to receive their dues and shares of the harvest in the common fields from the Big Team and the Commune. Those family which had more men than women at work, worked harder might receive more field produces and money at the end of the year. As PoPo's family only had her son, one single hand at work, he couldn't but envy other family, which had more hands at work and received much more than he did year in and year out. J became sympathetic with Uncle Treasure Root.

Dusk on the river was the most exciting moment of the day, when each household's mom or dad or children, stood on its own stone stairway, calling their ducks and geese home. Also, it was time for chickens and cats, loitering outside in the fields or lanes during the day. Some called with high pitch, some low, some mumbled as though angry if their pets did not come home, and some giggled singsong to allure them to dinner—some "Ar—liuliuliuliu. . . Ar—liuliuliuliuliu . . . ," some "Er-lu-Er-lu-Er-lu-lu-lu . . . Er-lu-Er-lu-Er-lu-lu-lu. . ." Different voices carry different scales and secret variations, secret "passwords," that the ducks and geese could identify and access, calling one after another, or at once. Their echoes rebounded, vibrating, rolling on the surface of the river, like music floating on the water, a delightful symphony in twilight. As the sun went down, smoke rose from every house's chimney.

By six O'clock, the farmers would come home for dinner. Each house had fish and shrimps over rice at least, because each family could scoop them right from the river or pond. In the river, there were plenty of fish, shrimps and crabs, big and small, submerging and jumping high and low, line by line, as though they were busy "writing a composition" ("鱼龙潜跃水成文"), as described in a poem, that J jot down in her diary.

The day was not over after dinner. Old people lit their candle lights, began evening gossip. The young went out dating, or visiting one another in the neighborhood. Some loved singing and dancing. Some were doing their rehearsals for performance. There was a village Performing Arts Troupe (文艺宣传队) organized by a young woman, who came from the city and settled down there. J watched their rehearsal a couple of times. Frequently, there were theater or movies shown in the village arranged by the "Big Team." During the Cultural Revolution, classical opera was abolished. Instead, movies were staged periodically. Some of the movies J watched with the folks in the village, as she noted in her diary, were 洪湖赤卫队 (*Red Defense Team on the Hong Lake*), 英雄儿女 (*Heroic Sons and Daughters*) and 刘三姐 (*The Liu's Third Sister*). Those movies became revolutionary classics in Chinese film history now.

CHAPTER 6

FATHER, MOTHER, GRANDMAS

J between her parents, 1953.

Theory and Practice: *Das Kapital*

J had time to study during her stay in the village. She felt more concentrated than in the city. Now distanced from home and the trauma of house-searching movement, she wished to comprehend the theory of Marxism intellectually and rationally, in order to understand why the government took away the property of her family; in what sense the propertied class exploited the proletariat; who the proletariat was in a strict sense; why she had to suffer the lot of deprivation and humility.

She set for herself a major task, that was, to crack the hard nut of Karl Marx's *Das Kapital*. She studied studiously line by line, paragraph by paragraph, concept one after another, the logic of thoughts, and the relation of ideas backwards and forwards. The theory of Economics was a hard subject, it wasn't like reading a novel. J worked hard, took notes. If she did not understand, she would stop, went back and forth, figure out the logic, the relation among "Wages, Price and Profit." Afterwards she was glad she did it. Marxism was not a mere slogan, pushed down her throat, as most of her peers felt, but a science, at least a philosophy, to be reckoned.

She even discussed with her father the validity of Marx's theory of economics, especially the key concept of surplus value and exploitation, which served as theoretical justification of class revenge, confiscating private property, that people around had a hard time to accept, and that J wished to understand. Her father confirmed that the theory had truth value in it. There was the truth of "surplus value," either to be reinvested or possessed by the individual factory owner. The boss owns the means of production as well as the products, while the workers did not, therefore, called "the proletariat."

J's father was a very capable and promising young business man. He had owned a factory before he was thirty, a small factory of paper production. He had a partner, Uncle Union, who was a little older than he was, loyal and respectable in Ningbo business circles. The factory was set in his house, a traditional Chinese

Uncle Union and J's father in 1940s.

residential house in a lane of "stone gate house" (石库门) . J still remembered toddling underneath the machines in the west chamber.

Uncle Union had two wives. The second one was married into the family after 1949, which was unusual, because polygamy was abolished after the Liberation. It was only because Uncle Union's first wife found herself unable to have children, she insisted to have her cousin marry her husband, so that the family could have children. Shortly after she came, the second wife gave birth to five sons in a roll! A happy family theirs was. J's father always envied Uncle Union, two wives and five sons, what a happy family!

The two of them worked together happily, Uncle Union supervised the factory production, and J's father worked on marketing and sales. Profit rose year after year. By 1956, the government enforced a new policy—公私合营 (merging all private businesses into state ownership). As Uncle Union and J's father had successful experience operating a factory, they were given positions as Vice-Presidents of the factory. Though he was paid more than the workers, J's father wasn't happy about the merge. He was a very active young man, always liked to do new things. He had an exceptional creative mind and intelligence that was well known in his business circles. He did not like the fact that he had to live by a fixed salary; whereas, before the merge, he said he "only need to pick up the telephone, and golden bars would come in [his] way and fill desk drawers."

He could have left Shanghai and gone abroad to the free world, and start his business there. It was his wife, then young and indulgent, who stopped him. J still remembered, one day when she was only five or six, she walked into the bedroom and saw her mother throwing herself upon the round table, crying, sobbing, begging J's father not to go to Hong Kong. She told J that her father was heartless. If he left for Hong Kong, he would never come back. He would leave them behind. J's father, who really loved his wife, gave up the opportunity. So it goes.

Later, he often complained to J, what if . . . what if her mother had let him go to Hong Kong in 1956! With the support of his Godfather there, who used to be a powerful businessman in

Shanghai, in a free world and free economy, he might have had a better future. He would have made a big fortune to support the family. They could have escaped the mob violence, the attack from those terrorists "United Action Red Guards" from Beijing, and stricken poverty during the Cultural Revolution. On this account, J believed him, she knew her mother was a selfish woman, in her father's word, "stupid, slow and stubborn." Nonetheless, he loved her. He was a traditional man, fooled by traditional Confucius doctrine that "a woman without brains is virtue itself."

From his father's "what ifs. . ." and "would haves," J learned a serious lesson—a wrong decision could affect one's fate, or fortune, a life time, even ruin one's life for ever. Nikolai Ostrovsky's maxim always rang in her ear, ***"someday when you shall look back and reflect on things past, you shall not feel sorry, shall not regret for what you decide to do today."*** That had become her guidance in life. She was very careful, deliberate in making important decisions.

At any rate, the study of that "Bible" of Economics must have rigorously developed J's logical reasoning, which gave her the best equipment to think for herself, and approach any subject with a strong analytical mind. (Nothing else could explain why she would receive an A+ in a course on Practical Logic, taught by a Jesuit Father at a Catholic university, only the first semester she entered an American university.) Later, she could crack the hard nuts of Henry James, James Joyce, and William Faulkner by reading the pages backward and forward.

She wrote in her diary: "To read an excellent book worths more than reading ten books that were commonplace." The book she considered best to be read during this period in the countryside was Engels' 《反杜林论》 (*Anti-Duhringnot*), instead of Stalin's 《论中国》 (*On China*).

To be reeducated by the peasants was necessary. J learned the process of threshing rice, the growth of vegetables, the nurturing of cocoons, and cocoons' spitting of silk. She witnessed how the peasants made a living, how hard they worked; and how kind, generous and hospitable the peasants were, what they need, like and dislike; what tradition and customs were good to pass down, and what ought to be left behind. Such knowledge was absolutely necessary for the young generation, the leaders and revolutionary successors in China. There ought to be no denying of that.

What went wrong was the end of that movement—the movement of "Go Up to the Mountains and Settle Down in the Countryside." Something went wrong in the end, as she reflected on the fate of her peers. It was wrong to put so many young people, for so many years, out of school! For many of her peers, they never had a chance to complete a junior high education, not for a life time.

The students need to come back to school to complete their education after their experience and experiment in the countryside, just like raising the ducks, geese, hen, roosters, and rabbits, it was only natural and productive to let them out in the morning, floating and swimming on the river, stretching their legs in the fields or lanes; but after dark, just like the peasants did, every house, as each school ought to, call them back, count the numbers, and make sure they were all in, and safe to lay eggs.

The Origin of Shanghai Opera

The peasants enjoyed classical opera, all sorts of opera. Next to Beijing opera, the most popular opera in the region was "Yue opera," or Shaoxing opera, now called "Shanghai Opera." It was originated in a small town in Shaoxing County, Zhejiang province. A group of Shaoxing sisters invented it at the turn of the last century. These Shaoxing Sisters transformed simple folk songs and folk music into theater. They played both male and female parts successfully, which became a competitive counterpart to Beijing opera. In Beijing opera, originally, men played both male and female parts. Delicate, lily-feet ladies were played by actors, exemplified by Mei Lanfang. In Yue opera, actresses played gallant marshals, scholarly gentlemen, or Emperors and patriarchal courtiers (see photos). Those original Shoaxing sisters invented their own individual style and established their respective school of

Cross dressing in Yue Opera,
Women play men's parts.

Yue opera troupes tour countryside. Open theater.

Peasants enjoy theater in the afternoon, 2004.

singing. Ten of them, with their respective unique tunes, became stars on stage.

At first, their theatre troupes toured in the countryside, staged in the open from village to village, entertaining the peasants as well as wealthy family. Many wealthy family built little stages inside their mansions or gardens. They would invite theater troupes to play on occasions, such as celebrations, ceremonies, or friends and family parties, as the custom was. The theater troupes were independent performing arts companies, they did not exist on patronage. They would set up stages in the open and perform on stage by the fields, so peasants could enjoy (see photos).

These innovative, adventurous, and independent Shaoxing Sisters gradually made their way to Shanghai. Their performance was superb—the actresses' cross dressing, long sleeves, silk costumes, images, voices, the rich variety of tunes, especially their elegance, expressive sentimentality, feminine mystique, a very refined sensibility, local color and dialect—attracted a wide audience in Shanghai. In the earlier period, most of the population in the city came from nearby provinces, a majority from Zhejiang, so the dialect clicked to their native ear.

The sisters were so successful that throughout the century, Yue Opera became the most popular opera in Shanghai. In the 1950s, with the support of Premier Zhou Enlai, it thrived. The ten sisters became celebrities in the country. During Cultural Revolution, however, gender crossing were criticized as "decadent," radical reform demanded men play male parts. Strangely, such a change of role play failed miserably, not that no men were interested in acting female parts, but that the genre might have its special mechanism of resistance. Its "South of the River," "Yue" femininity was extremely exquisite, subtle, sensitive and witty. Its refined sentimentality was too soulful, difficult and delicate, virtually impossible to be mastered by men. Unlike in Beijing opera, actresses replaced actors to play female parts, mostly succeeded to the star level, whereas in Shanghai opera, after a decade of "revolutionary" experiment, only one actor succeeded to be a star. Wasn't it strange? It must be a fascinating subject for gender specialists to figure it out.

After 1990s, women came back to play male parts, so the opera survived. The sisters played on world stage, in Europe and North America, became known to the West as "Shanghai Opera." There emerged a new generation of young actresses, charming, talented, and well-trained by their masters. They were well accepted by a national and international audience as super stars. J had the precious opportunity to go to theater, watching many of their performances and contests in Shanghai.

Watching some stage contests, J noticed something very special. By 1990s and 2010, the "Ten Sisters" reached their eighties, long retired from the stage. But they were professionally still active. In a national contest, the mentors were all present in the theater to support their pupils. Sometimes, three generations of actresses acted together on stage, the senior ones playing secondary roles. They were there to attract their fans in order to support the juniors. The survival and success of that opera, as many young actresses avowed, owed to its special master-pupil relations. Whether one could call it "female bonding" or not, J couldn't say; definitely, there was a unique tradition of high standard teaching—rigorous, strict, and demanding on the one hand, and on the other, devoted, caring, and sustaining. It was the tradition of such demanding and committed teaching and learning that the genre have survived and passed down from generation to generation with high standards and excellence. As an educator herself, J realized that something was missing in modern or colonial education.

The people from this part of the country were historically known for their excellence in teaching, not only the masters themselves, but also their wives were legendary figures. The most popular legend, *The Butterfly Lovers*, came from this part of the country, and was first staged in Yue opera, before it was adapted by other theater.

As far as the legend went, every peasant family knew the story. It was like a myth, existed in the collective consciousness of the Chinese people, about co-education and the barriers of social status quo. J knew the story when she was five years old, when Aunt Phoenix Letter, her father's sister, taught her to sing a passage from *The Butterfly Lovers*. To teach children sing Yue opera was a common practice in popular culture in Shanghai. Yue opera was more accessible than Beijing opera, that children could master. J had photos taken dressed in opera costumes. Unfortunately, the girl had a husky voice, wasn't born for singing, never pursued acting.

The Myth of Co-education

In old times (the written record of the legend dated 550 A.D.), only boys could go to school, not girls. Zhu Yingtai was a beloved daughter from a gentry family. She wished to go to school in Hangzhou, which was the Capitol of the Zhejiang province. Yingtai persuaded her father by cross-dressing and argument of equal rights. Her father was a liberal scholar. Seeing the intelligence and potential in his daughter, he secretly agreed with her feminist ideas, and was finally persuaded by his daughter.

Disguised as a young man, Yingtai went to school. On her way she met a young man, Liang Shanbo. Shanbo was also going to the same private boarding school. The two of them made friends, swore brothers. In school, they lived together, slept in the same bed. During the day, they studied together, with other pupils in class. Shanbo always protected Yingtai as a big brother. Yingtai turned out to be a better student. She helped Shanbo with his homework. Shangbo admired Yingtai for her intelligence.

Three years passed. One day, Yintai received a letter from her father, saying he was sick, asking her to come home. Before leaving school, Yingtai confided to the school mistress, who took care of their daily needs in school like a mother, that she was a girl and she loved Shanbo, wished to marry him. The mistress was sympathetic, promised her to serve as a matchmaker, to "tie the red knot." After Yingai left, she told Shanbo the truth, and advised him to go home and make a proposal.

Shanbo was so excited that he left immediately, not to go home, but to see Yingtai first. When he got there, Yingtai told him sadly, her father had already accepted a marriage proposal from the son of the County Magistrate, the Ma's. Shanbo had studied

Law in school, believed in his right that since he had the school mistress as witness of a matchmaker and the personal agreement of his betrothed, he could claim that his proposal was prior to the Ma's. He threatened to sue if the Ma's would not withdraw their proposal. Yingtai stopped him, not that she did not love him more, but that she knew better. She knew the wealth and power the Ma's family had, and how the system worked in and outside of court. She was convinced that Shanbo would never be able to win the law suit. His future career would only be ruined by his opponent. Shanbo went home with a broken heart. He was love sick, fell seriously ill, and soon died.

The Butterfly Lovers

On her wedding day, Yingtai refused to go, until her father promised her that on her way to the Ma's house to get married, she must stop by Shanbo's tomb to perform a ritual for the dead. Though it was a taboo in Chinese culture on a wedding day, her father once again indulged her, and let her go to the tomb to say good-bye to her lover. When she got there, she performed the ritual first, then threw herself hard to the tombstone.

A pair of butterflies flew out behind the tombstone, as the legend goes, and soared to the sky together, one after another. The lovers were united after death in their spirit. So it goes.

Educated Women in 1940s

That story incarnated the myth of the Chinese revolutionary desire in early twentieth century. Equal opportunity in education, co-education, revolt against the ancient tradition of parental arrangement of marriage, the immortality of Romantic love, its transcendence and revolutionary energy, unification of the soul after death somewhere out of Heaven and Hell—bespeak the millennium repressed desire of men and women in Chinese society. Not until the twentieth century could women go to school in public, and together with men, to college.

The traditional education system—China's ancient system of the Imperial Examination, which only men could take—was abolished in 1907. The Qing Dynasty fell in 1912. The Republic, supported by Western Powers, advocated Western democracy, urbanized the concept of equal rights for women. For Chinese women, equal rights meant, first of all, equal education opportunity, prior to economical and legal rights. A modern generation of men supported women's equality without reservation, without debate over the cliche of "what does the woman want?" For centuries, and for the educated in Chinese society, men's ideal desire, as incarnated in that myth of *The Butterfly Lovers*, was a classmate, a soulmate. Educated men would die for schooled women, intelligent, knowledgeable, and challenging. Western democracy found its way in the heart of a young generation, the Modernists in the 1920s.

Of course, not all family could afford or would send their daughters to go to college. At least, some of those who went to college fulfilled the gentry dream, marrying their schoolmates. Most of the college educated women, not all of them graduated, joined mainstream social, political, and revolutionary movements, then turbulent and ruthless, throughout the 1930s and 1940s. During the Japanese invasion, women worked in the military, industry, journalism, media, government, hospital, and international relations. Many became teachers in schools. A female teacher would be honored to be addressed as "Sir" instead of "Madame."

For the college educated women, the most successful were the Song sisters—Wesleyan educated, spoke English, pale skin, married influential and powerful leaders of China. The Song sisters served as public speakers, a liaison between China and the West in war times, brought China foreign aids and international publicity, played an active role in society, economy as well as in government. Their success was the middle class model, individual success in acquiring money and power on behalf of and through the control and prestige of their men.

There were others though, especially those originally come from traditional aristocratic, royalist, warlords' family, patriotic and anti-imperialist, disillusioned with the Republic, or depressed in patriarchal domestic life, escaping marriages by parental arrangements, resolutely joined the Communists in the North. For J's mother's generation, two of her mother's cousin sisters, one cousin brother, and her mother's own brother, who was a returned student from America, all rebelled against their own class, left their family in Shanghai, joined the People's Liberation Army during the Civil War (1945-1949).

As the expression was in Chinese, the women revolutionaries "fought shoulder to shoulder" with men as "comrades." Their ideal of equality with men was to become comrades-in-arms. Their role models was not the Song sisters, but the women revolutionaries. The most honored was not Mao's wives, but Zhou Enlai's wife, Deng Yinchao, a well educated, well respected senior revolutionary and a leader in the party. Also Kang Keqin, wife of Zhu De. She was a Red soldier, a four star military General, said to be capable of shooting with both hands. The two both succeeded in their marriage, therefore, respected as virtuous wives in traditional Chinese ethics as well as modern.

Comradeship became a new model for an ideal relationship between men and women after the Communist Party took over. By 1949, the communists won the Civil War, drove all Westerners out. Protected by the 7th fleet of USA, the Republican Party and its followers exiled to Taiwan. Madam Song endured the downfall of the Republic. She stayed with her husband Chiang Kai-shek, till he passed away twenty years later. Then she moved to Long Island, New York. She lived a long time before she passed away. America was where she ultimately belonged, a life time Christian was she. There was a classical Chinese saying in describing a superbly beautiful woman—"倾国倾城的貌," meaning "the beauty of her features could well ruin a country and ruin a town." So it goes.

J's mother and her two elder sisters, growing up in 1930s and 1940s Shanghai, all had the opportunity to go to college in 1940s. In college, they studied Law, the Constitution, Jurisdiction, Legislation, and Government. As they were raised in American missionary schools, they followed individual liberty against patriarchal, parental control. In a mythical sense, they were tempted by the devil, tasted the apple, initiated men's fall. They lost Paradise, had to suffer the consequences of sexual freedom. Two of them got pregnant before marriage, and dropped out of school. Both got married by their own choice, without the approval of their parents. J's mother never regretted. What she studied at college would have been useless under the new regime. After 1949, the old constitution was abolished, and the new laws were completely different from what was taught in college.

Her two elder sisters left Shanghai one after another, one landed in New York, and the other in San Francisco. Viva in San Francisco became a successful business woman. She successfully raised her three children in America. Mona in New York worked for American Airline, said to be promoted to staff director before her retirement. She was the orthodox, prudent, honorable daughter in the family. Shortly after her emigration, she married a clerk at the Bank of China in New York, much to the disappointment of her father and brother in Shanghai. She was the beauty of the family, meant to marry either one of her two rival suitors in long standing, both were sons of top officials in the government, powerful family in China. So it goes.

Engaged at Birth

Grandma had three daughters, as none had lived up to her expectation, she kept a close eye on J. She hoped J would turn out to be better, at least knew better in her relationship with men, and in control of her own life. J used to be warned not to be fooled by men. Grandma had two nieces, who were both rare beauties in society in 1950s Shanghai. When they came to visit, Grandma asked them about their dating activities, warned them against pregnancy before marriage. When her two nieces safely married without the scandal of getting pregnant before the wedding banquet, Grandma awarded them with big dowry—twelve blankets each as wedding presents. After their marriage, the two nieces stayed at home, just let their husbands support and adore them. They were not the role model for J to follow.

J looked around, who could be her role model? What kind of relationship would she want with men in her life? She had to be careful, as Grandma bade her, careful not to be fooled and lost, like her mother. J did not have much interest in marriage and family life anyways. She always thought family was a mistake, one did not have the choice to belong, to be related by blood, and to live together as families, only to bear the "curse" for centuries. Whereas with friends, one had choice to be together.

One thing she feared was to fall into the trap of family life, a houseful of people, noisy and crowded, too much trouble and gossip. She wouldn't be able to focus on her books and study. Housekeeping and babysitting were the kind of work every woman could do, that she wished to escape, not that she couldn't handle, she had already learned it and did it after the house-searching, (didn't she?), but that she wanted to spent her time focusing on her study, to complete her higher education. Her goal was *"to pursue truth, beauty and wisdom, to become a learned person,"* those were the words she jotted down in her diary. She was startled at herself, seeing those words and looking at herself now.

As for men, if she had to, she would take one by the time she must have one. She was not raised to go after men, but let the men

*Grandma Eura
holding J, 1953.*

come to her. The government policy at that time strongly encouraged late marriage and birth control. The legal age for women to get married was twenty-five, men twenty-seven. J was only nineteen. After all, she was betrothed to Gentle Wonder, Grandma Eura Yao's grandson, before the age of three.

Grandma Eura was J's Grandma's best friend. Gentle Wonder and J were born the same year. Two grandmas decided that they would like to see their grandchildren to be a pair, so that their two family eventually would be united, become one after their life time together.

J and Gentle Wonder became engaged. A picture was take a wooden boat on the playground of the People's Park, J sat at the head and Gentle Wonder on the end, looking at each other full of curiosity. It was from that photo and the location that J could tell she was about two. When she was three, Grandma moved out of her apartment in the Horse Racing Court Apartment, overlooking the People's Park. As for the two little children's engagement, their parents seemed to have no objection, either they did not wish to object to the Grandmas' wishes, or the Grandmas did not even bother to ask their opinion. So it goes.

When they were little, J's father always joked with Gentle Wonder to call him "father-in-law." Gentle Wonder sometimes did, being an amiable and sweet boy. When she was teased in turn, J was too shy to call Gentle Wonder's parents "mammy and daddy-in-laws." She never did. By custom, it was only appropriate for a girl to be reticent and reserved as she was. She was not sure if she would like to marry Gentle Wonder someday. He was handsome

J, Gentle Wonder, his "Mammy and Daddy-in-laws."

and gentle, had good manners; but being a few months younger than J, J took him only as a younger brother, not a big brother.

J loved Grandma Eura very much, loved to visit her. In 1950s, the Yao's still lived in the old quarter of the town. It was the Grandmas' arrangement that Gentle Wonder, his younger brother, and J went to the same kindergarten, that special kindergarten founded by Madame Song Qingling, which took in children from family of the former industrialists and capitalists in Shanghai. After school, if her father did not come to pick her up, J would go with the Yao brothers to their house, which was close by.

At the Yao's house, children must take late afternoon tea, milk and cookies, whether they wanted or not, because dinner was going to be very late, usually after 8:00 or 9:00pm. Ordinary family in Shanghai had dinner at 5:00 or 6:00pm. J did not know then, it might be European life style in old Shanghai. Decades later she traveled to Paris, where dinner was served quite late, around 9:00pm.

Grandma Eura 1964, recovered from a breast cancer surgery.

Grandma Eura, her daughter, her grandson and Jimmy, 1964.

Around 1960, Grandma Eura moved to a condo in a special apartment building for privileged residents from overseas and foreign countries. She bought that condo with US dollars. The apartment had five bedrooms and a large living room, which was used for dining room. Across the hallway, lived a young Russian couple, experts from the Soviet Union. They had two children, who looked like dolls to J, as caucasians were few in 1950s and 1960s Shanghai. The Russian family left Shanghai before the Cultural Revolution.

Gentle Wonder had three elder sisters and a younger brother. Grandma Eura's elder son's family also had five children, three daughters and two sons, about J's age. They lived not far away, often came over. Family gathering was frequent before the Cultural Revolution. Their second daughter was selected to join a ballet school in Beijing, seldom came home. J just filled in the place of ten children.

Gentle Wonder's parents worked in the same factory. They went to work and came home together everyday like "comrades-in-arms," a happy couple. When they came home, they always had the courtesy to stop by Grandma Yao's room before they went into their own. Gentle Wonder's mother was a respectful daughter-in-law, a virtuous wife, but she was strict with her children, seldom praised or indulged them. J was afraid of her. Once she made a startling observation about J. "Don't you know," she said to some guests around, "this girl is so quick that if someone steps on her tail, her head will shake." J was not even sure if it was a compliment.

Grandma Eura was J's Grandma's classmate in grammar school. She was a good student, often helped Grandma with her home-work. They were best friends ever since. Grandma Eura looked like a caucasian. She had snow white skin, green eyes, and a high nose. She was always clean, carefully dressed, and her hair always neatly combed and tied up. J still remembered her photo hung on her bedroom wall, when she was young, with wavy long hair, Shanghai style. She looked more elegant and attractive than the photos of those 1930s' movie stars, that were reprinted to entertain sentiments of nostalgia in the popular market after the 1990s. She might be a Eurasian from some Russian refugees. Her origin was obscure. Grandpa did not like Grandma to be friends with her, but Grandma ignored him.

She married a wealthy business man after his wife died, and survived by two sons and two daughters. She herself did not have children. Her husband passed away before 1949, left her a fortune and a loving family. Though none of the children was her own, she had brought them up, cared for them, loved them dearly as though they were her own. After the death of her husband, she had suitors, some distinguished, handsome and wealthy gentlemen in Shanghai. One had a large mansion with a swimming pool in the West Side suburb, and invited the children for a visit. Grandma Eura did not want to remarry. J heard her telling Grandma that she did not need the support from men. She had enough money left by her husband to do what she wanted. As her husband loved her so much, she just wished to fulfill his wishes—taking care of his family.

So she devoted the rest of her life to make the family happy together. It worked indeed, blood or no blood relationship made no difference. The eldest daughter married a banker, moved to America, brought some family money with her. Later it was this "Big Aunt," as the children called her, who helped the family when they needed after the house-searching in 1966; and later after 1980s, when some of her nieces and nephews came to New York.

Grand Ma Yura's family was the most traditional of all the family J knew of, growing up in Shanghai. Grandma Eura kept rituals of all the birthdays and death days of the Yao ancestors, seriously and ceremonially. On such occasions, sometimes J was there, a variety of dishes were served on the table, candles and incenses lit. The children were told not to touch the table and chairs, not to disturb the spirits of the dead ancestors, imagined to be sitting at the table dining, until the incenses were burned out. Then they could have a feast.

Of the ten children, four boys and one girl were about J's age. The four other sisters were three to five years older than J. They were polite and kind to her, but was not as close as Gentle Wonder was. Gentle Wonder and J were Grandma Eura's pets. At the dining table, J and Gentle Wonder were allowed to taste Grandma Eura's special dishes. The other children were well behaved not to transgress, well taught by their mother.

Gentle Wonder's parents had a different education philosophy. They did not pay much attention to their children's homework and grades from school. Instead, they encouraged activities. They liked to take the children to travel, watch circus and movies instead of opera, swim in summer, and sports in winter. Gentle Wonder's eldest sister was a champaign swimmer in Shanghai Swimming Team, and also played basketball in high school. Gentle Wonder's younger brother played violin day and night. Eventually he became a professional violinist in Singapore in 1990s. Gentle Wonder did not like to read books as much as J did. He had a beautiful voice, loved music and singing.

Around 1960, Gentle Wonder's family got a black and white fourteen inch television, a gift from an aunt in Hong Kong. Television was a luxury even in Shanghai, few family had televisions then. J was invited. She would go at least once a week to their house to watch television. Usually she went on weekends. The program ended very late at night, often by 11:00pm or midnight.

She took the bus home by herself. It was safe those days, no violence in the streets at night.

When the Cultural Revolution came, the Red Guards threw the Yao's family out of that spacious condo, moved them back to their old house, took away everything, including the television. The Yao's could no longer occupy the whole house which used to be theirs. The Red Guards pushed the ten of them into a quarter on the west side of the house on the second floor, which consisted of two joined rooms with one entrance, sort of a suite. Grandma Eura and her step daughter used the small room, with a bed and a dressing table in it. Gentle Wonder's parents and five adolescents slept in the large room, divided by a wardrobe in the middle. Their long time housekeeper, Zhang Ma, soon died of a heart attack.

When called to register in 1968, imaginably, Gentle Wonder did not hesitate. He registered, together with his elder sister Gentle Vicky, to go north to Jilin Province, to "settle down in the countryside." So it goes.

Gentle Wonder and Gentle Vicky
in uniforms going to Jilin in 1968.

CHAPTER 7

BACK TO THE CITY

J's "Hamlet Complex"

J came back to the city a year later, when the movement of "Go up to the Mountains and Settle down in the Countryside" was almost over. Her parents, after twelve years of divorce, decided to get remarried to each other. Her father's Godmother, who was her mother's aunt, had passed away, leaving all her legacy to her adopted son in her will, i.e. should the government return her assets posthumously. The adopted son, being a traditional man, fulfilled his filial duty well enough. He supported her in her later years, took good care of her in the hospital, and buried her at his expanse. Few relatives came to the funeral though. This time the closest relatives all advised J's mother to remarry her father, expecting the inheritance to come back to her family.

Another temptation was the housing condition. J's mother was incessantly harassed by her proletariat neighbor, who moved into her flat after the house searching, a family of five. They occupied formerly J's bedroom. Another couple moved into formerly PoPo's room. Three family shared the bathroom and a kitchen. The wife of the proletariat family was a shrew, creating all sorts of conflicts, constantly bullying her neighbors. When J was there, J would step out and spoke to her sometimes. After J and PoPo left, J's mother was afraid of her, found herself alone unable to protect her teenage son. She wished to move to a place where she did not have to be bothered by her neighbors. Yet privacy in housing was a luxury in Shanghai.

J's Father no longer lived in their old house that he bought with his golden bars when he first married, which was in another part of the city. After the divorce, he immediately followed J's mother, moved to her neighborhood, only a couple of blocks away. Thus he left his own mother living alone in a small room in the old house. Even he chose to be close to his children, by law he was only allowed to visit them once in two weeks on weekends.

The place he moved into was a big old house, Western mansion inside, Chinese architectural design outside on the gate, facing Central Huaihai Rd.. The front gate was carved with stone sculptured dragon, green and red tiles on top, so the house was called "the Dragon Gate" in the neighborhood. Inside the gate, there was a traditional garden, with rocky hills, a pond, and a pagoda in it. Behind the big house in the front, there was an extension of sort, a four-story building with balconies on the east side. It was someone's private mansion before 1949, but in 1960s, housed twenty-four family.

J's father lived in a two bedroom unit at the back extension, sharing a living room, the kitchen and bathroom with another family of five, a couple and three children. He asked his neighbor to exchange housing with J's mother. His neighbor happily agreed, as they found they could have an extra room just by moving J's closet wall to the center of the room to make a two bedroom unit. It would be perfect for their family of five. They came to talk to J's mother. J's mother liked the idea that she did not have to share the bathroom and kitchen with other family, could have a private entrance, closed and safe. So she agreed. J's father was triumphant, bragging to everyone: "Look, fighting against the Japanese invasion only took eight years. It took me twelve years to get my wife and children back!"

J, however, was not excited about the reunion. She suffered terribly from her "Hamlet Complex"—the depression, suppression, and difficulty to tell the truth of adultery of one's own mother. J's mother used to have a lover, who was her colleague for years in that housing management office. They must have started an affair soon after J's mother went to work in 1956. Some Sunday morning, J's mother took her to a Park. There she met her lover. A couple of times, they took her to movies. In1962, J's mother succeeded in

Two GMs, one Christian (L), one Buddhist (R), 1952.

divorcing her husband, accusing him for a possible love affair with her wealthy aunt, who was her mother's cousin, some twenty years older than her husband. As there was no substantial evidence, J's father denied his wife's accusation.

The old lady was quite a character, as Grandma's sisters all were. She ignored her niece, gave a big banquet at Park Hotel, invited all her relatives and J's father's relatives. When they came to the party, she announced that she had decided to adopt J's father as her son. The adoption hurt the feelings of her two nephews, who were her legal inheritors. They were J's mother's age, grew up with her like siblings. J's mother, encouraged by her relatives, insisted on divorcing her husband. Secretly, with the help of her lover, she moved to a better district, only a couple of blocks from her lover's place. J's father appealed to the Supreme Court, but the court was not sympathetic with him.

J's father did not know his wife had an extramarital affair until after the divorce. When he learned two years later, from Jimmy's nanny, he felt sucked. He did not blame his wife; instead, he

Father, Mother, and Grandmas, 1952.

blamed the Woman's Liberation. He never wanted his wife to go out to work, if she did not go out to work, she wouldn't have spent all the time with a lover at her work place! No one in the family wanted J's mother to go out to work.

It was in 1956, the government called for all housewives to go out to work. Jobs were assigned. For educated women, the government need them to work as school teachers and in other professions that required certain level of literacy. J's mother was not interested in teaching or taking care of children, so she chose to work as a bookkeeper in the local housing office. When she came home breaking the news, the house was in chaos.

J still remembered that evening, two grandmas were having a fit at once. Neighbors came in and out to persuade and appease them. Usually, the two grandmas hardly talked to each other, seldom agreed on anything. Now on this account, they both agreed that J's mother should not go out to work. Even PoPo thought it was absurd. She asked J's mother how much she could make every month, and what was the worth of that money, why she would need it. If she need more pocket money, her mother wouldn't mind giving her some extra, if that three hundred RMB a month was not enough. Grandma gave her that stipend for housekeeping, because she chose to live with her daughter's family. She moved into her son-in-law's house in 1954. Three hundred RMB a month was at least twice the ordinary family expanse in Shanghai in 1950s.

The old ladies yelled and cried to threat J's mother. The Buddhist Grandma was afraid that she might die without her daughter at her bed side. She had asthma, was bedridden whole winter long. She had five doctors come home to visit her, one German doctor, two physicians of Western medicine and two experts of Chinese herb medicine. The German doctor left Shanghai in late 1950s. In emergency, two private nurses in white uniform changed shifts day and night, attending at her bed side. Who was going to make those arrangements and talk to the doctors?!

The Christian Grandma was a widow, she raised two children without ever going out to take a job. She was a strong believer in her son's ability to support the family. She gave birth to a daughter first. Six years after, as her husband was aging, she still did not have a son, she went to the Church and adopted a son. When her son was only sixteen, she sent him out to work in the streets of Shanghai. She would never let her daughter go out to work. Not for a life time her daughter ever worked out of the house. She kept saying to J's mother: "You will have a son. Why don't you have a son? You will, you will."

After the divorce in 1962.

J's mother was quiet, just said to her families that it was government policy, she couldn't say "no" to the assignment. Overnight there were few housewives left in the city from then on. That was how Women's Liberation was accomplished, for J's mother's generation at least, everyone could get a job if she wanted to. Women became economically independent at a mass level. So it goes.

Ar Niang was happy with her own daughter, who did not go out to get a job. Aunt Phoenix Letter was a traditional woman. She was perfect by appearance, character and virtue. She had such a gentle nature, quiet and modest, just the opposite to her hot tempered mother. She was of few words, soft spoken, easy-going, and kind to all. No one ever found any fault with her. Only J's mother thought she was not smart enough, did not know how to make won-ton. Aunt Phoenix Letter never said one harsh word to his brother's wife throughout all those years of family trauma and drama. She was almost a Saint. Maybe it was Aunt Phoenix Letter's spontaneous, always content, good nature that convinced

Aunt Phoenix Letter,
J and cousin Ancestor Pride, 1953.

J's father of that Confucius saying—"a woman without brains is virtue itself." He loved his sister.

As their father died young, their widowed mother had Aunt Phoenix Letter married out young, to the son of her late husband's best friend. This friend and her later husband were colleagues, while they both worked at the Customs House in Shanghai in 1920s. The family was well-to-do, Aunt Phoenix Letter never had to work. Her husband loved her, was extremely kind to her and her families. He would do anything his wife asked him to. J called him "Fufu." They had three children, one daughter and two sons, a happy family.

They lived in Hongkou (虹口), the East side of the city, which was occupied by the Japanese before Liberation. J's mother never paid them a visit, as she never liked to go to the old city, where there were no modern toilet facilities. So J had never visited them till after the divorce, J's father got to take his two children to visit his sister's family for New Year. It took about an hour or two to get there. On the bus, J's little brother curiously asked his sister:

"What language do the Hongkou people speak?" The little boy already got the idea that Hongkou people were different, as though they had lived on another planet. J told him, they spoke Shanghai dialect, and they were closely related to the family.

Fufu also worked at the Customs House in Shanghai. After the Liberation, the government trusted his expertise in overseas shipping, and offered him a senior position with the China-Poland Shipping Company, one of the very few international corporations after 1949. In mid-1950s, this company moved to Tianjin, another seaport in the North. By custom, not all Shanghai wives would go with their husbands to live in the North. However, Aunt Phoenix Letter moved with her husband without complaint. Her eldest son, old enough to take care of himself, did not wish to go. She let him stay with her mother-in-law in Shanghai. She herself would come back visit them and her own mother once or twice a year. Ar Niang often called her back when she was sick. On such occasions, J got to spend sometime with her. It was Aunt Phoenix Letter who taught J sing Yue Opera, a passage from *The Butterfly Lovers*.

When the Cultural Revolution began, Fufu was under some pressure, but he was not persecuted or purged yet. Since his work involves the partnership of a foreign company, there was some protection. One day, Aunt Phoenix Letter ate a rotten tomato and had diarrhea. Something went wrong, she suddenly died in the hospital. Fufu came home, couldn't bear his grief. Without the company of his wife, he couldn't and did not want to live. Under the hard times, he couldn't predict the future. He took his own life.

His younger son Ancestor Pride was left alone at home in a strange city. Without his mother, he did not know what to do with his own life. He had a serious nervous break down, from which he never recovered. He was in his late twenties. Though he had a job in a factory, being disabled, no woman would marry him. He moved to live in the dorm and received a minimum wage from the payroll. J's father sent him money once a while. They wrote to each other. In 1994, he wrote to say he wanted to come to Shanghai for a visit, and asked to stay with his "daddy-uncle." J's mother said no. So it goes.

"Now this one is yours."

J's mother had given birth to a son before J was born, a huge infant it was, weighed thirteen pounds, but it was still born. Before giving birth to this dead boy, her first born was a daughter, a snow-white with twinkling dark eyes. All neighbors praised that awesome good-looking baby. When she was eighteen month old, one day, the mother was working on her sewing machine, heard a goggle from the baby's throat. She immediately found the baby had swallowed a thumb tag dropped from the wall paper. The wet nurse was with the baby, but she neglected. The two women immediately called a tricycle to take the baby to the hospital. On their way, the tricycle chain was broken. It was a bad omen. By the time the driver fixed the chain and got to the hospital, the baby had no breath.

J's father cried his eyes out, PoPo said; but he never blamed his wife. Three years later, he told PoPo, he saw a little girl in a dream, a voice said to him: "Now this one is yours. Take her." Soon his wife was pregnant again, and they had J, the third child. When J was old enough to be carried out in the lane, the neighbors missed the first born, the girl baby with pale skin and dark twinkling eyes. J was dark skinned with Mongolian eyes. Someone in the lane made a comment that J did not look as pretty as the first born baby girl. When Grandma heard the story, she ordered the servants in the house to offer two RMB to the neighbor not to say J was "not as good-looking." J became very special in the lane.

J's mother never mentioned the two first born and still-born babies. Anyhow, J did not remember she spent much time with her mother as a little child. She only remembered, her mother used to ask her to wait for her at the bus stop No.24 by the Big Ben, about three blocks from home. Usually after 5:00pm, when her mother arrived, they would take the bus to West Nanjing Rd., a central street in Shanghai, where her mother grew up. There they would go to Nanjing hair salon There they would go to the hair salon (南京理发店) to have her hair permed, or the best shoe store (蓝棠), to try leather shoes, and a special children's dress store (红装) to measure her size and have her dress made. J's mother liked pretty dresses, shoes, and hairstyle. She told J she grew up without the

J's hair permed, 1955.

money and freedom to have what she wanted. Now she had her salary to spend as she wished. Her salary was her pocket money.

Later when they moved to the flat, there was room available for her to hire a dressmaker to work at home. J's mother dismissed Grandma's old tailor, hired a new tailor introduced to her by the cook. The old tailor was a vegetarian, a Buddhist, a good person, but old fashioned. The new tailor could cut fashionable, modern style. He was a bearded tall man, full of smiles, and had a good sense of humor, liked to tell jokes. He would come everyday, work eight hours a day in their house for two weeks long seasonally, at least once or twice a year. The cook fed him well. The two of them were good friends. So he liked to come and work for J's mother.

J did not like those occasions going with her mother. Her feet was fat and wide, hard to fit the ready made shoes, so they had to order them. Often she had to come back more than once to try the samples. Her mother was a perfectionist for the dresses they ordered. J had to do the sittings more than once as well. When her mother had J's hair permed, she looked different from other girls, inviting envy and criticism from the girls and teachers in school.

Nana (L) and J (R), 1959.

They would give her trouble, calling her names, spat on her. Once the urchins followed her after school, pushed her, she fell, scratched her knees, blood all over her leg.

She came home, did not tell her mother what happened. She went to the neighbor sisters, who were her good friends. Nana, two years older than she was, in a higher grade in the same school, had a group of boys following her. The following day, Nana ordered her friends to beat up those urchins from J's class. That stopped the harassment.

Her mother seldom checked or bothered about J's homework. By the time the report cards came in, sometimes she looked at them. If there was anything short of 100, she would be displeased, pointing it out to J: "How come you got 97? Where were the other 3 scores? Someone took them?" Or, "Look at you, 99, what's wrong with you? Always careless! Weren't you?" She never praised J. She was content that J was a good student all the way through school; and that she never had any problem with the teachers. The teachers were always full of praise.

She herself was hard working, always outperformed as a bookkeeper. At the end of one year, while other bookkeepers accounted 2000 households, she did 6000! She often worked over time on weekends. Maybe during those weekends, she and her lover could be left alone in the office, enjoying a good time together.

When the Cultural Revolution came, J's father wrote to his ex-wife's boss, reporting the love affair, and asking for investigation. Normally speaking, J's mother was divorced, and her lover was a widower, it was perfectly legal for them to have an affair. There should be no problem for them to get married, which they were planning. There was some concern about the class difference. J's mother's class background and identity at work was classified as "capitalist." It was not honorable for a man from rural, peasant class background to marry her. If he did, maybe it meant the end of his promotion at work.

Things were different when the Cultural Revolution started. Such an affair became simply unacceptable. He and J's mother had difficulties to see each other. J served as a liaison to deliver their notes and letters, some money and valuables to be in his trust. One day after dark, at the No. 76 bus stop at the Peace Temple, J waited for

Aunt Modest, 1965.

his mother's lover for a while, then he came. He looked very sad and depressed. He said to J: "You are such a good girl, strong and solid. *I wish your mother were like you.*" Obviously, he was disappointed with J's mother, who couldn't endure the torture, confessed their relationship to the Red Guards. He felt betrayed.

The Red Guards beat him up, and tortured him for confession. He immediately hang himself in his apartment, without a word of good-bye. What he said to J were his last words. That was in the winter of 1966. So it goes.

At the same bus stop, a few days after this man committed suicide, J stood there waiting for her mother. When she came off the bus, J almost fainted. Her mother's face was bruised all over, one eye googled out, blue and purple all over. J wished she could forget that horrid sight. But she could always see it.

J's mother came home after work, attempted suicide. J's father came, full of patience, instructed PoPo to watch her carefully. He himself examined the drawers and dressers, took away any ropes, scissors and knives his ex-wife could lay hand upon. At that time, J did not know it was her father who was the informant. Soon afterwards, she received a warning from a relative, Aunt Modest. Aunt Modest worked in another housing office under the same housing bureau in Shanghai as her mother did. She had a friend of Red Guard at work, who informed her. Aunt Modest did not wish to add grief to J's mother, who was her cousin sister-in-law and a close friend. Therefore, she cautioned J to be careful, not to tell her father if there was any secret in the family.

J was shocked beyond grief. The great distress and trauma her mother and her family suffered was because of her father, who reported them! It costed an innocent life! After the death of her mother's lover, the family was completely cut off any financial aid, they could have received from him. He died without leaving a word. He was a bachelor without any relative in Shanghai, which meant, whatever J's mother put in his trust couldn't be retrieved. For the money and jewelry taken away from house-searching by the Red Guards, there was the expectation that once the government recognized its fault, it would give them back. It did ten years later.

J was furious at her father, but her father wouldn't know why J changed her attitude towards him. After the house search, he had stopped paying his alimony. So the first action J took was to demand alimony from him. At first, he was reluctant, complaining that his wages were less than J's mother, and now he had two mothers to support. His wealthy Godmother's house was searched too. As she never worked, did not have any income. J wrote to his father's work place, reporting him. It hurt his feelings. He was furious with J now, saying J was worse than her mother. He was afraid of his boss, so he promised to pay ten RMB a month. Although it was only half of the alimony the court ruled in 1962, out of his less than fifty RMB a month salary, even his boss could not ask any more. So it goes.

Now her mother should have agreed to remarry her father! Heaven forbid! J was indignant, a moral indignation arose in her good conscience. Could you imagine to sleep with someone who murdered your lover? What kind of a woman was she? J couldn't overcome the moral plight, not that she was sympathetic with her mother's lover, far from it. Although she delivered letters for her mother, it was difficult time, and she had to be sensible and helpful. In fact, she never thought the man was acceptable, being from a different class origin. J was taught in school and society, in Marxist theory, love couldn't be true between two people from different class background. In this case, the theory might be true, as her mother betrayed him by confessing to the Red Guards; and the man hesitated to marry her, left her to suffer alone in a difficult time.

Maybe J was too serious. She always had such a strong sense of moral justice. It became her tragic flaw. She always wanted things to be right. If things couldn't be right in reality, at least she had to think through and fix things right in her mind. Simply put, she felt at least her mother ought to know what was right and what was wrong. Her mother could have chosen and married someone else, things would be right. It was absolutely wrong to remarry her ex-husband.

Yet by a second thought, J speculated, her mother could be excused, provided she did not know it was her ex-husband who reported to the Red Guards, and caused the death of her lover. Now the dilemma J faced was whether she should let her mother know the truth that her father was indirectly responsible for the death of her lover, or not. To tell her or not to tell her? That was the question. It was a critical moment, now or never. If she chose not to tell her, what if she got to know afterwards one way or another? Would she feel guilty? Would she regret for her decision to remarry her ex-husband?

If she chose to let her mother know the truth, it might blow up a chance for the family to be reunited. Her teenage brother needed a father. Her own life and reputation in the future might be at stake. As Aunt Pearl, her mother's best friend since grammar school, who urged her mother to remarry her father, sensitively suggested to J, a young woman from a divorced parentage was somehow less respected in respectable society. For the sake of J's future husband's family, better to have an integral parentage. If her mother remarried her father, no one would ever mention the divorce by the time when she was to marry. J had no idea that Aunt Pearl had her own agenda until a few years later.

J turned to Grandma Eura. Grandma Eura decided, she would tell J's mother the truth, which she did. To her surprise, J's mother even did not have a fit. She did not change her mind, as if nothing had happened. In her heart of hearts, J was disappointed with her mother's conscience. So it goes.

A Room of One's Own

The whole family moved to J's father's place. The first night they moved in, J played a game of traditional wedding custom. By tradition, after the banquet, wedding guests were free to enter the bedroom of the bride and bridegroom, to tease them and horseplay. The bride and bridegroom must not decline the requests or demands of the guests. Not until the guests' wishes were fulfilled would they leave the bride and bridegroom alone to consummate the marriage.

Though no guests came to horseplay that night, J used the occasion to fulfill an important wish. She jumped into the center of her parents' large bed, which was the same old bed they first married in, J used to sleep in-between her parents when she was a baby. Tonight, she would not get up and get out of the bed, unless her parents gave her what she wanted.

Her wish was to have a room of her own. Her mother never agreed to let her have the other bedroom by herself, but to share with her brother. Her brother used to sleep with his mother. Now he was left out from her mother's bed. J did not want to share with him. She insisted that he could sleep in the living room. J wouldn't get up from her parent's bed until her father was exhausted coaxing her, then told her mother to let her have what she wanted, so that they could go to bed on their wedding night, precisely, their second wedding night.

So out of the closet into a room of her own, J enjoyed great privacy, that few of her friends had in Shanghai at that time. Shanghai was an open city since the mid 19th century. People from all over the country and of all walks came to make a living. The housing condition was notorious. "Seventy-two rental family packed together" in one building was common. "72 Rental Family" was staged in a drama in the 1950s. Although after 1949, the government implemented very strict registra restrictions, not everyone could live in or move to Shanghai as a resident, the city was still over-populated. Young couples arrived at legal age to be married had to apply and register at the local housing office. The waiting list could take two to three years long.

After the Cultural Revolution, the government implemented a radical feminist policy that application must be submitted at the local office of the woman's family residence to prove that the woman's family did not have room for the bride and bridegroom to be. The policy was meant to ease a traditional social problem. In Chinese culture, traditionally, the mother-in-law and daughter-in-law relationship was always difficult. Whereas, the mother-in-law and son-in-law relationship was traditionally affectionate. As it turned out, mostly, men married into the women's family were treated like honored guests, while women were free from the Confucius tradition of serving the in-laws. It was a radical but reasonable measure. City people welcomed the policy.

Her mother's intention not to let J have that bedroom was that secretly, she wished to save that room for her son's marriage. Her husband reminded her that there was nothing she could do about it. By the time, if J chose to stay at home, the government policy would dictate that that room was hers, since she was nine years older than her brother.

(Years later, after J left for America, her brother had quite a few girlfriends interested in him. A significant factor of his desirability was that he had a large room to get married. He himself did not want that room to get married. He begged his sister to help him come to America. Her sister arranged a student visa for him. The interview officer at the American Consulate in Shanghai was easy on him, seeing that he had white skin, blue eyes, and curly brown hair, looked like a caucasian. America was where he belonged. J's cousin brother, same age, very shy and timid, was denied his student visa, and unbelievably, delayed for forty years before he eventually got an immigrant visa to come to America.

So Jimmy came a year or two later. Shortly after his arrival, he married a white woman, six years older than he was, like an elder sister. When he called long distance to tell his parents he wanted to get married, his father just said: "Congratulations to you!" His mother was anxious to talk to J, asking if she had checked out the girl's family background, what her parents were and did, if the girl was intelligent, good-looking, had a good character. J replied: "What do you do? Who were you and your husband? Whatever her family background is, whoever wants to marry your son must be a dummy. How brilliant do you want her to be? We are in America. We are nobody here."

On the wedding day, after her brother and his bride registered in the city hall, J gave a small party at the Hilton in San Francisco, to entertain her American family. The same day in Shanghai, J's parents gave a big banquet in Park Hotel. J's mother was dressed up, as though she were the bride there.)

J's bedroom was a large room facing a tennis court, there was nothing blocking the view. J was not interested in having the room for marriage, not yet, but for study day and night. Now she could stay as late as she wanted, no one ought to bother that she did not turn off her light. After dinner while the families were noisy outside, she took a nap. When she woke up at nine or ten o'clock, everyone went to bed. She would study till daybreak. She always felt more focused at night.

One good thing after the move was that she was relieved of her housekeeping family duty. She did not have to take care of her brother, and manage the tight budget as before, now that her father became the housekeeper. She could focus on her education. She never forgot the birthday wish she made in 1969. She never forgot PoPo's admonition in 1967: *"What you store in your brain no one could take away."*

Also, with a room of her own, she could entertain her friends and visitors in her own room, as she liked, free to chat. Unlike before, the whole family only had one room. After her mother came home, it was dinner time, she couldn't bring friends home. Currie was the one who often called after or around dinner time. J just had to go downstairs, stood outside of the house in the lane, chatting with her for hours till midnight. Her mother kept calling her from the window above, asking her to come upstairs to eat dinner and go to bed. When boys of her age came to visit, her mother always made sure to be there. When they were leaving, she'd walk them out through the stairs and hallway, so as to avoid the neighbors' possible gossip.

J got a typewriter, 1974.

Those days, visitors—girl friends, boy friends, relatives, neighbors, acquaintances, classmates, coworkers, even strangers—did not have to call first before they came to the door for a visit. Cell phones were not invented yet. Not every household had a telephone either. Even those family who used to have telephones had their service disconnected or phones demolished by the Red Guards during the house searching movement. People just drop by and say hello. If it was meal time, the host would be obliged to entertain the guest, whether he was prepared or not, had or had not dishes to serve. It's up to the guest to decide whether to stay or leave. If the guest did not choose to leave, it was impolite to ask the guest to do so.

J had more visitors than her parents. Her girl friends, as well as some male friends—uncles, cousins, and girlfriends' boyfriends, and boyfriends' friends—liked to call on her. They all enjoyed talking to J about study—books, poetry, music, painting, calligraphy. They also exchanged their ideas, their family and heart affairs. J found herself to be in a position of a "counselor" of sort. Books might have given her the wisdom and ideas to help her friends. In return, her girlfriends made stylish clothes for her now and then, and male friends brought her books and movie tickets.

Most of them would leave before dinner time. Some forgot time, would keep the conversation going till late at night, ten or eleven o'clock, when her father would come out coughing loud out of her bedroom door. That was very annoying.

Three of her girl friends were stunning beauties, pale-skinned, tall and slim, with large eyes and high noses, curly long hair. When they walked in the streets, people would turn their heads around looking at them. J did not have that kind of beauty. PoPo once told her honestly, her looks could be rated "five on a scale of ten." She knew that. Her pretty girl friends liked sewing and dressmaking. Often they would make fashionable cut dresses and try on J first, so she was never behind the fashion. She had plenty of stylish clothes.

She even did not understand the importance of being good-looking. The way she was educated in school and society consistently taught her, one's looks were not as important as one's soul and mind. To be simple was virtue itself. She did not like to spend time dressing up or having her hair curled up. Once her mother received some bonus, gave the money to J to buy a kind of new cloth material, to make a pair of pants and a jacket to wear on her birthday, as she was approaching twenty now. J used the money to buy a good amount of coffee, because coffee would keep her awake at night. Her mother was exasperate, telling her father that J was hopeless for a young lady. So it goes.

The Portrait of an Artist

J made friends in the new neighborhood. She got acquainted with two sisters about her age. Their looks were in sharp contrast, one pale, one dark. So were their character, one soft and sweet, the other strong and tough. Their father was an oil painting artist. Mr. Claude used to have a large studio, "Orient Studio" on Huaihai Rd., well known in Shanghai Art circles. Unfortunately in 1959, he was "capped" as "Rightist," and sent to the Blue Sea, a remote region, for "thought reform" in the labor camp. When he came back ten years later, he was given a job to repair shoes in a co-op. His family of four lived in one room, which was the kitchen in a house.

He worked there everyday, diligently, never complained. When he was home in the evenings and during weekends, he kept painting. Sometimes he would go to the suburbs to paint nature, and came home with a series of landscapes, that looked so refreshing in the darkness of that bedroom of four. He was always optimistic, spirited, fresh and healthy, that J admired, as though everyday was a fresh morning for him. He believed in his art —"Impressionism." At that time, Impressionism was not introduced to China yet. He was truly an avant-garde in China, to paint impressionist paintings. Indeed J heard the word "Impressionism" first from him. He told J, as long as he painted, he was happy. To make himself happy, he had to paint every day. His family all supported him and his work. (Forty years later, one of his daughters opened a gallery in memory of her father's work on Huaihai Rd. in Shanghai.)

Mr. Claude came to paint a portrait for J, which J hung on her bedroom wall. Against a purple background, J had a distanced, subtle and ironic smile. "How typical," J's mother sneered, "玩世不恭"! She meant to say, that portrait betrayed a typical impish attitude J held towards life, always playful, not serious about life, career, and the world outside of her study. "It catches your soul," Olympia recognized, "something so remote and mysterious, nobody knows what it is behind the smile." Only uncle Quixote knew what it was. "好高骛远," he said, always crave for things that were far far away, high up in the sky.

Once Mr. Claude gave J an oil painting of water lilies, with a little poem he wrote himself in classical verse form.

鹧鸪天

不懂事故不当家, 不惭才拙学涂鸦.
省得烦恼那些事, 对景着意调铅华.   1975年6月21日

The poem said that he'd rather not to think about worldly gains and losses, housekeeping routines. Let him forget all the troubles in ordinary life. Whether he had talent or not he did not know, he just wanted to devote himself to his Art, facing the beautiful scenes, using his brush to mix his paint. J understood his philosophy perfectly with a kindred spirit. Maybe it was his own attitude towards life, that was reflected in J's portrait, or maybe he saw a kindred spirit in J too. At any rate, it fortified J's faith in the world of Arts and Letters, despite the dreary routines and setbacks in reality.

J wrote a poem for one of Mr. Claude's landscapes he painted and had given to J to hung on the wall. The poem celebrated the sharp contrast between the withering branches and fallen leaves over the brightness of the water pond, which looked like a clear mirror reflecting the ruins of sunset.

题壁上任先生画

池塘明镜映枯叉, 摇曳浮萍满树花.
红顶白墙残照里, 芦苇青青帔落霞.   1976年10月1日

Mr. Claude was pleased that J understood the basic elements of Impressionism. He liked J's poem. A few days later, he gave J an interesting poetry book, 《稼轩长短句》 (*Ji Cassino Short Sentence*). The poet Xin, Qiji was a patriotic warrior in Song dynasty, persecuted by those traitors in court, lost the favor of the Emperor, had to resign. He went into exile, suffered many adversities in his life, but he composed many poems. At least six hundreds survived throughout the centuries! All were published in that book!

Mr. Claude always encouraged J to keep up with her study despite the difficulties and hardship in life. One day he said to J: ***"Soon this country will be in want of people who have special talents and knowledge, you bet."*** He was a prophet.

The Idle Class (逍遥派)

Olympia, J, Apple, Klever—"Idle" in 1972.

By later 1971, some of the 1960s graduates gradually returned to the city one way or another. Some were sick, others just did not feel like to go back after they came back for a visit. They stayed at home, became unemployed. A leisured class, called "逍遥派," ("The Idle Class") began to emerge in every corner of the city. These young people were cynics, who were not interested in politics or social movements any more, but in a carefree Bohemian life style. They played guitar, piano, violin, mandolin, learned oil painting, brush painting, calligraphy, sculpture, foreign languages, played chess, bridge, poke games.

Though these people were called "The Idle class," few were really idle. Most people knew that they had to learn a trade or a skill in order to survive. One must have a special skill, or some professional knowledge, a unique talent—"一技之长," as it was called in Chinese, in order to find an occupation, "a way out" of idleness, or simply have something they love to do. Some took interest in medicine, photography, or sculpture. Some chose to learn carpentry, mechanics, and electronics repair. Even fixing bicycles could make a living.

Others were busy studying mathematics, physics, and biology, try to make up what they had missed in high school. Olympia came back from the North for a visit, she brought back three textbooks of mathematics, physics and biology. She shared with J. She became J's math teacher. Later when she went back to the north, she got a job as a school teacher in the city of Changchun. A decade later, she was recognized as a national model teacher.

To have a teacher was the most important and fortunate thing. Most people learned a trade or a skill just by luck, from someone around, a grandpa, grandma, an uncle, aunt, a big brother or sister, or a neighbor, who were willing to teach them, or "take an apprentice." There was no private schools available at that time. Aunt Modest's elder daughter, Cousin Angela, five years older than J, supervised J's practice of PiPa and calligraphy, so J resumed her practice every day seriously in good company. Neither of their family could afford the tuition to hire a teacher for them, to advance their practice, and turn them into specialists.

It was Grandma Eura's idea that J ought to resume her lesson of English, which might become useful knowledge in the future. Grandma Eura knew that J's mother had sent J to an English tutor, when J was ten years old. The man was a returned student from Germany, gave private lessons at home. He used a textbook by a Danish linguist, Otto Jespersen, called *Essential English*. It was composed in the form of conversation by a group of non-native speaking pupils, who were taking English lessons from a tutor, Mr. Presterley, in London. J's tutor himself was like Mr. Presterley, teaching several pupils at home, and taking afternoon tea and biscuits served by his wife, in the middle of his lessons. He wore golden laced spectacles, looked very solemn.

The first volume of the textbook opened with five foreign students on a tour in London, through the River Thames, the Parliament, the Big Ben, the Buckingham Palace, the New Hyde Park, the Piccadilly Square, and so on. It must be a very effective textbook. Decades later when J arrived in London for the first time, she was surprised that the city was so familiar, as though she had been here before.

She only took tutorial lessons for one semester. Just before the tutor wanted to teach her typing, she stopped going, because she was preoccupied with other extracurricular activities. She was selected to play basketball for her school and undertook the editorial for the school wall paper. She was too busy. Besides, it was boring to take the bus all by herself, twice a week, to take English lessons. She did not have particular interest in English. The tutor told her that if she felt bored, he would take her to movies; and that because she was such a promising student he had ever had, he was reluctant to let her go. A decade later, another English teacher was to agree with him. It was not a sheer compliment, but some potential J did not know she had herself, discovered by a teacher.

Entering junior higher, she was assigned to a class that studied Russian as a second language. She liked Russian better than English, because the pronunciation was more regular and closer to Pinyin than English. She would have liked to continue learning Russian, but there was no teacher around and available. By that time the diplomatic relationship broke down. The Russian language was considered to be less "useful" than English in China. Who could teach her English then?

A Child Genius

Grandma Eura thought of Aunt Pearl's son, Wise Bright Wang. Wise Bright was known to be a child genius. His father, a respectable engineer, took good care of his education since a child.

He was a "model" student in grammar school. After school when everyone was gone, he would stay as a volunteer to clean the bathrooms. When he went out with his mother into the streets, she would sat in a tricycle, paddled by an old man in front, Wise Bright would just run on foot by her side. It was because he felt ashamed, unethical and "bourgeois" to ride in it, let an old man paddle him.

He was among the selected few in the whole city of Shanghai to enter a special junior high school in 1964, which belonged to the Shanghai Foreign Language Institute (now the International Studies University). He was enrolled in an honors students program of "Experimental" education, given the opportunity to study a foreign language in its proper environment and at an earlier age. He was assigned in a class to study the Spanish language. He and his classmates, Spanish majors, lived in a Spanish style house, ate Spanish food, and everyone spoke Spanish, no Chinese.

His mother was very proud of his admission. He was one year older than J, so he had received two years of classroom instruction in junior high, when the Cultural Revolution started and threw the students out of school. For some reason, he did not go to the countryside. At home, his father paid close attention to his "continuing education," taught him several subjects himself, as comprehensive as possible—math, science, piano, and foreign languages. He studied English, French, Japanese, though his study of Spanish was discontinued. He was prepared to take an exam to join some research institute in the military in Nanjing.

One day he bought a textbook of Japanese home, his father was annoyed, blaming him that he was not focused enough. He had not mastered his French yet, now he turned to Japanese. His father asked him to return the textbook, and punished him to stand outside the door for hours. When Wise Bright came in, he suddenly became nervous. He was trembling, kept begging his parents to "forgive him." He started hallucinating. Maybe he had what was called today a "nervous break down." He was hospitalized for a while, before he was recovered. So it goes.

He was very happy to teach J English. His parents had no objection. His mother was fond of J, as she was classmate and best friend of J's mother since grammar school. The Wang's used to live in a Chinese style house near J's kindergarten on Central Nanjing

Rd., later moved to their Western style house on West Nanjing Rd.. They owned all the two dozens of Spanish-style houses in that lane. After the house searching in 1966, their family of six, which included their grandma and three children, was packed into one large room, the former living room. Wise Bright's mother, like J's mother, worked in a local housing office, usually was not at home during the day.

Wise Bright the genius.

When J came to take lessons from Wise Bright, his father would make sure he was there. He would sit in his little corner, listening. He would make sure Wise Bright prepared his lessons, and did everything right to teach J. After class, he would either join them or listened to their chat about the books they read.

Once J brought Wise Bright a book of *The Reference Material to the Controversies over Hairui's Resignation. Hairui's Resignation* was a historical play, the criticism and controversies over this play, published in major newspapers in 1960s, had started the Cultural Revolution theoretically. Maybe the book was what we would call "sensitive material," Wise Bright returned the book shortly, telling J that his father wouldn't let him read it. Another time, when J mentioned Tolstoy's *Anna Karenina*, Wise Bright was eager to read the novel. J said it might not be a good and appropriate book for him to read. His father was pleased and praised J's thoughtfulness.

The English class went well. Wise Bright took J through Volume II and Volume III of *Essential English*. Then Wise Bright fell ill, J stopped going to class. A few weeks later, Aunt Pearl and her husband came, asking J if she loved Wise Bright. J said no. J's mother testified that she had asked J before, J had no interest in any one around. J's father went further to remind Aunt Pearl that J was already engaged to Gentle Wonder, the Yaos. Aunt Pearl was upset, she told J that it was not a shame if a girl admitted that she was in love with a boy. She herself was the one who fell in love with her cousin/husband first, and asked to marry him. J felt insulted. Being sensible, she only suggested to Wise Bright's father that if his son was depressed, maybe he could take him to travel somewhere, for a change, that might cheer him up and make him happy. Wise Bright's father said he was planning a trip to Hangzhou.

J stopped going to Aunt Pearl's house afterwards. J's mother lost her life time best friend. On this account, she couldn't blame J, as she knew that Aunt Pearl had her intentions; yet her daughter was not easily manipulated. She must have secretly read J's diary, which she sometimes did, to be convinced that J was not interested in Wise Bright. The Wang's was a perfect happy family in the eye of everyone. Unfortunately, J had never envied their children, so well protected, they were somewhat too naive for J. She loved Liberty, not boys, wealth, or social status.

A year later, Grand-Aunt May Fourth, who lived in Aunt Pearl's neighborhood, came to tell J's mother that Wise Bright took his life in his own hands. He had committed suicide twice. The first time, he turned on gas in the kitchen. The second time, he jumped from the roof top of their house in the middle of the night. His parents, afraid to disturb the neighbors and lose face, wouldn't call an ambulance immediately. They waited till daylight. By the time he was taken to the hospital, it was too late. What a genius wasted! How much education invested in him! So it goes.

"The Honor is Mine"

J's mother turned to her elder brother for J's English education. Uncle Quixote, after all, was a Professor of English at Shanghai Foreign Language Institute. He was a very interesting figure. Being the elder son in the family, he received the best education affordable in Shanghai in 1930s and early 1940s, all the way through St. John's High School in Shanghai to St. John's University in New York. In New York, he often ran out of his allowance. He would go to the Central Bank and demand the teller to give him more money.

The teller was a young China man, who made friends with him. One day he visited Uncle Quixote in his room, saw a photo of a beautiful young lady. Uncle Quixote told him it was his sister Mona. He was impressed. Neither of them could have, or would have imagined that eventually Mona would marry this man in New York. Uncle Quixote always thought it was a mistake. How could the most beautiful sister in his family marry an ordinary teller! He was so sorry for his sister. That was another story.

What he learned from American culture was to give his mother a surprise on her birthday. It must be in 1939, on his mother's forty-year old birthday, he spent a fortune to send a wire home. The wire was written in English, when it arrived in Shanghai, no one could read English at his mother's house. It caused a great stir in the family. At first, everyone was worried that something unexpected might have happened to Quixote in America. Grandma's two brothers went out, ran all over the city to find people to interpret the wire. After much ado, they were told, the wire contained only one sentence: "Many Happy Returns of the Day!" Grandma's families were practical people, did not even know how to appreciate that romantic gesture on Uncle Quixote's part. Grandma was not pleased, she was hard to please anyway. Uncle Quixote, on the other hand, laughed at the ignorance of Grandma's brothers.

Quixote returned to China before the end of the war, WWII. Instead of serving the government then in power, as his father had planned his career for him, he rebelled against his father, mother, sisters and everyone in the family, joined the Communists in Guangzhou. During the Civil War (1946-1949) that followed, he served in the People's Liberation Army as an English interpreter. Maybe he made the right decision to return to China. Had he stayed in New York, he could have become nobody and nothing, maybe a beggar in the streets, Grandma said. He could be less than the teller in Chinatown.

He wouldn't want to work as a teller in Chinatown anyways. Even to be a banker in America wouldn't interest him. He majored in Political Science. China was under Japanese invasion. As an educated person, he must serve his country. He was very young, had his ambition, ready to start his career as a diplomat. So he returned to China to "report" himself to his nation. His father had already arranged a position for him through his friends of leaders in the government in Chongqing, but he turned it down. He did not like the Republicans. When the Civil War broke out, he joined the People's Liberation Army instead. Maybe he made a right decision. The Communists won the war, and took over China in 1949.

In early 1950s, Uncle Quixote came back to Shanghai a veteran, which gave him a safe social status, safe from his family history and class background. Strange enough, when it came to marriage, for all his American education, he was least independent and romantic. He was the only one in the family who accepted his father's arrangement for a marriage. Maybe he wished to make up with his father after he came back to Shanghai, maybe he wanted his father's money, which he did have a share.

He was not a healthy man. He had a lung surgery in the army, some of his ribs were removed. A chronicle asthma would seasonally keep him in the emergency room for days. He was frequently on sick leave from his teaching duties, but still received his full salary, which was over one hundred thirty RMB, considered high by the living standard in Shanghai.

His wife was a little crippled. She came from an old warlord family in Beijing. She did not care to socialize with relatives or friends in Shanghai society, only kept close company with her own mother and a brother. While most women had a job, she never worked inside or outside the house, just let the nanny run the family business. Although she did not know anything about home economics, she was absolutely a virtuous wife. She was quiet and obedient, kept her husband in good company, drinking lunch and dinner, sometimes from lunch to dinner. Like him, she also suffered from asthma, frequently fell ill. They could understand and feel for each other.

The two of them gave birth to a big and healthy baby daughter in the winter of 1957, and subsequently, two very attractive boys in early 1960s, only one year apart. The two boys were pale skinned, had big bright eyes, very handsome. When Uncle Quixote took his sons out in the streets, people couldn't believe they were his children. He was so proud of it. To show off his progeny, he would tell everyone the joke that a tricycle driver in the streets asked him if he could be sure that if he was really the father of the two boys.

When Grandma was alive, she did not want to see Uncle Quixote, because he only came to her for money, incessantly, endlessly and shamelessly. She called him "脱底棺材"(a bottomless coffin), meaning an asshole, that could never be satisfied with the need for money, like a coffin, only contained a dead body, without life or hope. Ever since he was a teenage, when he had money in his pocket, he would spend every penny he had, then beg and borrow from anyone around.

When he went to boarding school, his nanny dressed him well with clean shirts, T-shirts, pants, ties, socks, handkerchiefs, gave him a watch, pencils and good stationary. When he came home, he would be left with nothing. He said other students did not have these things, so he gave to them. His nanny had to buy these supplies out of her own pocket money, to avoid Grandma's reprimand.

Once PoPo was so happy and excited telling their neighbor's nanny that the young master in her house was going to college in America! The neighbor's nanny sneered at PoPo, told her not to get excited too soon. A young master in her house already returned from studying in America, learned nothing but riding a motorcycle! By the time Uncle Quixote came home from America, it was worse —he learned nothing but drinking. He became an incurable, addicted alcoholic for a life time!

After studying Kingston's *China Men*, J began to speculate what could have possibly happened to Uncle Quixote in New York. As she knew better now, she realized that racism in America at that time might have hurt him badly. It must have hurt him so much, deep down, inside and out. He must have lost his self-esteem there. Later in his life, he would incessantly babble about his ancestors, forefathers, relatives and their connections, the glories of their past. He was house proud. Maybe he relied on his family names to sustain his ego. In today's words of psychoanalytical theory, his American education might have "emasculated" his manhood, imaginably.

Grandma said, had her eldest son been an accountable man, she wouldn't have to have divorced her husband. She could have lived with her son and his family. It was the custom in Chinese society. With him "the bottomless coffin" around, sooner or later, he would ruin Grandma's assets. By contrast, J's Christian Grandma was fortunate. She sent her son out to work as an apprentice immediately after he graduated from high school. The following year, he brought home all the food needed for the celebration of the New Year. Since then he always supported his mother. Maybe that was what Grandma saw in her son-in-law, and chose to move in with J's family in 1954.

Uncle Quixote's wet nurse, Buddha Heart Mama, once came to see Grandma, holding Uncle Quixote's daughter in her arms. Grandma did not even turn around to look at the baby. J felt so sorry for her little cousin sister. The nanny complained to Grandma about Uncle Quixote's wife, being mean to her. Grandma gave her money, cursed her son for having such a "shit" of a wife. She couldn't care less for warlords and the names of the in-laws.

A couple of years later, Buddha Heart Mama fell into the river in the countryside, died of famine. That was during the period of the "Three Year Natural Calamities" in China. All blamed Uncle Quixote and his wife for that, for letting the nanny go live in the countryside. His wife must have been not kind and generous to her husband's wet nurse, who raised him almost like a mother! What kind of family breeding she had!

Mona in New York heard the death of the old nanny, she was grieved. Buddha Heart Mama was also like a mother to her when she was a child. Knowing the famine and food shortage during "Natural Calamities" in China, she asked favor of relatives in Hong Kong to mail boxes of butter to Shanghai frequently, sometimes with money. It was a great relief to the families, though J did not know, at that time, American laws forbade citizens to send food or money to mainland China. Many families lost touch across the Pacific. Letters were few.

One day J's mother was very excited to receive a letter from her sister Mona. She told Grandma that Mona's son Victor was ten years old now, a good boy. Every morning, Victor rode a bicycle to deliver newspapers in the neighborhood. Grandma had a fit. She blamed Mona, said Mona must be "out of her mind"! Stop it! Let a ten year old boy deliver newspapers in the streets! Even our servants' children wouldn't have to do it! Maybe, Mona was giving her son a "good breeding," J's mother appeased Grandma; let her son learn to make his own money, so that he wouldn't grow up like their brother Quixote! So it goes.

After Grandma's death, Uncle Quixote approached J's mother for money. Sometimes he came to complain about his wife, incapable of housekeeping and taking care of the children. When she started knitting him a sweater, she could never finish it. Knitting was a common pastime craft for Shanghai women. J's mother would remind her brother cynically, that his father had "raised the red lantern" to find him such an invalid wife from an aristocratic family! Then she would let him have her children's clothes, which Uncle Quixote gladly took. All those years, even he enjoyed a high salary, it was never enough for him. He depended on his sisters and relatives abroad, sending him foreign currency to survive. Even his wife's old nanny in Hong Kong would send them children's clothes twice a year. So they never had to buy any clothes for their three children.

His family lived in an apartment building only a few blocks from J's house. Six of them—husband and wife, three children and a nanny—only had one medium size room. They were very close, seldom had fights. Once his wife came to J's mother crying for help. It turned out that in the middle of the night, she woke up only to find her husband in bed with the nanny!

The nanny had worked in his father's family before. His father's third wife, the Pintan actress, kicked her out after she found her husband involved with the nanny. To help cover up his father's scandal maybe, Uncle Quixote took her in. She became the boss in the family. Uncle Quixote's wife did not know what to do, except for crying. She wouldn't go home and have a fight with her husband, with her traditional virtue and "good breeding."

During the Cultural Revolution, Uncle Quixote was taken under custody by the Red Guards for "隔离审查" (isolated for investigation). For months, they kept him "inside," interrogating him for his family history and connections, pressing him for confession after confession. The Red Guards did not beat him, seeing him being so thin, ribs missing in his lung, his back hunched, an invalid. Instead, they fed him well with pork-chops. He gained twenty pounds when he came out of detention.

As universities were all closed for years, professors had a long period of vacation, enjoying themselves at home. At home he was busy drinking, entertaining a group of his close colleagues. J was introduced to two male and two female professors of English. Lady Emily was educated at Oxford University in England, spoke Oxford English. Lady Viola was married to a celebrity and a journalist. Uncle Lindsay was a Shakespearean. Uncle Earnest was a linguist, a first rate translator, and a very patient and good-humored teacher. They were frequent guests at Uncle Quixote's dinner table. The dinners usually would last four hours long. While they drink, they would talk stories of the past. Sometimes they spoke in English. J was interested in their company. At least, she had a chance to listen to professors' talk.

Uncle Quixote was fond of J. All those years, he spent more time with J than with his own children. He would come to J's house in the morning, got J out of the bed, took her out for coffee, or lunch, visiting his friends, then brought J home for dinner with his family and friends. Other than his incurable weakness, he was a very sweet man, affectionate, communicative and humorous. J liked him.

He did not teach J much English. Instead, he taught J how to make coffee, taste wine, and improved J's culinary skills. J sometimes cooked for his guests. On such occasions, he would threw out a phrase or two at J. For instance, when his guests were taking their seats at the table, and someone asked J "May I sit beside you?" J was taught to say: "The honor is mine."

Some afternoons, he would come to sit in J's room, talk to J about poetry. He taught J how to appreciate Mao's poems. Mao was a great poet! He also taught J to laugh at the follies of money and the moneyed, and despise the economic, business mentality of J's parents. He frequently forgot about dinner time to go home. Then he would send J to get wine for him, and buy him some cooked pig's ear (cheap meats) to go with the wine, until his son came over to ask him to go home.

At his dinner table, he and his colleagues would talk about politics, family history, life abroad, anything but money. Under table, he borrowed from everyone. Usually a fortnight after his pay day, he began to borrow here and there, his colleagues, neighbors, relatives, and even from servants. As everyone was hard up those days, he would give them back as soon as he had money. On his pay day, the 6th of each month, his house was full of guests, and dinner was richly served.

One time at dinner, Uncle Earnest mentioned that he was taking private pupils at home. J mentioned to her girlfriend Pinnacle. Pinnacle's parents both passed away soon after they were beaten up by the Red Guards, and thrown out of their mansion. After their mother's funeral, the four siblings, eighteen, nineteen, twenty and twenty-one years old, were left alone at home. They had eight elder brothers and sisters by their father's first wife, who lived in Shanghai and nearby, one in Hong Kong, but no one came to comfort them. The four of them did not cry, did not go to bed the whole night long, just sat there, clicking melon seeds (嗑瓜子). They did not know what to do next, and how to go on living by themselves. The next morning, the husks of melon seeds piled up inches thick, and covered all over the floor. J was sympathetic.

Pinnacle became the housekeeper. She cooked for the family, made four seasons of clothes ready for her sister and two brothers, and managed to pay all the bills. They had an income from Hong Kong, from his father's funds, left in care of their eldest brother there, who sent them a monthly allowance in Hong Kong currency. They could afford paying tuition.

J got the idea to have Uncle Earnest teach them English, and take care of their education. Like J, the four of them, had more or less studied English previously, so their levels vary. Uncle Earnest offered three classes for the four of them separately. Soon after,

Pinnacle let her boy friend and other two relatives join the classes, that made Uncle Earnest busy.

J did not envy them their English classes. Who would envy these orphans? She knew her mother couldn't afford the tuition. At that time, she still had Wise Bright teach her English. One day Uncle Earnest asked J why she wouldn't come to study with him. He offered to teach her alone free of charge.

"The honor is mine," he said. Uncle Earnest loved teaching. He quoted Confucius' belief that for a teacher, nothing was more delightful than teaching a good student. A good student J was, everyone knew, and he knew. He discerned J's intelligence and potential. He even predicted that ten years from now, he couldn't be sure how the other students of his would turn out, but J alone would be the most accomplished.

"Never mention the money," he was Uncle Quixote's type; "money is irrelevant when it comes to learning." He was Uncle Quixote's close friend. Whether Uncle Quixote asked him to do him a favor, or he was willing to take over Uncle Quixote's duty to take care of J's English education, J did not know. Uncle Quixote often asked Uncle Earnest to help him, including writing his confessions to be submitted to the Red Guards at the university.

It was not for nothing Uncle Earnest took J in as a pupil. He made a contract with J: J must major in English, come to class regularly and complete all homework and assignments on time. According to his experience, he said, the quick ones wouldn't work hard, like Uncle Quixote; and the hard working ones were mostly slow and dull, not quick enough, like himself. Eventually, the diligent and less intelligent would succeed. The world belonged to a majority of the slow and steady people, while the quick but not hard working seldom would succeed.

So far, it was only a fable of "The Turtle and the Rabbit." J never liked the turtle as she knew she was not a turtle. She liked to take naps sometime. But she was not that arrogant rabbit either. The rabbit was born to be able to jump and run much faster than the turtle. It was not a fair competition for the rabbit to use its genetic superiority or biological advantage to race against a slow creature like the turtle. J never liked to race with anyone. She liked to go at her own pace. She would make it, sooner or later, one way or another. In the Chinese zodiac, she was a dragon, dragons had a strong will, and will power. Dragons were supreme creatures, wouldn't compete with earthlings.

Uncle Earnest had something more in his mind. He saw J was bright and promising, but he was afraid she might be spoiled by Uncle Quixote. He wanted J to make a commitment, work hard, be serious and persistent in English study. "Intelligence plus Diligence is better, but rare." He was so confident, in this case, "success is guaranteed." He intended to take J as an "apprentice," or a disciple, to become an English Professor and a professional translator as he was. Five years later, he was proud to say he had a foresight.

CHAPTER 8

ENGLISH STUDIES

The English Major

It was on January 28, 1971, J first went to Uncle Earnest's home to take her English tutorial lesson. At first she went once a week. Later, as Uncle Earnest saw J was quick to learn, making fast progress, he encouraged J to come twice a week. Uncle Earnest, with his wife and two children, lived in a one bedroom apartment in Carlton Apartments. The building had housed well-known writers in 1930s and 1940s, such as 张爱玲 (Ailing Chang). Chang left for America in 1950s. She kept writing, couldn't make a decent living. One day she was found dead for a week in her apartment in Los Angeles in 1960s. In 1990s, however, her works were rediscovered and well received in Shanghai and Taiwan. Carlton Apartment was located one block behind the Park Hotel downtown.

The upper left corner of the room was Uncle Earnest's study. Several bookshelves lined against the wall, and a large desk set by the window. He sat in his desk chair facing the window. To the right of his desk, a single sofa chair was for his guest. It was quite comfortable to sit in the sofa and talk to him face to face. When a student came, Uncle Earnest would let the student sit at his desk,

Uncle Earnest at his desk, 1973.

and he himself in the sofa. At the back right corner of the room was a full size bed. His wife often slept in the bed, taking her nap.

Under Uncle Earnest's instruction, J soon completed another sequence of textbook, *Discovering English*, which was published in England, four volumes. This textbook was for college students. In other words, after completion, J ought to have a command of college level of English as an English major (maybe for non-native speakers).

Every week, J had to memorize twenty five to fifty vocabulary, make sentences with useful words, idioms, paraphrase key passages, and write an essay to be corrected. Uncle Earnest corrected J's writing scrupulously. J must pay attention to every red mark to understand the correction, so not to make the same mistakes again. He knew grammar inside out, syntax, sentence structure, parts of speech, transitive verbs and intransitives, and the right propositions for right verbs and so on. J took notes. He knew much more written or "bookish" English than Uncle Quixote. Uncle Quixote spoke English fluently, as he had lived in the English speaking world, had first-hand experience with Western culture, that Uncle Earnest did not.

In China, translation and interpretation used to be divided into two separate professions in foreign language study or training. Interpretation works on oral proficiency and quick response. Whereas, translation requires strong literacy in both languages, not only the ability of reading and comprehension of English, but also the command of the Chinese language, writing skills and styles, literary expressions and linguistic sensitivity.

During the period when China was isolated from the English speaking world, there was less demand for interpretation than translation. To be trained or hired as an interpreter, one's family background had to be cleared. Overseas family relations would be regarded as a taboo for a diplomatic career, even to serve as an interpreter. So teaching and translation were certainly more practical for J's future career. Considering her interest in literature, certainly she was most promising in that line of profession.

Uncle Earnest had a more comprehensive, planned curricula for J. Beside the textbooks, which helped J to have a standard command of the language, he assigned supplemental reading materials every week. Ambrose Bierce' "An Occurrence on the Owl Creek Bridge" was the first piece all his students read. Washington Irving's "Rip Van Wrinkle" was another. J's favorite piece was Edger Allan Poe's "Eleonora." She was overwhelmed by the sweetness of Poe's sensibility. Conan Doyle's detective stories challenged J's intelligence and analytical reasoning. Tales from Shakespeare by Charles Lamb was enjoyable for his prose style.

She read at least over twenty such short pieces. Uncle Earnest believed that the language and style in short stories were most refined, precise, and effective in teaching writing. His teaching philosophy was that good reading yields good writing; and good writing comes from imitation. When his school age daughter came home asking for help to write an essay, he simply dictated a sample essay for her. By so doing, he set a higher standard for his daughter, so that next time the child knew how to write. It might be old fashioned, but turned out to be an effective method.

There was no textbook for these supplemental reading material, as Uncle Earnest had only one copy of the book on his

J at Uncle Earnest's desk during tutorial, 1973.

shelf. He would select the pieces he wanted to use. Then he had his wife type those texts word by word, page by page, make copies on ink paper, (there was no copy machine then), to distribute to his students. His wife was a Eurasian, half English, could read and type the English texts. She enjoyed typing the texts for pastime. For two or three years, she persistently did all the typing and copying. What an amount of work!

Typewriters were not available for purchase those days. It was rare to see at people's homes in Shanghai. Around 1974, Uncle Earnest got a used typewriter from his friend. He brought to J's house, so that J could begin to type herself. J mastered the key board in one afternoon, with ten fingers, two hands. All those years, Uncle Earnest himself could only type with one finger, his right index finger. He was amazed that J could learn so quickly. J was instructed not to read the text from line to line, for the sake of speed.

After the short stories, Uncle Earnest gave J a well selected book to study for writing—*The Familiar Essays*. The book was published in England, a gilded hardback. It was a fine selection of the works of all those classical essayists from Francis Bacon, Addison, Steele, Swift, Johnson, Goldsmith, Defoe, De Quincey, Thackeray, Stevenson, Hazlitt, to Charles Lamb. Uncle Earnest patiently taught J to appreciate the beauty of diction, rhetorical troupes, personal voice and style. He himself wrote in the style of Thomas Hardy. J liked William Hazlitt.

The familiar essays opened a world of Ideas—philosophy, history, ethics, morality, satirical sketches, current affairs, social life, mannerism, politics in London, the Whig and the Tory, and gentlemen's education—for J to speculate, tackle them analytically, and reason with logic. J felt, to approach the mind of these great authors in their original native language was quite different from her experience reading Russian, French, and German authors in translation, something more personal, intimate, witty, and humane, stylistically varied, and rich with sense of humor. Maybe it was from studying that book J began to appreciate the English language.

When she came to class to discuss her readings with Uncle Earnest, she would prepare questions to initiate the conversation. Occasionally, if Uncle Earnest failed to answer her questions right away, she would ask to be excused to "wash her hands." Thus she let him sit there, have a few minutes to smoke a cigarette, think about the answers to her questions. He answered her questions mostly to her satisfaction. In J's mind, that was the standard of a great teacher. Later, when J became a teacher, she would encourage her students to ask questions. She would tell her students not to be afraid that she, the teacher, might not be able to answer their questions; or she might be embarrassed or lose face. She would tell her students, if she did not have immediate answers, she would think about their questions and get back to them next class.

There was one essay that talked about the Oxford education. At Oxford, students learned most from discussions of their thoughts and ideas, individual responses to books and lectures in tutorials. They wrote essays under the guidance of those "bulldogs," as tutors were called "bulldogs" at Oxford. An Oxford man used to be "smoked and smoked into a scholar" through tutorial instruction more than indoctrinated in classrooms and lecture halls. J thought it was funny, as she spent three hours in the afternoon, twice a week with Uncle Earnest for years, sitting at his desk, while he smoked cigarettes after cigarettes, though not cigars, and she, sipping green tea, face to face. Was he a "bulldog"? Would he turn her into a "smoked salmon" afterwards?

Funny wasn't it, eighteen years later, J was hired as a "bulldog" at Harvard to teach Expository Writing. That was her first job out of graduate school from Buffalo. At Buffalo, she taught her own class for four years as a Graduate Teaching Fellow. It was exceptional in an English Department to let a non-native speaking candidate teaching native speaking undergraduates reading, writing, and even Introduction to Literature, as J did. Buffalo was unique. One reason she chose to go to Buffalo after she completed her M.A. at Stanford in nine month (and had a job in San Francisco for three years), was that she read in its university catalogue that it "had preserved the Oxford tutorial system." When J got into the doctoral program, indeed, tutorials were a major requirement, preparing for the Comprehensive Exam, as well as thesis writing. Nowhere could she have received a graduate education as substantial.

After the *Familiar Essays*, Uncle Earnest handed out a series of type written essays by Ralph Emerson for more advanced reading. From the notes J took, she could tell that she studied at least six essays, those on *Art, Friendship, Intellect, Prudence, Self-reliance, and Spiritual Laws*. The style and the syntax were hard, the voice alien, the prose archaic, the poems not poetic, the thoughts so demanding, hard to follow; and the humor, if any, not as delightful as what J was used to. She did not know Emerson was an American, of German descent, till years later she came to America and took a graduate seminar on Transcendentalism at Stanford. Professor Gelpi enjoyed her research and class report on Theodor Parker. He asked why she wouldn't stay at Stanford for doctoral study. J was less interested in feminist theory than post-modern fiction. Unconsciously, Emerson's thought and Transcendentalism, the spirit of "American Adam," had left a strong impact on the formation of J's mind and attitude towards life. An "American Scholar" was she before she came.

To have something enjoyable and delightful, J read Oscar Wilde's *Lady Windermere's Fan* with Olympia's uncle, Uncle Bull, which was his nickname. Like Uncle Quixote, Uncle Bull was also a St. John's product from Shanghai to New York. He returned to China on the eve of the Liberation. During the Korea War in the early 1950s, he served the People's Liberation Army as an English interpreter. He visited J quite often, came to chat in English with her. He taught J to role play the dialogues from the plays in practice of oral English. Later when J came to America, she found that no one spoke English as those upper class ladies portrayed in the plays. No one ever said: "The honor is mine."

The Art of Literary Translation
(貌似神似)

To study English conversation was unreal, as there were no native speakers around. There was no linguistic environment or situation to speak the language. At that time there were no tapes, or DVD to listen and practise oral English. To learn professional translation, on the other hand, as Uncle Earnest planned, was more feasible and practical.

After 1972, the Shanghai Translation Publishing House began to give Uncle Earnest work to translate technical materials for industries. A medical doctor was studying medical translation with Uncle Earnest. She always had a huge amount of material to be translated, so he was devotedly working with that woman doctor, engaged with medical translation. J was not interested in medicine.

Once Uncle Earnest showed J a long narrative poem published in a medical periodical. The poem was written in memory of Hippocrates the Greek, Father of Western medicine. The poem related Hippocrates' influence on the history of Western medicine. J thought it was appropriate to translate it into classical verse form in Chinese as the subject was classical. Uncle Earnest thought it would be impossible, not even to give it a try. J insisted, as she was challenged. She did it anyway, translated into Chinese classical verse form, seven words a line, half a sentence all the way through that long poem. Uncle Earnest was astonished. When he showed to his friends at the publishing house, no one recognized it was translated by a young lady over twenty. The style looked "out of an old man's pen, sophisticated," they told him. He was so proud of his pupil J.

There was a good reason that Uncle Earnest took J as an "apprentice" to learn the trade of translation. He said, in Shanghai, during the twenty years of his teaching experience, he seldom encountered a student majoring in English, who also took a genuine interest in Chinese, and whose Chinese literacy and literary sensitivity were as rich as J was gifted with. (Indeed, after 1980s, English majors' Chinese literacy in China, as well as in Taiwan, declined drastically, worse than ever before.)

For Uncle Earnest's generation and the previous generations, translation was an Art. Many of the World Masterpieces, as mentioned before, were translated by men of letters, who had a classical education in Chinese. Not afterwards. Before contemporary Western translation theory was introduced to the Chinese academia, in practice, translators believed in three words —信，达，雅—truthful to, identical with, and elegant expression of the original. Under such principles, there were translators who believed in "literal translation" (直译, direct translation) and those who believed in "literary translation" (意译, translate by meaning). Literal translation aimed to be as close as possible to the appearance of the original words and texts. Literary translation, however, sometimes depended on paraphrase, in order to bring out the connotations and implications of meaning, depending on the translator's literary style.

(Later when J participated in directing doctoral theses on the subject of Western translation theories at Fudan University, she would tell the graduates that these theories were for cultural studies, not necessarily applicable to the study of translation skills.

Nowadays in China, universities admitting graduate students for translation studies clearly indicates whether the program aimed at training translators or at researching on translation theories. The difference between theory and practice was always a problem in communication between the East and the West.)

In translation, J was a perfectionist, and very ambitious. Synthesizing the literal and literary translation, she set a high standard for herself—striving to match the appearance as well as the substance (貌似神似). That was the ideal Uncle Earnest wished to accomplish. The first few pieces Uncle Earnest had J translate were short stories. J did very well. There were not as many red marks in J's translation as that in J's English composition. Later ones were philosophical essays. Gradually, J had more and more surprises for him. Some blissful expressions, coincidences, a marvelous phrase or sentence, that matched the appearance as well as the substance of the English original, that he wouldn't or hadn't thought of, were beyond his imagination—would send him to Heaven. He said it made him "jealous," but that was the joy of teaching—"the purple (pupil) is out of the blue, succeeds blue" (青出于蓝，而胜于蓝). That was a bliss in teaching in Chinese tradition. Later J saw that in her students as well.

Uncle Earnest had two manuscripts translated and were under press review in early 1965, one was a biography of Rembrandt and the other a biography of Picasso. The Cultural Revolution suspended their publication. Western artists were judged to be decadent, have "bourgeois taste," or "corrupted." When the manuscripts came back from the press, Uncle Earnest trusted J to edit them, of all his friends of translators, editors, publishers, colleagues, and pupils. He expected the day would come when these two manuscripts could be resubmitted to be published. It came true, both were published in early 1980s.

The Research Paper

To be able to do some translation work regularly, either technical or literary, or get a job as a translator at the Shanghai Translation Publishing House was a "great expectation" for J. The other expectation was to teach English. Uncle Earnest had a plan. He assigned J to do a research project. It was for J to write a research paper, equivalent to a Master's thesis. The subject was a critical study of William Hazlitt, whose writing J had liked. The research was in preparation for the occasion of Hazlitt's bicentennial birthday in 1978, a couple of years in advance. Uncle Earnest expected there would be a bicentennial celebration in Shanghai in memory of this revolutionary Romanticist. J could submit the research paper to an academic press.

Where to do this research? She was not a college student, had no access to university libraries. Even in university libraries, resources were very limited. Uncle Earnest sent J to the Shanghai Library, which reopened recently. It was just across the street of Uncle Earnest's apartment building, situated on Nanjing Rd. next to the People's Park, inside the building of the Big Ben. It was a colonial building, British style in formerly the British section.

As J walked in, she was awed by its marble stairs and sculptured ceiling, large wooden tables and benches. The atmosphere was so solemn and serene. It was another world from the crowded, busy, noisy streets and city center outside. J fell in love with this world—the world of books, knowledge, immortal learning and writing. She never imagined, this could be the world for her for a life time. Only after she came to America, she pursued such a life as her dream.

There was no access to the shelves. The books could be read only in the library, but not to be checked out. Every day for a couple of months, J rode a bicycle for thirty minutes to go to the library in the morning, and came home after five or six o'clock in the evening. She looked through many volumes of *The Complete Works of William Hazlitt*, at least thirteen volumes. Twice a week she came back to report and discuss with Uncle Earnest. Though the more she read, the less she felt she knew, she still completed the project.

She did independent research of Hazlitt's life and work, including the 19th century historical background, English politics and international movements, the influence of the French Revolution (1798). She examined his criticism of the government policy on warfare and the Bill against the Jews, his writings on despotism and democracy, and his attacks on the liberals. She took notes of his literary criticism on Shakespeare's characters and his aesthetic theory on poetry. She surveyed and analyzed a good amount of the existing criticism of Hazlitt available in the library, before she finally came up with her own assessment.

Afterwards, under Uncle Earnest's guidance, she produced a thesis on William Hazlitt, forty-severn pages in Chinese. Uncle Earnest's wife copied the thesis word by word with ink paper underneath, made three or four copies, ready to be submitted to the academic world. For some reason J couldn't recall now, the essay was not published. Maybe by 1978, J already got a job at a university, busy teaching. Maybe J was leaving for America, did not submit for publication. At any rate, by completing that project, she acquired independent research skills and useful skills analyzing data and ideas in depth. The experience itself was absolutely necessary for advanced study.

Now as she pulled out these three copies from a large envelop in her closet, and reread the pages, she couldn't believe her eyes that what she wrote about Hazlitt—his upright, undaunted, uncompromising character, his firm critical stand, his superior insight, independent, lonely mind, and his tragic fate—in a way, left a visible mark in her own career as a literary critic in the English speaking world. Was it tragic or classic?

College Entrance Examination

By 1976, J's father wished she could stop English study now. J had passed the age of twenty-four, ought to get out of her study, and get a job. Her peers who went to the military farms in the North sent money back to support their family now. It was a shame that J still depended on her parents for a living, her mother told her flat. When J told her that she wanted to have an academic position, her mother laughed at J: "Where would you teach? At a university? Who would hire you?" J told her, Uncle Earnest knew a young woman, who had worked as a waitress in that Green Willow Village restaurant on Nanjing Rd.. She had no college degree, but she was well versed in French, got to teach French at a university. Her mother was cynical, doubtful, but secretly, she wanted her daughter to succeed in her studies.

J's father was jealous of Uncle Earnest, for having a very affectionate relationship with J. He was afraid that J might fall in love with a married man. He went to report to the police that Uncle Earnest was corrupting J with his Western knowledge. J blamed her mother: "Told you not to move here! See, now the police was stationed inside our family!"

The police officer came in to visit J. He asked J what she was reading. J showed him a *Beijing Weekly*, which was an official periodical in English. He looked at it and examined some of the books on the table J was reading. As he couldn't read much in English, J explained to him there was nothing decadent, corrupt, or counter-revolutionary that she was studying. She was translating medical information, scientific knowledge, useful to society. After Nixon's visit in 1972, the government encouraged people to study English. The police officer did not find any fault with J.

He went back only reported to the authorities that in this neighborhood, there was so and so's daughter, talented, had good English knowledge. Soon after, he came back to deliver a message that the District Authorities recommended that J get prepared to apply for college, as the National College Entrance Examination would be reopen to the public, hopefully in a year or two. The country was in want of talented and knowledgable people now!

In the neighborhood and among the relatives, J's father made himself a laughing stock, that he did not wish his daughter to read books and study English! For most parents in Chinese culture, it was unthinkable, absurd, and perverse! One of J's neighbor, also a father, paid a special visit to J, simply told her to ignore his father and keep reading her books and studying English. China needed Western knowledge now.

J's mother, however, wanted J to prepare for the College Entrance Exam. She got J two more tutors, one was her friend's daughter. She was J's age, a "Workers, Peasants and Soldiers'" research student (graduate student) in the Philosophy Department at Fudan University. She would teach J Political Science. Political Science was a priority and a significant part in College Entrance Exam. Another tutor to prepare J for mathematics, physics, and biology was a distant relative. He was a young man over thirty, worked in a factory.

This young man, whose name J couldn't recall, had got acquainted with one of J's Grand-Aunts, Grand-Aunt Rainbow. Both of them were performing Taichi in the park. Grand-Aunt Rainbow was J's Grandfather's elder sister. She must be over seventy in the 1970s. She was a rare beautiful lady, well preserved for her age, active in mind and body. Her daily activities were well planned and scheduled. At that time, she was studying the Japanese language together with this young man. She was fond of J, especially knowing J was also studying a foreign language. J sometimes visited her in her apartment on West Nanjing Rd., admired her taste and intellectual curiosity. She showed J poems, calligraphy, good tea and French curiosities. She was a remarkable woman, elegant and soft voiced, speaking a Suzhou dialect. Her story was unique.

Grand-Aunt Rainbow was married at a young age, had two children. Strangely, she did not like babies, so she gave them away. Later her husband left her, went to Hong Kong, but he still provided for her and sending her money every month throughout the decades. She never wanted to go to Hong Kong. When people told her that her husband might have married another woman in

Hong Kong, she chose to ignore, simply did not want to believe it. She did not want to hear anyone speak ill of her husband. Past the age of seventy, she met this young man in the park, and liked him. She adopted him to be her son. J saw them very affectionate together in her apartment. This young man, being recently adopted, was eager to be introduced to the relatives. He was well prepared to teach J math, physics and biology.

Post-Graduate National Examination

Uncle Earnest was opposed to the idea. He believed J had completed the curriculum of a college education as an English major, ought to obtain a position to teach English at college level. If she entered college, by the time she graduated, she would be assigned to teach English in a remote region, who could tell where it might be.

His advice was to skip the national college entrance examination, and instead, take the examination for graduate study. Send in that Hazlitt paper, they got to admit her, he believed. Indeed, if it were in American universities, a strong research paper might get her into a graduate program, as it did years later. J's paper on the stream-of-conscious novel got her into a graduate program at Stanford.

The graduate schools in China admitted very few students. Usually, only full professors, distinguished big names, took one student per year. After the Cultural Revolution, only a handful of full professors survived. Mostly they already had their favorite students in mind among their former graduates, or recommended by their colleagues. That was the first year open to the public. Previously, post-graduates, as they were called in China following the British system, were recommended within departments. Most research universities were only ready to admit one to three students for graduate study in English.

Among the top four universities, Beijing University, Fudan University, Shanghai Foreign Language Institute, and Beijing Foreign Language Institute, only the last one would admit ten students for graduate study. Compared with one to three at each of the other top universities, it was a fair number. An outsider of the loop might have a chance to get in, J thought and applied.

In order to prepare for the postgraduate exam, J went back to the Shanghai Library, got books of American Literature, a literary history and an anthology. She began to study the major authors, periods, and genre in American Literature. However, when she took the exam, there was only one question on Literature. It asked about a bestseller novel—Seagull's *Love Story*. She was disappointed that the school even did not care to mail her the exam guideline, as they ought to. The examiners completely ignored a "little girl" in Shanghai.

Anyway, she got to the top twenty final list. She went to Beijing to take the oral exam for the final. Staying in the dorm, she met the other finalists, a group of young men, no woman. There was another woman candidate, but she lived on campus at home. Among these young men, the man who scored the highest was a peasant from a small town. He was also an autodidactic. J admired him, but was too shy to approach him. He seldom talked to anyone, not as communicative and sociable as the other men.

The others were mostly instructors of English already teaching at universities. They were graduates before 1966. A couple of them had served in the Ministry of Foreign Affairs, and had experience abroad. They were big brothers, all married men. They were attracted by J's presence. They treated her friendly like a little sister, took her to lunch and dinner, came to chat with her in the evenings. One asked her if she knew an English word "man-killer," J said no, she had never come across the word. Another warned her never to marry a foreigner, or a caucasian, because he would leave her any time.

The one who gave her the best advice was an English instructor from Hangzhou University in Zhejiang. When he heard J mention her cousin's visit from USA, and she came with Nixon, he was excited. He said: "Silly girl, why do you want to come here?

If you are interested in American Literature, go study in America. Ask your cousin to help you!" He also informed J that the Beijing Foreign Language Institute was primarily for the training of interpreters to serve in the Ministry of Foreign Affairs. With her bourgeois family background and overseas relations, she wouldn't have a chance. That good man even paid her a visit later when she returned to Shanghai. He wanted to make sure that J wrote to her cousin for help.

J was not selected after the final. She was hardly disappointed. As soon as she found out that the food was awful and the dorm life was impossible for her, she wouldn't want to be there. In the dorm, there was no hot water; only once a week there was hot water to take a shower. She couldn't imagine how she could live in Beijing for two years. Then where? Uncle Earnest was right. She could be assigned to teach in a college in a remote region. She might not be able to come back and live in Shanghai.

The examiners encouraged her that she was very young (by the academic standard in China), she could come back next year. J said no, she did not wish to come back. Then they asked the Ministry of Education in Beijing to give her a letter of recommendation to the Education Bureau in Shanghai to assign her a position to teach English at any university, as there was a shortage of English instructors at that time. As Mr. Claude predicted, the time had come that the country was "in want of people who have special talent and knowledge" now.

CHAPTER 9

LOVE AND DUTY

First Love: Another Autodidactic

While she was preparing for the exams, J's father urged her to get out and get a job first. The Neighborhood Committee could assign jobs available in collective workshops, which manufactured all types of parts for various industries. Even though the standard wage was only half of the pay in the factories, the work condition and work environment very poor, for many unemployed youth, left idle in the city, or returned from the countryside, a job was a job. The ones who were politically active, frequently attending meetings and participating in social activities, had good relations with the cadres in the Neighborhood Committees got assigned first, the others later.

J went to volunteer at the Barefoot Doctor's clinic in the neighborhood. The national physical examination for women's health was going on, the clinic needed assistance. After a while, she got assigned to work in a workshop, which produced small wiring parts for semiconductor industry. The workshop was set inside a residential house in a lane, dark and small. The workers were mostly women in their forties or fifties, with a group of new comers of the 1960s high school graduates.

The first day, J ran into trouble with a supervisor. A group of boys came to her aid, arguing with the supervisor to give J an easy way out. J thanked them for their support, and made friends. The "gang leader" of the boys turned out to be a 1966 senior high school graduate. He had received full six years of curriculum instruction by the time he graduated, that made him stand out. Supposedly he knew better than the rest of boys, who were younger than he was. His name was Summit, five years older than J.

As they talked, it turned out he was also an autodidactic and an English major. His father used to work for a British company in old Shanghai. He became fluent in English without going to school. He liked to read books. Unfortunately, he died early in 1950s. He was survived by his wife, a daughter and four sons. One day, out of school during the Cultural Revolution, Summit discovered a big suitcase of books left by his father underneath his mother's bed, many in English. He read every one of them. Like his father, he taught himself English and translation. Considering the fact that he had no one to teach him (无师自通), J was utterly impressed. She admired him.

His Chinese knowledge was excellent too. When J mentioned that she enjoyed classical verse, he immediately obtained books on prosody, and taught himself. In a couple of weeks, he mastered the form, and wrote poem after poem to J. They echoed each other's poems, which was a classical mannerism of communication between friends, also a dating game in traditional Chinese culture.

His mother did not have a job. His elder sister was married and lived in Qindao, a city in the north. His elder brother worked in Tianjin. Two brothers got jobs in Shanghai. Maybe they did not have a father in the family, somehow the three brothers managed all to stay together in the city, no one went down to the countryside. That summer when J first got to know him, his mother was not at home, she went to spend the summer with her daughter in Qindao. Summit was the housekeeper and the cook for the family.

He worked evening shift from 2:00pm to 11:00pm. Although he had already prepared dinner ready for his brothers before he came to work, he would still ask leave from work for an hour, on top of that half an hour break time, during 6:00-7:30pm, went home to have dinner with them. For that he got his wages deducted every shift, criticized by his supervisor, and looked loose in the workshop. It hurt his opportunity of promotion and transfer to better jobs.

Imaginably, others would not do that, ask leave for an hour every day at work! He did not mind. He must keep company with his brothers, he told J, and dinner time was the only time. Otherwise by the time he got off from work, and went home after 11:00pm, they already went to bed, he wouldn't have the time to talk to his brothers and learn what they were doing during the day. His mother asked him to keep an eye on his brothers. Family was that important to him. J understood. She took his absences from work rather as his merit. It was Bellring's mother who gave her daughters and all the girls around that good advice. "Girls," she said; "do not judge a man's character by how well he treats you, if he was after you. Watch how he treats other people around, then you can tell his nature and temperament."

Another time, they were sitting on a street bench, J was showing Summit the pictures from America in an album. Pictures from America were curiosities then. A street scum approached them, grabbed J's purse and took the album, ran away. Summit rapidly ran after him, caught the guy, got J's album and purse back. J, who had never had a big brother or father to protect her like that, adored him as a hero.

They fell in love with each other. For him, it was love at first sight. For J, it was her first love. They thought it was a right match in the tradition of the Liang Shanbo and Zhu Yingtai, Summit and J. Or, they were "comrades-in-arms," as they worked together in the semiconductor workshop, and both wish to change for better. They shared a common goal to become English teachers and translators. They were "predestined," as the Chinese would say, meant for each other.

Summit asked his mother to inquire about J's family, and if possible, make a proposal. His mother came back warning him, "this girl was not someone you could handle, a spoiled princess. You'd better be careful." Summit did not mind that he was dating a girl from a bourgeois family. He knew J was not the type of girl anxious for money and status quo, but he wanted to make more to take care of her. So he asked J to give him two years' time. He hoped to get a professional job, move out of the neighborhood workshop. He was so confident that he swore to J if he couldn't get a better job, he would not ask J to marry him. J admired his sense of honor and responsibility as a man, though she never worried about his job, because she was in the same situation, wasn't she? From the tradition in Zhejiang culture, a man's talent and ability were far more important than his social economic status at the moment, not to say the country was in want of knowledgeable and talented people now.

The Legend of *The White Snake*

This time it was not a "rich girl and poor boy story." J's parents did not have any objection, seeing Summit was an amiable fellow, a good cook, gentle and polite. He brought lake crabs and cooked them in the kitchen. J's parents was pleased to know that his family was originally from Shaoxing, a respectable region in Zhejiang province for its scholars and learned wits. As culture, cuisine, customs and dialect vary from place to place, province to province, people from the same region would be easy to communicate and live together. At least, the cuisine was similar, which was important in Chinese family life.

As rare among the young people, Summit also enjoyed traditional theater. Shaoxing Opera was sung in his mother tongue, and Suzhou Pintan he often listened by the radio at night. Once *The White Snake* was on the radio. The story was another popular legend in that region, that everyone knew. The White Snake and the Blue Snake were both goddesses. One day they came down to the West Lake in Hangzhou for sightseeing. The White Snake fell in love with a young scholar, Xu Xian (Promise Fairy), married him. Shortly, the White Snake was pregnant. The Blue Snake stayed with her, protecting the White Snake from mortal attack. Xu Xian was a traditional Chinese scholar, good for nothing in protecting his woman.

As the Laws of the Almighty in universe forbade a Goddess to marry a mortal man, the White Snake's mortal indulgence incurred the wrath of God in Heaven. A powerful Monk in the mountain called Fahai, (法海, Boundless Law), whose power was as immense as the ocean, was determined to destroy their forbidden relationship. At first, he arrested Xu Xian, advised him to become a monk like him, so that he might acquire the spirit to resist the temptation of women and wine.

The White Snake had her magic power. She flooded Fahai's Golden Mountain Temple with a war. She was aided by the Blue Snake and some ocean spirits from the underworld. A war between Heaven and Hell took place. Fahai appealed to the God of War in Heaven. Warriors from Heaven came to his aid. While Fahai was fighting, Xu Xian escaped from his temple in the mountain. The White Snake, being pregnant, weak in strength, lost her magic power. She retreated, and went home. On her way, she met her husband, and delivered a son. Eventually, Faihai was more powerful, captured the White Snake and sucked her in in a crab shell. He placed the crab shell in the dungeon underneath his Thunder Pagoda. The White Snake and Xu Xian, her husband in the secular world, were severed for ever.

This was the version sung in Suzhou Pintan. Summit knew another version from Shaoxing opera, which had a happy ending. The Blue Snake rescued the White Snake. The three of them and their children lived happily after. J argued with him, later she found herself might get mixed up with the story in another play, *The Magic Lantern*, in which the husband raised his son. When the son was eighteen years old, he told him the story of his mother and where she was. The son came to the temple in the mountain, broke in the dungeon with a magic lantern, and rescued his mother.

The Thunder Pagoda stood by the West Lake in Hangzhou, J had visited. *The White Snake* was a historical legend, adapted to all sorts of fiction and theater. Its English version became an American fairy tale now. In this case, the snake and the woman became one, and the Chinese fairy was a seductress, it was just perfect for Christian readers. Only specialist in translation theory might be able to account for the transfiguration.

Personally, J never took fancy of this fairy tale. She was not sympathetic with the White Snake. She did not see how Fahai could have let go the White Snake to live in the human world. A snake was a snake. She was at best a goddess, and at least a fish of sort. In J's mind, it was transgression for the White Snake to seduce a mortal man and live in the secular world. Fahai was only executing the will of Heaven. Summit, on the other hand, cursed Fahai and praised the Blue Snake. At any rate, both of them were too young to understand the sexual desire of beauty and beast. Neither of them could possibly perceive the hidden agenda of its mythic allegory.

"The Conscience does Make Cowards of us all"

As girlfriends often tell their heart affairs to one another, J told Pinnacle about Summit. Pinnacle, who was always conscious of status quo, thought it was not the right match for J. Pinnacle's father was an "Oil Baron," a shark in the oil business. He was found to be the most wealthy man in Shanghai during the house search movement in 1966. From his house, the Red Guards got four millions, sheer bank notes.

Pinnacle's father had one daughter and eight sons by his first wife, all big and tall, grown up and married. Except for one, none was well read and well educated. Most of them behaved like brutes. Pinnacle's mother was his father's private nurse. She married him after his first wife passed away. Maybe from her mother, Pinnacle learned to be ambitious in marriage. At that time she was engaged to the younger son of a cotton industry baron. Later they broke apart. She went to Hong Kong, where she eventually married a wealthy man, at least twenty years her senior.

Pinnacle was "class conscious." She was not easy to make friends across board in school, as J was. One day she approached J to say hello. It was only because her mother's best friend was

Grand-Aunt May Fourth, who on the bus the weekend before, happened to mention to her that her elder sister's granddaughter was in her school. J did not know who she was in Pinnacle's eyes then and there. At any rate, Pinnacle made friends with her, and became very close. In many ways, she took good care of J.

Pinnacle immediately told Uncle Earnest about J's love for Summit. Her siblings and Uncle Earnest's other two boy students were all apposed to the idea that J fell in love with a stranger who worked in a neighborhood workshop, and whose family was not "who's who" in Shanghai.

Uncle Earnest, who was equally conscious of status quo, stormed into J's room. He was furious and mad, sat there for six hours, gave J a lesson of "stop it, not do." The reasons were multiple. First, he did not want J to be distracted from study by involving with boys yet, until she set out on her career. Secondly, by the time if J was ready to get married, (still there were two or three more years to go for the legal age of marriage), he would find her a good match, a college graduate at least, well educated, an academic. At least, J must get his approval in matters like this. Third, he had gone to her workplace, watched Summit from a distance, found him not handsome, "he looked like a ghost." Fourth, he did not have a decent job. How could he let this man ruin his Pygmalion? J told him Summit's English was good enough, could help him with his translation and teaching. He started to abuse Summit's writing.

He was really anguished when J told him no, she loved Summit. He threatened of murder. J was immovable. In the following weeks, he confessed his passion for J, for years repressed and unspoken. J was embarrassed. She wrote him a couplet: "此情虽非古来稀，终背人情逆天意" (This sort of love, incidentally, did occur in history and legends; but it was against the Law, and forbidden by the Will of Heaven). He went home loony, couldn't eat and sleep well, wanted to commit suicide. His friends, those two lady colleagues, came to comfort him, reminded him of his family responsibilities. He insisted to threaten J with suicide. Then the two ladies turned to J, asked J to help him.

Once more, J was caught in a moral dilemma of "to be or not to be"—whether to say to him, a man who taught her for years, free of tuition, to whom she owed so much, "go ahead, do what you want, I do not care," even knowing he wouldn't really kill himself; or to promise she would not see Summit again. "The conscience does make cowards of us all/ and thus the native hue of resolution/ Is sicklied o'er the pale cast of thought."

Under the circumstance, J decided she had no right to ignore Uncle Earnest, let him sink into agony and abyss. J recognized how jealousy could destroy the best in a man, including his love. As for Summit, he was still young, he could find another girlfriend. So J promised not to see Summit again. After all, J had only got to know him for a short period of time, less than a year or so.

She told Summit she would soon leave for America, so they'd better say good bye for now. Summit got a fever, was hospitalized for two weeks after J parted with him. His best friend Big Wave ran into J in the streets, told her about the blow Summit received. Big Wave warned J not to let him see her again, otherwise he might hurt her. If Summit did not hate her as much, Big Wave did. He was Summit's sworn brother. Summit had mentioned to J, if he died early, Big Wave would take care of her. So it goes.

Uncle Earnest's wife, on the other hand, was grateful to J. She never displayed her jealousy, or said anything harsh to J all those years. Her marriage survived. Even after J left China, there was more sexual freedom in society, extramarital affairs were common place, divorce was easy; for instance, Uncle Bull divorced his wife, married his pupil more than twenty years younger than he was; yet for the next forty years, Uncle Earnest never fell in love with another woman or had an extramarital affair.

After 1990s, his wife was paralyzed and bedridden, Uncle Earnest undertook all the house work, and took care of her himself. In 2004, J went back to Shanghai to teach at Fudan University. She invited Uncle Earnest out for lunch. He asked J if she could recognize the sweater he wore, that was a gift from J thirty years ago. J couldn't recognize it.

J made a fair decision. It was tragic, but like in a tragedy, there was a tragic necessity. She had no remorse or regret. She had no guilt towards Summit either. He got married a few years later, had a son, who grew up and was educated in America. His son already bought his parents an apartment in Shanghai, and himself another one in Manhattan, New York City. Summit had a granddaughter now. He was proud of his son. J asked him if she had not told him she left for America, would have he come after her, and raised his son in New York? That was another story.

After that emotional trauma, J felt that she had paid a huge emotional debt to Uncle Earnest. She had sacrificed her love for Summit to save his peace, if not really his life. He could not say she was ungrateful now. At the same time, she realized that her life and career might have been too dependent on Uncle Earnest, his knowledge, his instruction, and his mentoring to make it—to find a way out in life, to become an English teacher and translator, so much so that she couldn't function without his guidance.

She couldn't deny Uncle Earnest's apprehension that Summit might not be a right match for her future. Summit was a family man, he was talented, good humored, and gentle. But he had no ambition at all. "Ambition" might be a negative word, what J had in mind was a lofty ideal, at least a public spirit, that was what education was meant for, and that was somehow missing in Summit. He inherited a traditional "South of the River" (江南) poet's attitude towards life. His philosophy was that reading, writing and learning were his personal hobby, for pleasure sake and pastime. For him, it was vulgar to use one's poetic knowledge to make a living or pursue a career. J knew she herself wouldn't be satisfied with that, or with family life only.

She analyzed her own feelings for Uncle Earnest to see if she could have taken him as a lover. She really did not love him so much as a man or sole life companion. J loved him for what he had done for her, his gentleness and affection as a father figure and a friend. J wanted him for what was in his head, his language, prose, his knowledge and instruction, not his body. He had a big head, once J bought a winter hat for him, he had to exchange for the largest size in the department store, though his height and weight were only medium. He was not handsome at all.

Knowing he was in love with her, she wished to distance herself, to cool down his feelings. She wanted him to know that she gave up Summit to consent to his wishes, to follow his instruction as he wished, and as she promised him in the beginning—to work hard and be persistent. She would keep her promise. As for a love relationship, it was simply forbidden and impossible in Chinese society at that time, even if she were willing. There was no privacy for extramarital love affair. She gave up her regular attendance of class, she needed a break now.

Difference and Mutual Influence

J had her bosom friend to rely upon in distress. Knowing J's emotional trauma, her friend Currie invited J to visit her in Dalian, a beautiful sea port in the North. Currie's parents came to Shanghai from the North in 1949. They came to take over the Bank of China. They were senior revolutionaries, cadres in Shanghai. With that class background, Currie, after working two or three years in a military farm in the Black Dragon River region, was selected to go to college to study Pharmacy.

The university was in Shenyang, another city in the North, not far away. Currie got an assignment of internship to work in Dalian, so she invited J to meet her there. J was invited to stay with her aunt. Her aunt had a large house, modern style. Her husband was mostly away from home, serving in the military, a high officer.

Currie and J were classmates and good friends ever since 1965. During the Cultural Revolution, the "Red Five" and the "Black Puppets" were naturally and unnaturally separated. Currie was unaffected, still went to school and walked home together with J. As the two of them walked together across the school courtyard, it sent a signal to the Red Guards that J was a friend. Others looked at them with strange eyes. People in school couldn't make sense of the two extreme differences—one Red, one Black, one dressed in northern provincial padded coat, looked like a peasant; and the other, fan in hand, handkerchief loose hanging out of her pocket, dressed in vogue, obviously a bourgeois city girl—should be so close and good friends. Pinnacle just shook her head.

What most people did not know was that Currie, who looked provincial, was extremely intelligent. She was interested in science and technology at an early age. The first year she entered junior high, she was only thirteen. She already knew how to play with camera, radio, and semiconductor like toys. She would take them apart and put them together. She knew how to fix lamps and bicycles with her slim fingers. She was the one who made a large model cruise ship with electric wiring, on behalf of the class, to be exhibited in school. Math teachers loved her.

She was not interested in language arts, sports, singing or dancing. Even the daily ten minutes physical exercise, for that every student had to be there 7:45am before class started, she would sometimes skip, either stay in the classroom or arrive after it was over. She did not care for school or grades at all. If she did not feel like to go to school, she just stayed at home. No one could persuade her. Sometimes, J might come to the door, and call her out.

Currie had a philosophy that success in one thing depends on the negligence of many other things. She quoted Confucius to teach J: "有所不为才能有所为," one must not do everything in order to do something. She criticized J for being involved with too many social activities and too many friends. J couldn't behave like Currie. Only now she realized the wisdom of Currie's philosophy. While she pursued her American dream, she neglected many other things, such as the pursuit of money, power, even sex and marriage, fancy cars and a big house. She was often criticized by her family and friends for being "unrealistic," "unpractical," and "immature." Only Currie could understand her and always encourage her to be more focused on her study.

Currie was an individualist, who had her own ideas. She told J she wanted to study physics, and she wanted to get a Ph.D. in physics someday. That was the first time J ever heard the word "Ph.D." J had no doubt of Currie's aptitude and potential. She ought to get a Ph.D. in physics, and have inventions. Currie went to college, but did not have a chance to study physics and go on for a Ph.D. What a genius wasted! J told Currie that she would get a Ph.D in America for her sake, to fulfill her wish.

Currie liked J because J was like a book, full of ideas. Also, J understood her as no one did. She could talk to J about her feelings, her emotional trauma. She was sensitive and nervous by temperament. Whereas, at home, feeling was regarded to be sentimental, "bourgeois taste," not talked about. Everything must be rational and politically correct. Currie felt relaxed in J's company. J was her emotional cushion.

J was sensible enough, stopped going to her house after the Cultural Revolution started. She was afraid that Currie's family might have a problem with her bourgeois family background. Currie kept coming to visit J. She couldn't care less for what people would think and say. J wouldn't ask her to come upstairs, to avoid "corrupting" her in her family surroundings. Therefore, as mentioned before, the two of them always stood chatting outside under a streetlamp.

One day, when Currie was in the military farm, J went to Currie's house to tell her parents that Currie wrote to say she was ill. Her father was at home. He came out all smiles at J. He even asked J to sit down, and he talked to J for a while. He told J that he had read some of the letters J wrote to Currie in the North. He believed J was a good influence on Currie. J was flattered as well as embarrassed, a senior revolutionary cadre thought she was a good influence on his daughter!

As it turned out later, both her parents and her three siblings liked J. For the next forty years, they remained J's loyal friends. There weren't any "class conflicts" or disagreement in political opinions, that caused any problem in their relationship. Her folks were simple, sincere, and solid people. They were from the North, but they were not dull. They were refined in their sensibility and intellect. They might be provincial in the eye of city people, but they were very sophisticated in their taste and judgement.

They had a different attitude towards money. They spent money according to needs and necessity. They were not as calculating as the Philistines in Shanghai, or as indulgent as the happy-go-lucky hedonists among the wealthy. For instance, Currie would wear her old padded coat cover for years and years, never thought about a change of fashion or design. Yet she would buy a huge chunk of Russian cheese in Harbin, which costed her a fortune, to mail it to J, only because J wanted cheese to make a tasty casserole on her birthday. Without Currie, J would never have known the true value of things money could buy. Once she became financially independent, she adopted Currie's life style and economics to a certain extent.

So this time, when Currie invited J to visit her aunt, she happily accepted. Though Shanghai was a coastal city, it was the first time J took a cruise on board a ship. It was the first time she saw the ocean, first time set out to sea. The effect was cool. The vast and infinite waves washed away the nuisance and troubles in her life in Shanghai, her sadness and her loss of love. She wrote a poem as a letter home.

家信

北上何所求? 寻我知心友.
浊水从此逝, 轻舟出海游.
波尽知天阔, 潮退见绿洲.
我材必有用, 携书登高楼.　　　　1974年7月11日　于大连

(A Letter Home

Why up north do I travel?
To see my bosom friend, who knows
　　my heart and mind.
The muddy rivers disappear
　　behind me hereafter,
A light boat, out of the mud,
　　sailing towards the ocean.

At the end of the waves,
I know how wide was
　　the boundary of Heaven,
When the tides retreat,
I see Oases emerge.
Nature's gift must have use for
　　Nature's glory,
Books lift the waves to reach
　　the pagoda high above on shore.　　July 11, 1974, Dalian)

The writing of that poem restored her peace of mind. The ocean purified her feelings. She left everything behind and looked forward. Uncle Earnest wrote several poems to J to ask her come home. He consented that for the sacrifice J made, he would direct J on the right path to become who she was meant to be in the near future.

J had a wonderful time in Dalian. Every day, Currie's aunt served elegant breakfast and dinner. There were always four dishes for breakfast—sausage, tomatoes, eggs, and cucumbers, with white buns or porridge to go. At dinner, shrimp and vegetable dumplings were made as tiny as a thumb! During the day, Currie's cousin sisters took J to the beach. J picked up big bags of bright colorful shells to bring home. She made ash trays, necklaces, and other decorative pieces to give her friends as presents.

Currie told J that at the college, the students did not read many books, mostly lab work. Frequently, they had to go down to the countryside to work in the fields. She did not think there were many intelligent people even at a university. She was not interested in Pharmacy. The pressure she had at the university was not academic work, but the requirement to join the Youth League, then the Party. It was an honor to be a member. Everyone was making efforts to join, and almost everyone was accepted. She alone did not apply. She valued her privacy. She did not want her university authorities to investigate her family background, her personal life and life style thoroughly before they accepted her, as routine procedure must require. She did not want to attend political meetings, observe all the rigorous discipline, participate in activities she did not care, and sacrifice her individual will. She had no interest in politics, just content to be a plebeian, have her own way in life. She finally got away with what everyone did.

Theoretically speaking, it was unthinkable, wasn't it? The daughter from a revolutionary family had no revolutionary passion. Had her family and school education failed her? Or she failed them? J tried to understand Currie. Though her family and relatives were from the North, Currie was a daughter born in Shanghai. She was interested in city life and its modern life style. From her family background, Currie stepped out. She was open to difference, curious of the best of Shanghai, that J stood for. She had a scientific mind, which wouldn't follow empty words and political propaganda. She trusted her own eyes, experience, and experiments. She spoke and acted by heart, instead of theory and language from books and newspapers. There was no revolutionary incentive in the city environment.

She was a modern individual, a product of where she was. Though she was selected to go to college as a representative of "the Workers, Peasants and Soldiers College Students," she was alienated from her constituents. She was born and grown up under the maple trees in a Western style mansion, at the West Side of Shanghai, a bourgeois district. She was alien to the working class in another part of the city. She couldn't relate to the peasants in the North, less than J could in the South.

Currie returned to Shanghai after graduation. She got a job in a hospital. Chemistry was never her cup of tea. She had no ambition to advance her study in medicine. In the 1990s, she found her passion for stock exchanges. There her gift in mathematics worked, she made a fortune. By then, China was modernized, no one criticized "bourgeois life style," or Western fashion anymore. Currie changed her life style! She wore high heel shoes, carried brand name purses. Dancing and dating all night long, she toured all over the country, staying in four star, five star hotels. She laughed at J for looking so "provincial." Coming back from America, J looked like a "country pumpkin," or an earthy "turkey" in her eyes. They were still best friends, understood each other, as in old days.

J wondered if one's class background, family origin, and economic status could forever determine one's class consciousness, political lineage, and dedication to the revolutionary cause. Rather, it was public education, social environment and popular values that played a more significant part in shaping the mind of the modern individual. Karl Marx might not have anticipated the high mobility in the 20th and 21st centuries. With economic reform and high mobility in modern society, the original concept of class, origin and identity, either in Marxist theory or by feudal tradition, could no longer sustain its stability. The class structure in China was soon to be challenged by economic reform. The proletariat became

Currie (R) and her twin sister (L), each had a son in 1980s.

business owners and bourgeoisie. Many sons and daughters of revolutionaries and army officers were turned into industrialists, real estate owners, and financiers. So it goes.

Higher Education Reform

Universities had been reopened five years later in 1971. At that time, admission was very limited. Criteria was based on recommendation only. College students must be workers, peasants and soldiers, directly coming from factories, communes or farms, or the military. Family background must be Red, and Red only. The selection was very exclusive, only a handful of people could go to college.

Higher education was experimental at that time. It underwent radical reform from curriculum instruction to textbooks. Much reading requirements and classroom instruction were cut or downsized for ideological or pragmatic reasons. The period of college education was shortened from four years to three years, while a requirement was added to prolong the time period for field work. Political Science was given as a priority in performance, academic subjects secondary. The books students read were reduced to a minimal amount. Bookish knowledge was not valued.

By 1975-76, "The Workers, Peasants, and Soldiers' College Students" graduated and placed in positions that required professional knowledge, they found themselves ill-prepared, incapable to keep up with the professional demand in every field. They proved to be academically and professionally incompetent, not up to the standards of college graduates admitted and graduated before 1966. Most of them had to be sent back to be "reeducated," or take continuing education classes. "The Workers, Peasants and Soldiers' College Graduates" was no longer a label of honor and distinction in society than a pitiful synonym of "the inadequately college educated." Fortunately, the number was small. The "selected few" became a "lost generation," victims of 1960s radical reform. Simply, these people failed to compete with the professionals at work in an increasingly competitive new economy.

In English Education, the situation was worse. The time "The Workers, Peasants and Soldiers' College Students" were in school, they were given to study what was "politically correct" according to the limited, radical, revolutionary dogmas during the Cultural Revolution. "Down with" every author or book that had something to do with "the bourgeois" or "the revisionist." They did not study the English language as it was spoken and written in the West. As for English Literature, their knowledge was limited.

J heard a joke from Uncle Quixote's colleagues who came for dinner. In an English exam, there was a question to ask the students to identify the name of "Shakespeare," one student's answer was "an herb medicine." It could be a joke, used to describe the English majors' ignorance of English Literature at that time. Their English textbooks were written by Chinese professors, who translated Chinese revolutionary ideas into English for the students to learn. They read very few texts in the original.

Their knowledge of Western culture was even poor, as they were totally isolated from the capitalist, bourgeois culture and the

English speaking world in school. At home, few had contact with the West, exposed to the influence of Western culture, since their family background was exclusively Red, proletariat and grassroots, no connections overseas. China was isolated from the West for a long time during the Cold War. No one was to blame for their ignorance. So it goes.

By 1976, the Cold War began to thaw. After the first visit of some Chinese American Nobel Prize winners in Physics came, the government recognized the merit of studying abroad. It agreed to let those Professors of Physics conduct interviews and select a few promising students to study science in the West. Soon with the help of these scholars, the government sent the first group of Chinese scientists to study in the West, namely, to America, Canada, England, and Germany.

These scientists were China's best. They were not selected from the generation of "The Workers, Peasants and Soldiers' College Students," but from graduates before 1966. Some of them were returned research students from the Soviet Union in the 1950s. After they studied in the West for a semester or two, all reported they were far behind the progress in their respective fields and professions. One in New York committed suicide. After he saw how much behind and out of touch with the progress in his field, this man was utterly depressed and shattered. He gave up. All reported lack of English proficiency, cultural knowledge and oral skills. Most of them only had reading proficiency to survive their degree requirements or carry on their research in the labs or library.

Only a couple of months after J worked in that workshop, a large oil company in the suburb of Shanghai got the permission to recruit English instructors to train their staff to work with foreign experts. A citywide recruitment exam was announced and held by the faculty at the Shanghai Foreign Language Institute, the highest authority in foreign language teaching in Shanghai. J was recommended by the District to be registered to take an oral exam. The candidates at the exam were all past middle age, who learned the English language either in 1940s, or graduated before 1966. J was the youngest. She saw Summit was there taking the exam too.

When the results came out, J scored the highest, and Summit, the second. From then on, they were both transferred from the workshop to work as English instructors in that oil company in the suburb. In the morning, big shuttle bus would drive them to the campus. There the work environment was very pleasant, bight and clean. They sometimes ran into each other in the hallways, but they just say hello, exchanged a few words, and kept a distance from each other. J was as good as her word.

A year or two later, Summit got a job as an assistant of lexicography. He worked with a large team of famous linguists, translators and professors in Shanghai. They were making a new English Dictionary. A couple of years later, he got a position as instructor of English at a university. It was the Shanghai Marine University. So it goes.

"Good Afternoon, Sir!"

J was transferred to Shanghai Jiaotong University to teach in a special program—the "Study Abroad" program. It was the second group of government sponsored students, selected from all over the country through rigorous criteria. They were mostly top research students and professors in Physics and Engineering. They had passed rigorous exams not only in their special fields, but also in technical English. Family background was less important this time. Over two hundred students were gathered in Shanghai Jiao Tong University to advance their English study for one year, to be better prepared for study abroad. J's job was to teach them English conversation, Western Culture, how to take the test of TOEFL, a little grammar, and everyday writing; thus prepare them for research and study in the West.

It was a period of faculty shortage in English education, called "青黄不接" in Chinese, "simply no supplies between the famine season and the harvest time." Any English instructor who meet the qualifications, succeeded in an exam, and could perform the duties would be hired. Moreover, the government would allow the recruited faculty to establish legal residency in Shanghai, which was a very attractive incentive for many, therefore, very competitive. J did not need the residency, but got one of the ten positions offered by a major university in Shanghai.

The university hired these nationwide recruited instructors for a special program to train researchers to study in the West. Among the ten new faculty, a couple of them were senior instructors, who were graduates of 1940s, already on faculty in the Foreign Language Department at Jiaotong University. The rest were all middle aged, graduates before 1966, who had been teaching English in other universities or working in foreign ministry, anxious to be transferred back to Shanghai. J was the only one without a college degree, but she was well accepted, loved by all her colleagues, students and supervisors.

She met with a group of junior faculty in the Foreign Language Department. They were about her age, the recently graduated "Workers, Peasants, and Soldiers' College Students." They were studying *Essential English* for continuing education, that was the first textbook J was given at the age of ten, to begin her first English lessons, with a tour in London, as mentioned before. That was the textbook, those junior faculty told J, put them in direct touch with the West. J understood why she was wanted there. She helped them with their studies, and made friends.

The class J was assigned to teach had about twenty-five to thirty students, except for one woman, all men, aging from thirty-five to fifty-three. All came from research institutes, they were university faculty, some senior professors, renowned scientists. J was only twenty-five, shy and timid. Especially, every time when she came to class, she would be shocked by the courtesy the students paid to her. As soon as she stepped into the classroom, they all stood up, "Good afternoon, Sir!" They would stand there, until she said: "Sit down, please." When she announced the class was over, all would stand up again: "Good-bye, Sir!" J told them there was no such formality in Western universities, they could do without it.

Then after class, they became quite casual with J, patted her on her shoulder, rode their bicycles on her side, as J rode her bicycle home. A couple of bold ones would call on her at home. Some made friends with her, only to find her and meet her again in

"Good Afternoon, Sir! " J (L4). Shanghai Jiaotong University (上海交通大学), 1979.

第六机械工业部出国预备生英语培训班结业留念 1979.7.5

Commencement of Study Abroad, July 5, 1979. J (R2)

San Francisco, when they came to Berkeley a year or two later.

One class J always remembered. Whenever American feminists asked her about gender equality and women's status in China, she often thought of that class she taught. As a practice for conversation, she asked her students to talk about their daily activities from morning to evening. Almost all the men said, the first thing they did in the morning was to go to the vegetable market. For most of them, the first thing they did after work was to prepare for dinner. What did their wives do? J asked. They said their wives had a nine to five work schedule mostly, and they themselves as university faculty had a flexible schedule, so naturally, it was their job to do the house work as much as they could. There was one man who did not have to cook dinner, his wife was also a professor.

J taught that "Study Abroad" class for one year before she left for America. In the middle of the academic year, there was a dramatic episode. Jiaotong University belonged to the state system, could only take transfers from state system employers, not that from the co-op system. J's employment status still belonged to the co-op system, the neighborhood workshop she first entered the work force.

Aunt Modest, always resourceful she was, got a great idea. She suggested that J's mother retire. At that time, there was also a government policy to solve the unemployment problem for the1960s graduates, which allowed unemployed youth to replace their parents' positions, if the parents were willing to retire. It might be a good incentive to encourage early retirement, while solving unemployment of "The Idle Class" in the city. J's mother's housing office belonged to the state system. J's mother was willing to take a retirement now after so much torture and humiliation at the work place, and let J have the benefit of replacement.

Her office authorities were very supportive by then. They had to do something to compensate J's mother for the torture and persecution they put her through during the Cultural Revolution. Her colleagues always liked J, saw her grew up, knew she was a good student. Now they were proud of her to be able to teach at a university. They let J come in to work for one month in January. January was during winter break at the university, when J did not have to teach class. As soon as her first paycheck was stamped from her mother's housing office in the state system, Jiaotong University gladly accepted it, thus the transfer went through.

For the month J went to work in her mother's housing office, she met those Red Guards, who had come to her house and took everything away; who beat her mother at work, and humiliated her in public. Some felt guilty now, some were envious of J's accomplishment, all wanted to make things easy for J. After the house-searching, J's mother's job was no longer bookkeeping, but construction. She carried a cement bucket to assist the construction workers to build house, or mend houses from door to door.

The construction masters decided that it would be a waste of time to teach J practical construction skills. They decided to let her work in the kitchen and in the dinning hall. J learned to make steam buns and wrap dumplings, serve the workers at meal time, and clean the kitchen afterwards. Her mother's master invited J home to have dinner. They lived in the east end of the city, in a crowded, industrial district. J spent a weekend with his wife and daughter. J got to know the workers personally, and saw how they lived and worked, thus she was "reeducated by the working class" as part of her practice in that work place.

CHAPTER 10

LEGACY

"A Woman's Place is in the House and the Senate"

J did write letters to cousin Ambrosia in Washington D. C. after they first met in Shanghai. Ambrosia was a pioneer in normalizing US-China diplomatic relations in early 1970s. The first time she came to China was as either before or after Nixon's visit. She did not inform the Chinese authorities in advance that she had relatives in Shanghai. With the address her mother gave her, she immediately found her mother's wet nurse, Good Mama, who still lived in the house, where Aunt Viva left with her three children twenty years before. The place was called "Lafayette Lane on Lafayette Rd.," later changed to "Restoration Lane" on "West Restoration Rd." (West Fuxing Rd.). With the help of Good Mama, Cousin Ambrosia got hold of Uncle Quixote and the whole family on J's mother's side, invited all to dinner in Jinjiang Hotel.

(Some forty years later in 2014, the two cousins, J and Ambrosia, met again in that neighborhood in Shanghai. Taking a walk in the streets, they happened to pass that "Restoration Lane" on West Restoration Rd. (West Fuxing Rd.). As they walked into the lane, they found some of the buildings were preserved as historic sites, protected from demolishing. Some important people had taken residences there. Two women's names looked familiar.

One was 何香凝 (He Xiangning), a pioneer revolutionary at the turn of the twentieth century. She was Sun Yet-Sun's comrade. The other was 史良 (Shi Liang), a woman lawyer under the Republic, and after the Liberation, served as Minister of Justice. Shi Liang was the attorney who settled J's Grandma's father's large estates after his death. The estates was divided equally among four daughters, two sons and the wife. Whether Grandma and her sisters were benefited from a feminist attorney was another story.

J asked Ambrosia if she remembered she had lived there in that lane in her childhood. Ambrosia said she could recognize the place, only because she had visited Good Mama the first time she returned to China in early 1970s, but she couldn't remember the house number. Good Mama had accompanied Aunt Viva to her husband Uncle Fortune's hometown in the North in 1942, where Ambrosia was born. After Aunt Viva left China with her three children, Good Mama had lived there and waited day and night, over twenty years, only to see them back from America! It was Ambrosia, a daughter in the family, who made it happen. Good Mama said, she could close her eyes now, once she had seen them back. She passed away only a couple of years later.)

J missed that family dinner, as she was not at home that evening. The next day, she went to the Jinjiang Hotel to meet Ambrosia alone. As they were strangers, they did not have much to say to each other. Ambrosia could fast speak nine languages, yet only a few sentences in Chinese, only in Shanghai dialect, with a foreigner's accent. So they somewhat talked in English. Ambrosia was quick and vivacious, alert and fast paced, very sophisticated and diplomatic. She asked J what she would like to have from America, J said she needed an atlas of the globe. It took her some time to figure out why J wanted an atlas of the globe. She sent to J in the mail shortly after she returned to USA.

The second time she came back, she was with the Delegation of Young Political Leaders. She wore a T-shirt, which says: "A Woman's Place is in the House and the Senate." She might be doing some research on women's status in China. J did not know then, in the United States, the 1960s generation was going through "Women's Liberation," and struggling for equal status with men.

After she returned to the states, in a letter, Ambrosia asked J what she thought women in China needed most. J quickly replied: "Laundry machines and refrigerators." It was true that in China, the masses of women all had jobs and had to work outside of the house, what they needed most was to save time on housework. In 1970s, there weren't so many leisured wealthy housewives, or housekeepers as these days. Now as she reflected, it

Ambrosia and J first met in Jinjiang Hotel.

might not be the desirable answer for Ambrosia, and what her education and cultural background had prepared for her to comprehend. The Americans expected to hear "sexual abuse," "patriarchal oppression," "infanticide" "domestic violence" and "sexual harassment" at work and in the military, and "discrimination against the weak sex," as J learned decades later; but she was really unaware of issues like that growing up in China. To say the least, those were not popular and serious social problems in Chinese society.

On the contrary, in China, radical feminist power, represented by Mao's wife, Jiang Qing, with her radical agenda, had been a nightmare. During the Cultural Revolution, Mao became senile, lost control, and his wife Jiang Qing became a dictator. She took revenge on all her former enemies, political enemies as well as her rivals in the culture and movie industry. With the Gang of Four, she ruled China for a decade, people were fed up by radical feminism indeed.

Western feminists might argue that Jiang Qing was criticized because she was a woman. It was not true, there were so much more to it. Differences and special conditions in gender construction, historical formation, political power and intellectual tradition in Chinese civilization—all had to be considered, that were simply beyond the knowledge of Western feminists and their education behind "the Iron Curtain of Language," as J eventually figured out. J was to make their acquaintances and know their limitations twenty years later.

Ambrosia was not completely "melted" in the melting pot, she was raised by traditional Chinese values and life style carried over from her parents. She married her college boyfriend at Harvard. He was a year younger than she was. At home, she was a good cook for her husband, and dressed conservatively, to the taste of her husband, who was a lawyer. Though she had to travel abroad frequently for work, by average half a year, her marriage lasted over fifty years by now. She had a model husband, everyone in the family recognized. He adored his mother-in-law. Every five years, he would give her a new Cadillac.

From her letters, Ambrosia discerned that J had too much "creativity and imagination to be wasted in China," she promised to help her to come to America. At first, she introduced J to a man from Michigan, who was a philanthropist. The man came to Shanghai for a visit, called J up, and asked J to come to the Peace Hotel to meet him.

J took him out for a walk along the Bund. The man handed J two pages of his autobiography, which was readable in English. Only one phrase in it looked to J as odd, this man had no children "that he knew of." How could one "know not of" one had or had not children? J was totally ignorant of the life style and sexual relationship in American culture at that time.

With an American efficiency, the man asked J if she wished to get married. J did not get the message, because Chinese courtship was not like that. Why would she want to marry someone she did not know? That was beyond her comprehension and her upbringing. Then the man asked her if she did not want to get married, how would she be able to survive in America? J told him her Aunt Viva had a restaurant in San Francisco, she could work there, and use the library to advance her study. The man looked disappointed, but told J if she needed help, she could contact him after she came to America.

Did Ambrosia send this man to marry her? What kind of a feminist idea was it? A marriage of convenience? Or marry someone to support her so that she could go to college in America? It was news for J, educated under socialist China. Later J learned that in a capitalist economy, marriage might be a means of survival. In the following decades, China underwent economic reform, sexual revolution, and social changes. To go to America through marriage became acceptable. Unfortunately, there was something missing in J's education. She did not know that in America, "Oriental Wives Desire Romance" was a popular myth. Maybe, she was intellectually over-educated, and sexually retarded. So it goes.

Uncles and Granduncles in the North

In 1977, Ambrosia got visa for her parents, her husband and her sister. Before the normalization, few could obtain visa to come back to China for a visit. Aunt Viva and her husband, Uncle Fortune, their younger daughter, cousin Pagoda, and Ambrosia's husband Karl were coming to visit China. They had left China for over twenty-five years, now thanks to Ambrosia's arrangement, were coming back for a family reunion. Ambrosia was a daughter who made her father's dream come true.

Uncle Quixote felt sorry for J, as he learned about Uncle Earnest's romantic passion for his niece. As his friend, he could understand that heart's affairs were hard to reason, hard to control. He took it comically as a classic case, or a classic "curse"— "自古文人多无行." "Since time immemorial, men of letters never know how to behave themselves," said he. He promised J to ask

Uncle Philip and J (L);
his lovely daughter and
J (R), Beijing,1978.

Aunt Viva to take her to America. He sent his daughter Winter
Born and J together to meet Aunt Viva and her family in Beijing,
the first stop of their planned trip. Their second stop was Qingdao,
Uncle Fortune's hometown, before they would arrive in Shanghai.

Winter Born's mother had relatives in Beijing. The two
girls stayed at one of her Uncle's house, a traditional four-quarter
garden house. The Grand-Uncle and his wife both looked very
respectable, tall and dignified. They were warm and generous. The
Grand-Uncle served in the air force before 1949. In early 1950s, he
led a fleet of aircrafts, with a division of his air force, flew back
from Taiwan, across the straits, returned to China, where he felt he
belonged.

In Beijing J met another uncle, Uncle Philip, who worked
at the Ministry of Water Resources as an engineer. Uncle Philip
was older than Uncle Quixote, their fathers were brothers. Uncle
Philip was the eldest son and eldest grandson in a large family,
born by the first wife. Such a status ought to have placed on him

heavy filial duty and family responsibility. Yet he left home, joined the communists in 1940s.

After he was established in Beijing in early 1950s, he moved his mother from Shanghai to live with his family. His wife was a specialist in foreign languages, worked in Beijing Foreign Languages Bookstore, a nice and pleasant woman. They had a lovely daughter, a few years younger than J, a happy family. Strangely, their daughter never asked to come to America, while most cousins and relatives in the large family came one after another during the next three decades.

During the Cultural Revolution, Uncle Philip was ordered to "go down" (下放) to work in the fields, in the Blue Seas, a remote region up north, close to the Mongolia border. He carried his mother on his back, and went. Wherever he went, he carried his mother on his back, in the sand and across the river. A filial son, he became legendary. Unlike Uncle Quixote, Uncle Philip was a man of responsibility.

Unlike Sweet Oliver PoPo's son, that working class cadre in a factory, who was ashamed of his widow mother being a nanny of Grand-Aunt May Fourth, kept it a secret from his wife, another working class cadre in Shanghai, Uncle Philip was a revolutionary, yet he still preserved Chinese ethics, valued his filial duties. J respected him a lot. She became confused of "the origin of class identity" in Marxist theory. Its practice and rationale in excluding the children from wealthy family in college and school admissions after the revolution succeeded in 1949 was obviously a mistake, absurd. It wasted so much human resources and talents.

Uncle Philip's father was educated at Oxford University at the turn of the century. His wife, Uncle Philip's mother, went to Oxford with him, to keep him company. She came back speaking English with a Suzhou accent, very sweet, but with a high pitch, which impressed everyone in the family. Once Uncle Quixote taught J to mimic her accent, and made everyone laugh. In the 1950s, Uncle Philip's father lived in Shanghai with his concubine, a Beijing opera actress. J remember visiting him, the time he was translating the works of Mao Zedong into English for the publishing house.

During the mob violence, he was beaten and seriously ill, sent to the hospital. The nurses wouldn't admit him, not even let him into the emergency room, because they identified him as a "reactionary." Then came his daughter, Aunt Betsy, from Tianjin, dressed in military uniform, with a red star on her cap. Aunt Betsy was J's mother's age, the two were close as first cousins when they were young. After graduating from college, Aunt Betsy went north, joined the communists in 1940s, and married an army officer. She was a soldier during the Civil War. After Liberation, she was assigned to teach English at a military foreign language institute in the North. She was called home to see her father dying. She talked to the doctors, they immediately let her father in, but it was too late, he passed away shortly. So it goes.

A Legacy Recognized

On the day when Aunt Viva's family were supposed to arrive at the airport later afternoon, Winter Born and J did not get to meet them. They were told by the authorities not to go, because it was almost five or six o'clock in the evening, the government had assigned people to meet the guests at the airport, and escort them directly to the People's Grand Hall, to attend a state banquet, a big planned event for the celebration of the National Holiday.

It was September 30th, the next day was the National Holiday for the celebration of the founding of the People's Republic of China in 1949. October 1st was a big occasion in China every year. The Head of the State, Deng Xiaoping, was entertaining his honored guests from overseas and at home. The people in charge of the protocol from the Ministry of Foreign Affairs already made arrangement to meet Uncle Fortune and his families at the airport. A limousine drove them directly to attend the state banquet, held at the People's Grand Hall, which stood outside of the Tiananmen, the Heavenly Peace Gate.

The two of them from the family, Uncle Fortune and Aunt Viva, were seated at the first table, the head table, where Deng Xiaoping was seated. Next to Aunt Viva was a Minister of International Trade, his name was Ten Thousand Miles. During dinner, Aunt Viva kept complaining to him about the quality of things "Made in China." Pagoda, Ambrosia and her husband Karl sat at another table at the back, Table No. 52, or something like that. Ambrosia was not addressed as "Her Majesty." She was not an American Ambassador yet at that time, and her husband was not "his Majesty" in her honor, as he later claimed to be in another Asian country. That was a decade later, another story.

The next day, more surprises came. Aunt Viva, who got up early, and did not dress up well enough, went downstairs by herself to have her breakfast in the dinning hall at that Friendship Hotel. A waitress stopped her at the door, asking her if she had money. Aunt Viva would have given her a hard lecture on service, if it were in her own restaurant. She had such a good sense of humor that she came back to the room, told her families as a joke. Her daughter Pagoda took it seriously, said: "Told you not to wear polyester, Mom!"

Pagoda brought two huge suitcases of clothes, coats and sweaters for ladies, all American style, to be distributed among the relatives. J picked up a dark green wool coat with a squirrel fur collar, and some wool sweaters. When she returned to Shanghai, her girlfriends were excited to see the designs from America. No one criticized "bourgeois" fashion style anymore. Instead, young people wanted to be "modern" and have "modern" life style, like that in the West. Once again, fashion was behind them in the streets of Shanghai.

Winter Born was a better communicator than J. She communicated to Aunt Viva that she and J wished to go to America. She could take care of Uncle Fortune, as he was aging. Aunt Viva asked if they got their parents approval; if they knew that life in America was not easy. It was hard, one must work from morning till night, unlike the leisured life ladies led at home in Shanghai, served by nannies and servants. There were no servants for them in America. She also asked if their parents knew what they were doing, sending their precious young daughters to

America. Winter Born said yes, her parents would let her go. J said her parents were anxious for her to leave; they did not want her to be home. Aunt Viva took pity.

Uncle Fortune was busy with the talks for the next two days. When his host asked him if he had any needs or requests personally, he promptly asked Deng Xiaoping that his wife had two nieces, he wished to take them to America. One was an English instructor, he believed that her English was good enough to go to college. If he could sponsor her himself to study in an American university, someday J's American education would benefit the country, or the relationship between US and China.

There was no precedent at that time. Under the socialist regime, the government would issue a passport to a student to study abroad only sponsored by the government, not by private funding. The selected few must pass a strict background check, exclusive of any foreign relations or unfavorable family ties. J would never have had a chance. Uncle Fortune himself was sponsored by the government in China to study at Harvard University after the settlement of the Opium War. That was in 1910, still under the Qing dynasty. After undergraduate study, he was accepted in a degree program at Harvard Law School. Years later, he became the first Chinese student to receive a Law degree from Harvard and an expert in International Laws in China.

He told J that he used to ride a donkey, not a horse, to go to college at the Tsinghua Garden, now the Tsinghua University. After he returned to China, at first he tried to teach International Law at Jiaotong University in Beijing. However, there was no textbooks in Chinese for him to teach International Law in China. It was very difficult for him to translate laws in English into Chinese, and write textbooks in Chinese to teach Chinese students. Before long he was wanted by the government to supervise the Customs House. He liked J being a good student, and wished J could come to America to further her studies.

Deng nodded his approval. As rumor had it later, Deng spoke to his followers that he figured, if he let go one hundred students sponsored by their relatives with their private funding, only one returned to China in the end, it would cost China nothing. Why not? He was a pragmatist, well known for his saying for economic reform—"white cats or black cats," he couldn't care less about their color, only "a cat that can catch a mouse is a good cat." Ambrosia was that "good cat," fetched her parents back to China, to advise the new "Emperor."

Uncle Fortune was not a politician. He thought of himself as a statesman, a man of principle and vision, not an agent or follower of someone's politics. He was T.V. Song's senior school brother at Harvard. T.V. Song was a revolutionist; he was a royalist. After they returned to China, the Qing Dynasty was overthrown by the revolutionaries. Song became the Prime Minister of the Republic, invited his school brother, expert in International Law, to manage the Customs House in China. Song often consulted him on international laws, especially during the postwar period, with peace treaties and takeovers. Once he resigned and went to America, Song had to call him back. Uncle Fortune was a transcendentalist, always kept himself from party politics. He never joined Song's Republican party, led by Chiang Kai-shek. It was unthinkable for a high officer working in the government, impossible if he were not an exceptional man, possessed with superior knowledge and diplomatic talent.

Uncle Fortune got the worth of his American education. He learned, by international law, the protective tariff ought to be controlled by his own government, instead of the Englishmen, who ruled the Customs House in China. He was determined to take back that management. For the next twenty years, he managed diplomatically and firmly to get back the rule from the hands of the Englishmen. With his superior knowledge and tactful strategies, he succeeded. He was feared, but well respected, in diplomatic circles in the West.

For his past endeavor, the government in China remembered him and his historic efforts in protecting national sovereignty. That was why Deng Xiaoping honored him as soon as he returned to China for a visit after so many years. He himself was flattered by the honor he received. It was not the brand name of "Harvard," as the name was so mythologized these days in Chinese society from Taipei to Beijing, that J and Winter Born were benefited from Ambrosia and Uncle Fortune's distinctions, but from their virtual service, hard work, dedication and personal efforts—a legacy recognized. Uncle Fortune had his integrity. He remained independent from partisan politics, and with a touch of Puritan ethics, resisted bribery and corruption in China.

On the eve of Chiang's retreat to Taiwan, he refused to accept a bribery from the agents of Chiang to smuggle gold or some treasure out of his Customs House. Chiang murdered two of his assistants. He was furious, terribly hurt, refused to follow Chiang and Song to retreat to Taiwan.

The new government offered him a position with the Bank of China. He was not prepared for the new system and its laws. He did not want to live in Hong Kong and enjoy a traditional comfortable way of life like a lord. He immigrated to America. He did not take, or smuggle out, much of his personal assets, gold or treasure, as easily as he could have done, with his position in charge of the Customs House. His Harvard education taught him Puritan ethics. In Chinese, it was called "两袖清风"—he was a courtier, who "carried in his two sleeves only a breeze of wind," rare.

He and his families, who came after him as refugees in 1952, were naturalized as US citizens. At first, he served in the China Cabinet for the White House. That was in early 1950s, he advised President Truman to normalize diplomatic relationship with China. Unfortunately, wise counsels were often ignored, like "a breeze of wind by the ear," a classic case, or a classic "curse," Truman did not take his advice. He resigned from the China Cabinet, came to San Francisco. He lived in Chinatown, and led a quiet life at home. He was aging, reached the age of retirement.

While the wives of other high officers and wealthy men of the lost regime were playing mahjong in China town, Aunt Viva had to work outside of the house. She worked as a cashier at Safeway and waitress at local restaurants, to support her husband and the family, bringing up three children—Ambrosia, Pagoda, and Steel. The three children grew up with their parents at home without speaking Chinese. Though they came to America respectively at the age of three, five, and nine, their English proficiency turned out to be superior in public high schools. It was their father who taught them English at home. Ambrosia went to Berkeley and Harvard. Pagoda went to Berkeley and then Georgetown. She even passed the California Bar Exam in 1979.

Steel worked at the airport in San Francisco. When the day came in 1970, Uncle Fortune saw what he wanted to see taking place in US-China diplomacy, he wrote to President Nixon, in which he recommended the service of his daughter Ambrosia.

J and Winter Born accompanied Aunt Viva's family to Qingdao to visit Uncle Fortune's home town. The Mayor entertained them with a ceremonial banquet. Uncle Fortune's sister, over ninety years old, was still alive. She was a single woman, never married. She no longer lived in the old mansion on the hill, but moved to a shabby small house in town. She looked tall, straight, and clear complexioned. She used to know several foreign languages—English, French, German, and Japanese at least. She survived the mob violence during the Cultural Revolution. How happy she was to see her brother, Aunt Viva, and Ambrosia who was born in her house, came back from America! She saw her brother on television, with Deng Xiaoping in Beijing, before he arrived!

Aunt Viva and Uncle Fortune in USA.

Application for American College

Winter Born and J returned to Shanghai. Each submitted their application for a passport at their respective Police Stations.

In San Francisco, Pagoda was filling out the forms for them to apply for college. First of all, she needed J and Winter Born's English names. Neither of them had one. As Winter Born was going to take care of Uncle Fortune like an adopted daughter, Uncle Fortune named her "Diana."

J turned to Klever. Klever chose the name "Katherine" for J. But her mother said no, she couldn't have that name, because it was hers, her name at school, at that missionary school. In Chinese culture, the daughter having the mother's name was a taboo. They did not know, in Western culture, it was rather common the mother and the daughter could have the same first name. "Why don't you call yourself 'Jenny'?" her mother suggested. Coincidentally, "Jenny" sounded very close to that of J's Chinese name spoken in Shanghai dialect, as she was called at home and in the streets. Pagoda preferred to spell it "Jennie." So it goes.

The next thing she needed was transcripts. J had a junior high school diploma, but no official record for grades beyond the first year of junior high. Winter Born was five years younger than J. By the time she went to junior high, schools were reopen, class instruction resumed, so she had all the transcripts. After graduation of high school, she was assigned to work in a cotton factory. The work was heavy. She worked three shifts day and night, had no time to study English. She was happy to have a chance to get out and go abroad. Yet, was she prepared to go to college in America without speaking English? Why didn't her father teach her English all these years he was drinking with his friends?

Aunt Viva consulted a Chinese professor at University of San Francisco, who often came to her restaurant for dinner, and respected her family. Aunt Viva showed him J's letters written in English. He was Professor John Tsu, a man who knew what to do. He served as advisor to several US Presidents and in the White House on Education Committee. He contacted the Admissions and the English Department, then asked J to send in tapes reading passages of American literature and some writing sample, which J did promptly. The Admission's letters came, J was admitted as an English major, freshman, for Fall 1979. Winter Born was admitted to the Intensive English Program at University of San Francisco, starting in June 1979 to attend the summer school.

Winter Born left home in June. A few days after she arrived in San Francisco, she called home, crying over the phone, telling her mom she wanted to come back home. It was strange, J thought. Uncle Quixote and his wife did not tell J why Winter Born wished to come back. She might be homesick. She might miss her mother. Anyhow, she had a happy family in Shanghai, J thought. Something might be amiss. At least, J was warned before she got there, not to expect too much for life in America.

For J, her semester would start in the fall, which was good timing, because she could complete teaching the "Study Abroad" class. The one year training ended in July. Her students were preparing to leave for Europe and America. The university administration was disappointed with her, as her papers of transfer just went through its Human Resource in February. The Shanghai Police Bureau came shortly after, to inquire J's motive, behavior, personality and performance, in order to determine whether she deserved a passport. The university had never approved for any employee to go to Hong Kong, not to say USA, since 1949. J explained to them that since she did not have a college degree, in the long run, she would need to get her college degree to survive academically in a university. The Department Chair understood, and he gave his approval, contingent upon her completion of teaching the "Study Abroad" class, which was to end in July, 1979. She promised and she ended well.

J's mother was happy, making stylish silk and wool dresses for J to take with her, and buying tea, china, fans and all sorts of presents for the relatives in America. By the time after Ambrosia's first visit, the government had returned some of the assets, the banknotes and some additional currency in exchange for Grandma's diamonds. They never returned the thirty-six trunks the Red Guards drove away in 1966. So it goes.

Since J was fifteen, her mother always gave her two RMB a month for her pocket money. She still received two RMB when she reached the age of twenty-five. Maybe it was because J was not smart enough to ask for more. She never did. She never knew how to ask others for money, except for her father's alimony. This time her mother gave J two thousand RMB! It might be worth at least two hundred thousands now, something like twenty-thousand in US dollars today.

J gave it all to Uncle Earnest to thank him for the unpaid tuition all these years. She told him that once she was gone, she expected ten years to come "without seeing daylight," meaning life would be hard for her for the next ten years in America. She expected to support herself; studying and working at the same time, she would not be able to send any money back to China. She told him not to miss her, take good care of himself and his family. He said to J: "Child, wherever you go, your root will always be here, with me."

Farewell at the airport, Shanghai, August 23, 1979.

After the airplane took off, J saw a red crane sign at the tail of that Airline Japan, which lifted her from the ground of Shanghai to the ocean of clouds, flying to Tokyo, where she would change a plane to San Francisco. The crane was a sign of longevity in Chinese culture. J wrote a poem:

出国

骑鹤上金门,
潜云入太空.
人寰再一顾,
依依白发翁.　　　　1979年8月23日 上海至东京机上

(Leaving the Country

Riding on the crane's back,
　　flee to the Golden Gate,
Dash across the clouds,
　　delve into the outer space.
For a last time, I looked back at
　　the human world below—
Only my teacher, hair turning gray,
　　still lingering there.
　　　　　　　　　August 23, 1979,
　　　　　　on the plane from Shanghai to Tokyo)

J thought she would never come back to China.

End

ACKNOWLEDGEMENT

I am indebted to my classmate in Shanghai No. 2 Girl's School Ding Zhu Sheng and her son Tang Kai for safe-keeping a suitcase I left in China in 1979, and retuning to me seventeen years later in 1996. The notes and diaries in that suitcase supplied the material for this memoir.

I wish to take this opportunity to thank my friend Judith Evind for some of the old photos she scanned for me around 2000, that I discovered cleaning my mother's apartment in Shanghai, after she immigrated to America. It was Judith' interest in photography and her hobby of collecting old photos that inspired me to save memorable pictures, as these used in this book.

Special thanks goes to novelist Kathleen Guillen for introducing me to the rapid transformation of the literary market, ebook and online publishing. She opened for me the windows to the future of bookmaking and self-education. I am grateful to the editorial and technical assistance she provided me. Her generous assistance, in her "small ways," as she puts it in her novel *The Shadow of Daddy*, "makes America a better place."

Lorrie Nicoles read Chapter 3 and provided valuable suggestions for my revision. Professor Neil Schmitz in Buffalo, New York, read part of it with "sizzling" interest and offered rigorous critique for my revision. The Buffalo memories (pp 58-65) were added to address some of the questions he raised. I thank him for remaining a life-time teacher to me.

A READING GUIDE

The Education of Jennie Wang

1. Who is Jennie Wang? Who is the narrator? When and where did the author write the book?

2. What is the narrative function of the "Overture"? How does it help the reader approach the subject of the book? Identify its theme and comment on its narrative voice.

3. What are some of the positive and negative traits in J's character? Support your impression with one detail or action. Does J's character change throughout the book?

4. Make a list from the books mentioned in Chapter 3 that you know, have read, or those you might feel like to read or know more.

5. What textbooks and study methods J used in studying English? Could you tell the most important factor(s) that contributed to her success?

6. There are quite a few "story within a story" in the book, such as the stories of *The White Snake* and *The Gadfly*, that serve as meta-commentaries in the narrative. Could you speculate any allegorical meaning?

7. How is life in the countryside different from that in the city of Shanghai? Compare and contrast a small town that you

know with that ancient river town Nanxun, as described in the book.

8. In the "Introduction," the author cautions the reader that as often as not, she is being ironic. Could you sense some of the significant ironies in the book?

9. After reading the book, could you speculate the possible meaning of that quiz question Professor J raises for her students in the beginning: "How do you interpret Morrison's evocation in the opening chapter of the book: 'The heavy trees that sheltered the shacks up in the Bottom were wonderful to see'?"

ABOUT THE AUTHOR

Jennie Wang received her Ph.D. in English from State University of New York at Buffalo, M.A. from Stanford University, and B.A. from San Francisco State University. She taught Expository Writing at Harvard University and American Literature at University of Northern Iowa, where she was tenured as Associate Professor since 1998. She has published several books including *The Iron Curtain of Language, Novelistic Love in the Platonic Tradition,* and *China Men's American Dreams.*

She was appointed Professor of Comparative Literature and Dissertation Director at Fudan University in Shanghai in 2004 and Professor of English at Providence University in Taiwan in 2010. She returned to America in 2014. Currently she is writing her second memoir and working on several trans-Pacific bilingual book projects in California. (bilingualacademypress@gmail.com.)